You Can Hear Me Now

Nicholas P. Sullivan

JB JOSSEY-BASS

You Can Hear Me Now

How Microloans and
Cell Phones Are Connecting
the World's Poor to the
Global Economy

John Wiley & Sons, Inc.

Published by Jossey-Bass
A Wiley Imprint
989 Market Street, San Francisco, CA 94103-1741   www.josseybass.com

Jossey-Bass books and products are available through most bookstores. To contact Jossey-
Bass directly call our Customer Care Department within the U.S. at 800-956-7739, outside the U.S. at 317-572-3986, or fax 317-572-4002.

Jossey-Bass also publishes its books in a variety of electronic formats. Some content that
appears in print may not be available in electronic books.

Library of Congress Cataloging-in-Publication Data

Sullivan, Nicholas P.
    You can hear me now : how microloans and cell phones are connecting the world's
poor to the global economy / Nicholas P. Sullivan. — 1st ed.
        p. cm.
    Includes bibliographical references and index.
    ISBN-13: 978-0-7879-8609-4 (cloth)
    1. Cellular telephone services industry—Developing countries. 2. Grameen
Phone Ltd. 3. Information technology—Developing countries. 4. Telecommunication—
Developing countries. I. Title.
HE9715.D48S85 2007
384.5'35091724—dc22   2006032157

Printed in the United States of America
FIRST EDITION
HB Printing   10 9 8 7 6 5 4 3 2 1

Contents

Preface

[T]he people of Bangladesh are a good investment
in the future. . . . With loans for people to buy cell
phones, entire villages are being brought into the
Information Age. I want people throughout the world
to know this story.
                    President Bill Clinton, Dhaka, Bangladesh, 2000

In the Hands of People

I first got to know Iqbal Quadir in March 2002, traveling from
Boston to Monterrey, Mexico, for the International Conference on
Financing for Development. He was a fellow *business interlocutor*,
invited to represent the views of private businesses and foreign
investors, groups typically ignored by the Bretton Woods institutions (the International Monetary Fund (IMF), the World Bank,
and the United Nations), the conference sponsors. The invitation,
although largely ceremonial, signified a growing recognition that
private investment was a key driver of economic growth in poor
countries. The event took place in the shadow of the riots in Seat-
tle in 1999 protesting World Trade Organization (WTO) policies,
the follow-on antiglobalization protests, and finally, the terrorist
attacks of September 11, 2001.

The general thinking behind the invitation was that poverty was a root cause of antiglobalists' anger and anti-West terrorism, that economic growth reduces poverty, and that private investment was needed to spark *sustainable* growth. Aid alone clearly had not done the trick.

Growth doesn't always translate directly into poverty reduction of course, as gains are never evenly distributed. But studies indicate that on average every extra 1 percent of GDP growth—moving from, say, 2 percent to 3 percent growth—reduces poverty by 2 percent. Hundreds of millions have been lifted out of poverty in China and India alone since 1990, due to fast and steady economic growth driven almost exclusively by investment, not aid. Over the last decade in South Asia, where growth rates have averaged better than 5 percent per year, poverty fell in Bangladesh, India, and Nepal by 9, 10, and 11 percentage points, respectively.[1]

Quadir (pronounced "ka-deer") was the visionary and catalyst who created the framework for what would become GrameenPhone in Bangladesh—a cell phone company built by Norway's Telenor AS in conjunction with Bangladesh's fabled microlender, Grameen Bank. (In 2006, Grameen Bank and its founder, Muhammad Yunus, shared the Nobel Peace Prize.) In a country with a per capita GDP of about $1 a day, one of the lowest phone penetration rates in the world, and a government widely perceived to be the most corrupt in the world, GrameenPhone is a wildly successful business.

Thanks largely to GrameenPhone the penetration rate of phones in Bangladesh has increased fiftyfold in the last decade, to 12 per 100 people, although that is still lower than the rate in some African countries. GrameenPhone holds the dominant share (63 percent) in an increasingly competitive telecom market and is the best-known brand in the land.

A major factor in the company's success is its Village Phone program, which delivers phones to most of the 68,000 villages of Bangladesh, which have never before had phones. Grameen-Phone's method of distribution and its motto—"good business is good development"—could be an example and a motto for the power of inclusive capitalism.

"We put technology in the hands of people," as Quadir explains it. "Whatever people do with the phones, it's good for them, good for the country. Phones bring people together in collaboration, cooperation."

"A Magnificent Innovation"

The GrameenPhone tale I heard on the plane and at the Monterrey conference (where Quadir was a niche celebrity among a who's who of world leaders and international diplomats, including such opposites as George Soros and Fidel Castro) resonated on a number of levels, all set against the backdrop of the rabid antiglobalization discontent coursing through the poorer countries of the world and the richer countries' spotty record of success with foreign aid.

At the time I was on a personal quest, trying to make sense of the anti-WTO and antiglobalization protests. The global gulf between the haves and have-nots reminded me of America in the 1960s, when the gap between white and black, rich and poor, exacerbated by the Vietnam war and college deferments from the military draft, led to fiery urban riots that threatened to shred the social fabric.

I had been writing about entrepreneurs and technology for more than twenty years, and saw the nexus of the two as a potential solution to widespread discontent. In the late 1990s, I had attended massive Garage.com networking events in New York (run by former Apple "evangelist" Guy Kawasaki), where entrepreneurs came face to face with venture capitalists. I was struck by the fact that many of the entrepreneurs came from poor countries. They had traveled halfway around the world for a chance to meet money men in the West. They wanted to replicate the U.S. experience of the go-go 1990s. At the same time, I was moderating international Internet conferences for *Inc*.com (a sister company to

Inc. magazine), with legendary entrepreneurs as guests—and most of the participants were foreign.

I was clearly ready to hear the GrameenPhone story—and it was a great business story, one of the best I had ever heard. Quadir was a relentless entrepreneur who had spent nearly four years trying to kick-start a business against great obstacles. In an era when private-public and for-profit–nonprofit partnerships are seen as a way to solve vexing problems, the combination of a private multinational corporation and a world-famous social institution (albeit a for-profit bank) presented a great model. Joshua Mailman, a founder of Social Venture Network and the initial angel investor who put up initial seed capital for the project, refers to GrameenPhone as a "magnificent innovation unparalleled elsewhere," a new partnership model between a for-profit multinational (Telenor AS) and an indigenous nonprofit (Grameen Telecom) that will be a commodity in 2015.

In the aid-versus-enterprise debate, Quadir was being anointed as a model for creating entrepreneurial solutions. His notions of bottom-up development and the importance of spreading power at the bottom levels of society, his distinction between the "narrow and powerful interests" of ruling elites and the "encompassing interests" of the population at large, were extremely powerful. Quadir is an upside-down thinker—and a practitioner who has acted on his instincts.

Over the next few years I saw Quadir off and on. We were both living in the Boston area and shared similar interests, although we were at different ends of the spectrum. He had left GrameenPhone and Bangladesh in 1999 after being named a Global Leader for Tomorrow by the World Economic Forum. There he caught the eye of Joseph Nye, dean of Harvard University's Kennedy School of Government, who later offered Quadir a post as a lecturer. Meanwhile, I had returned to academia and was attending graduate school in a midcareer program at Tufts University's Fletcher School of Law and Diplomacy, studying international finance and development economics.

The more I heard about and studied the GrameenPhone story, the more unusual and important it appeared. Other companies had followed GrameenPhone and achieved both economic and social success delivering cell phones to developing countries, but very few had set a clear business goal of reaching into the most unreachable places. Micro businesses, yes. Social entrepreneurs, yes. But big, scaleable operations backed by multinational foreign investors—no. GrameenPhone was on the scale of a massive World Bank infrastructure project—except that the World Bank hadn't done it, wouldn't have done it, couldn't have done it. How *had* it been done? That's what I wanted to know, and what drove me to write this book. Was there a model that could be replicated?

Since the Monterrey conference in 2002, the pro-enterprise voices in the development debate have been gaining strength in numbers, powered by the positive response to C. K. Prahalad's *Fortune at the Bottom of the Pyramid* and his call to "eradicate poverty through profits."[2] A whole new ecosystem of development-through-enterprise advocates has sprung up, seeded by Prahalad's cohorts, such as Stuart L. Hart, founder of Cornell's Center for Sustainable Global Enterprise (and coauthor with C. K. Prahalad of the path-breaking 2002 article "The Fortune at the Bottom of the Pyramid"[3]), and Allen Hammond, vice president of innovation at the World Resources Institute (which offers a wonderful selection of blogs at www.nextbillion.net).

Ashoka, Omidyar Network, and Skoll Foundation are globally oriented nonprofits that back social entrepreneurs with resources. The Lemelson Foundation funds technological inventions and innovations in developing countries. The World Bank's International Finance Corporation is a critical backer and funder of private enterprises and private equity firms in developing countries, and the World Bank's Private Sector Development blog gathers news and ideas about "a market approach to development thinking." One of the first to publicly question the efficacy of aid from an inside perspective was William Easterly, former World Bank economist and author of *The White Man's Burden*[4] and *The Elusive Quest for Growth*,[5] where he championed enterprise over aid with the mantra, "People respond to incentives."

This book adds to the chorus. It is written for lay readers with an interest in globalization (and its discontents) and for entrepreneurs, policymakers, technologists, and innovators with a stake in business and economic development and poverty eradication. GrameenPhone was my entry point, and even though cell phones are spreading like wildfire throughout poor countries and bringing the benefits of information communications technology, GrameenPhone is my end point. As a joint venture between a multinational for-profit and an indigenous nonprofit, it is a model that signals a new approach in the attack on unmet human needs.

Acknowledgments

The people who made this book are the people whose stories I told. I would like to thank Muhammad Yunus, Tormod Hermansen, Khalid Shams, Iqbal Quadir, Inge Skaar, Gunnstein Fidjestol, and Trond Moe—all veterans of the early days of GrameenPhone—for sharing their time and memories with me. Erik Aas, the current CEO of GrameenPhone, completed the circle by giving me an inside look at today's operations.

Khalid Shams, Tawfiq-e-Elahi Chowdhury, and Abdul-Muyeed Chowdhury—three of Bangladesh's most esteemed civil servants, who started their luminous careers as Pakistani civil servants—gave me a true sense of what nation building means. Mohamed Ibrahim, chairman of Celtel International in sub-Saharan Africa, and Sam Pitroda, who helped bring village phones to India in the early 1990s, both took time to meet with me and recount their illustrious life stories.

This book would not have come to fruition were it not for John Taylor "Ike" Williams, director of Kneerim & Williams at Fish &

Richardson literary agency, who took me (and my "Bangladesh project") on as a client. He ferried me into the capable hands of Carol Franco, former director of the Harvard Business School Press. I was lucky enough to be her first client in her new life as a book agent, which gave me the benefit of her full attention and editorial expertise in shaping the proposal and book. Carol in turn led me to Susan Williams, executive editor at publisher Jossey-Bass in San Francisco. Susan is a wonderful editor with a strong track record in business leadership books who kept me on course during six months of intensive writing.

Crocker Snow Jr., who as editor of *The WorldPaper* and longtime follower of Grameen Bank and Muhammad Yunus was the first to bring Iqbal Quadir to the world's attention, initially introduced me to Quadir in 2001. Crocker also provided insightful comments on a draft of the manuscript. V. Kasturi "Kash" Rangan, Harvard Business School professor and cochair of the school's Social Enterprise Initiative, was kind enough to read and comment on a manuscript draft. Michael Chu, senior lecturer at the Harvard Business School and former CEO of ACCION International, provided me with a good understanding of the financial mechanisms behind commercial microfinance. Lee Aitken, longtime friend and a former editor at *Time*, *Vanity Fair*, and *The New Yorker*, made helpful comments on an early draft of the book proposal. Partha Bose, another friend who is both a business author (*Alexander the Great's Art of Strategy*) and international business strategist, provided innumerable book development and marketing ideas.

Abu Saeed Khan, noted telecom analyst in Bangladesh, and Sayeed Rahman, founder of the Bangla ICT Listserv on Yahoo, helped put the Bangladesh ICT revolution in perspective. Alex Counts and Susan Davis of Grameen Foundation USA put Grameen and its numerous offshoots into a global context.

I thank all for their information, advice, and encouragement, and hereby absolve them of any errors that may have crept into my writing. I also thank the friendly staff at Hotel Lake Castle, in the diplomatic zone of Dhaka, where I enjoyed many good meals and sleeps on my two visits to Bangladesh.

My ability to promote this book to diverse audiences will be enhanced immeasurably by a generous grant from the John Templeton Foundation, as part of its initiative to eradicate poverty through free enterprise. I thank Arthur Schwartz, executive vice president, for proactively encouraging and shepherding my grant proposal. Foundation founder John Templeton, it should be noted, was one of the original modern-day investors in emerging markets, betting on postwar Japan. The grant's institutional sponsor is the new Center for Emerging Market Economies and Enterprises at The Fletcher School at Tufts University, where I earned a midcareer master's degree. I thank Fletcher's Roger Milici for backing the project. Without my training at Fletcher in development economics and international finance, particularly from professors Jeswald Salacuse, Michael Klein, Steven Block, and Julie Schaffner and lecturer Michael Fairbanks, I wouldn't have been able to write this book with whatever authority and credibility I bring to it today.

Two longtime supporters of my writing are Claudia Cohl and Hugh Roome, my editor and publisher, respectively, at Scholastic Inc.'s *Home Office Computing* magazine. And I pay homage to Arthur Stern, a painting instructor at The New School, who taught his art students to "paint what you see" and taught me to "write what you see."

My wife, Debbie, was relentlessly supportive of and optimistic about this effort from the start, especially at times when things weren't going so well. She deserves a prize. I thank her and our daughters, Sarah J. and Lucy, for their faith in me.

November 2006   Nicholas P. Sullivan

The Author

Nicholas P. Sullivan has written widely about technology and entrepreneurship, for the most part tracking the impact of the information communications technology revolution in the United States. For the past five years he has focused on global development and investment, a path he followed after hosting international Internet conferences and radio programs for entrepreneurs while he served as editor in chief of *Inc*.com (a sister company to *Inc.* magazine). He was thereafter a United Nations–accredited *business interlocutor* to the International Financing for Development Conference (Monterrey, Mexico, 2002), and participated in several high-level dialogues at the United Nations. He compiles the annual Wealth of Nations Index, a ranking of seventy developing countries, is publisher of *Innovations: Technology/Governance/Globalization* (an MIT Press journal), and is a partner in the Global Horizon Fund, a private-equity fund of local funds in emerging markets.

Sullivan was a founding editor and later editor in chief of *Home Office Computing*, once known as the "bible of self-employment." As one of the nation's first high-profile telecommuters, he wrote the popular "Workstyles" column, which chronicled life and work in the information age, and the book *Computer Power for Your Small Business* (Random House/American Management Association). During that time he also served as a publishing executive at Scholastic Inc., dealing primarily with Fortune 500 telecom clients. He has chaired the *Inc.* E-Strategies Conference, the *Inc.*/Cisco Growing with Technology Awards, and the US West New Ventures Seed Capital Competition.

Recent publications include "Do BITs Really Work: Bilateral Investment Treaties and Their Grand Bargain" (*Harvard International Law Journal*) and "Clinical Economics" (*Compass*, Center for Public Leadership, Kennedy School of Government). Sullivan is a graduate of Harvard University and The Fletcher School of Law and Diplomacy. (www.youcanhearmenow.com)

Introduction

The Three Forces of External Combustion

You Can Hear Me Now describes a powerful economic revolution sweeping large swaths of what development economists call the *South*, a geographical area encompassing South Asia, Africa, and parts of the Middle East. (Latin America is also part of the South, but as the region is generally richer and communications better developed it is not a focus of this book.) While many in the West cry for more aid to governments of poor countries, private investment is breathing life into economies long stifled by corrupt, aid-drunk governments—and lifting hundreds of millions out of poverty.

You Can Hear Me Now shows the positive impact of information communications technology (ICT) on poor countries and describes a model for development that has the potential to address unmet human needs on a large scale. Focusing primarily on fast-growing cell phone companies, *You Can Hear Me Now* describes an inclusive capitalism that engages and enables many of the 3 billion who live on less than $2 a day—those at the "bottom of the pyramid."[1]

The most dramatic example of this new breed of business is GrameenPhone in Bangladesh. Starting service in March 1997, GrameenPhone now has more than 10 million subscribers, revenues pushing $1 billion, and annual profits exceeding $200 million. It has invested $1 billion overall in Bangladesh. Total foreign investment in Bangladesh from GrameenPhone and its rivals now tops $2 billion. To put that in context, Bangladesh received a mere $268 million in foreign investment in 2003, $205 million in the telecom sector!

In the villages where most of Bangladesh's 148 million people are living, GrameenPhone provides *access* (within a reasonable walking distance) to 100 million people through 250,000 village phones, each of which is owned and operated by a female entrepreneur who has taken out a microloan from Grameen Bank, co-winner of the 2006 Nobel Peace Prize. By leasing time to villagers for calls, these so called *phone ladies* pay back the loans and make an average of $750 a year, or roughly twice the average Bangladeshi's annual income.

Iqbal Quadir's inspiration for the business came when he was working as a venture capitalist in Manhattan in 1993 and his computer network crashed. Frustrated by his resultant lack of productivity, Quadir flashed back to his childhood in Bangladesh, then virtually free of phones, when he had spent a day walking ten kilometers to find a pharmacist, who himself was out walking to find medicine. Quadir concluded that "connectivity is productivity," in Manhattan or a rice paddy. Shortly thereafter, at age thirty-six, after eighteen years in America, Quadir quit his job and moved back to Bangladesh to help start a universal phone service in a country with just one phone for every 500 people.

After more than two years of hunting for foreign investors, Quadir teamed Norway's Telenor AS with Bangladesh's Grameen Bank, the renowned microlender. "Why can't a cell phone be like a cow?" Quadir asked Grameen Bank founder Muhammad Yunus, who agreed to lend money to women with a credit history so they could buy cell phones. The phone ladies pay back these loans by leasing time to villagers, just as they sold milk from the cows they had bought with Grameen Bank microloans.

Today the GrameenPhone tale of private investment importing information technology is being reenacted in dozens of the world's least-developed countries, connecting people to local and global markets for the first time and creating fertile ground for new spin-off businesses built by indigenous entrepreneurs. Cell phone companies such as Celtel in Africa, Orascom in the Middle East and South Asia, and Smart Communications and Globe Telecom in the Philippines are generating profits and wealth—while bridging the digital divide in ways impossible to predict. Selling prepaid calling cards in Africa is now a $3 billion business, with more than 200,000 outlets run by indigenous entrepreneurs. The cell phone itself has evolved from a simple talking device into a mini PC with Internet and transaction capability—allowing people who have never had bank accounts to make cashless transactions. *People who until a few years ago had never used a phone or bank are now transferring money by phone.*

Indeed, information communications technology has transformative powers in countries where phones and electricity have long been mere figments of the imagination. A woman who has earned enough selling cell phone services to rebuild her house in a Bangladesh village says that the phone is as magical as Aladdin's Lamp.[2] Bangladeshi jute farmer Munshi Rahman uses the phone to sell his crop directly to the highest bidder: "Gone are the days when we went to the market blindfolded to sell our crops at a price dictated by the commission agents. Now I have the choice of selling my crops at the market that gives the best price."[3] In a remote village in Sierra Leone, Emma Sesay went into an unexpected and difficult labor. She borrowed a phone to call her husband, who drove home with a midwife to deliver a baby boy. Sesay named the boy Celtel, after the phone company that had provided the phone.[4] As Sam Pitroda, an Indian expatriate who returned home in the 1980s to rebuild India's telecom network with domestically manufactured digital switching devices, says, "As a great social leveler, information technology is second only to death."[5]

By helping to build a profitable, sustainable, and scalable business in a country that most investors perceived as a "basket case" (Henry Kissinger, when U.S. secretary of state in the 1970s, said that Bangladesh was a "bottomless basket"[6]), Quadir is in the vanguard of an economic movement that is changing the developing world. Just as GrameenPhone would not have been possible without foreign investors, foreign investors would not have entered the country without a native entrepreneur such as Quadir and a connection to a local institution such as Grameen Bank (which brought with it both a rural distribution method and the political connections of Muhammad Yunus). Nor would Quadir have jumpstarted such a business without the falling costs of information technology. "Moore's law [that the data density on an integrated circuit will double every eighteen months] made this a very compelling business idea, however great the obstacles," says Quadir.

These three outside forces—information technology imported by native entrepreneurs backed by foreign investors—provides an external combustion engine of growth for countries long throttled by burdensome governments and markets distorted by billions of aid dollars.

The Need for an External Shock

Imagine the finely tuned markets in the West as running off internal combustion engines, constantly creating sparks and explosions that power the economy to steady gains. The poor markets of the South, in contrast, cannot create sparks internally but require external combustion engines, much like the steam engine that heated water in one chamber to produce steam that cranked a turbine in another.

Economists refer to this outside stimulus as an *exogenous shock*—an unexpected and uncontrollable shock to a closed system that alters the way that system functions. Skyrocketing oil prices or major currency depreciations for a major trading partner are examples of exogenous shocks that have major ramifications for linked economies.

In the case of GrameenPhone and other new businesses throughout the South (primarily in South Asia and Africa), the entrepreneur, technology, and investment all initially come from outside the country. The entrepreneur, like Quadir, is a native who has trained and worked in the West and returns with foreign money to deliver technology. The combustion fuels a virtuous chain reaction. Cash and profits lead to reinvestment. Spin-off businesses are created by new entrepreneurs. Ensuing competition creates a market for capital looking for the best and quickest return and forces government reform. Over time, as shares are traded and sold, capital markets deepen. With new liberalized policies and regulations set by the government, the country begins to live off internal combustion provided by its own technology, entrepreneurs, and capital. This is now beginning to happen in India, where entrepreneurs are now designing and building low-cost computers for low-income people and where the legislature recently (2004) passed a *right to information* bill, indicating a whole new level of government transparency brought about by the spread of information technology to hundreds of millions of Indian citizens.

Of course this pattern also describes the standard progression of development that every country goes through: GDP (gross domestic product, or national income) increases as the economy moves from subsistence agriculture to light manufacturing and urbanization to major industrialization and then to high-tech services. A country such as Malawi still operates at subsistence level. Bangladesh is beyond that, with garment manufacturing putting it on the first or second rung of what economist Jeffrey Sachs calls the "ladder of development."[7] And India, its own information technology revolution fueling heady growth, is a few steps further up the ladder.

In poor countries, growth is rarely natural and organic. Either leadership moves beyond the needs of narrow ruling elites and establishes new growth-oriented policies (as in Singapore, Taiwan, South Korea, and Chile), or new technology and resultant empowerment spark a shift that unlocks human potential to produce more and more with less and less (as in Eastern Europe before and after the fall of the Berlin Wall). The question is, What kind of shock will best break the vicious cycle of poverty in the least-developed countries and put them on the path to self-sustained development?

The knee-jerk answer for the last fifty-plus years, since the success of the Marshall Plan in rebuilding Europe after World War II, has been foreign aid. That charity has done little but distort markets, rather than unleash them. Perhaps if aid were targeted toward the particular needs of client countries and their citizens, it might achieve a better track record. But one-size-fits-all foreign aid is essentially laundered through governments that use it for large infrastructure projects (dams and large power plants near the capitals) that do little to provide long-term income opportunities for citizens.

That's why the GrameenPhone story is so important. In a very poor country long dependent on aid that has not been productive, GrameenPhone has shown that private investment, especially when used to distribute empowering technology tools, creates and disperses new wealth. GrameenPhone has been instrumental in putting Bangladesh on a new, sustainable, and upward trajectory of growth.

The Three Forces of External Combustion

Of the three forces of external combustion—information technology, native entrepreneurs, and foreign investment—information technology is the necessary first ingredient.

Information Technology

Technology has long been the key driver of change in all economies—from irrigation systems in ancient China to spectacles to light bulbs to steam engines to telephones to airplanes to hybrid seeds (the Green Revolution) to computers, a theme that is neatly chronicled in David Landes's *Wealth and Poverty of Nations*.[8] Even simple outboard motors were a boon to Bangladeshi fishermen in the 1990s, as were micro water pumps that irrigated rice paddies.

But information communications technology has distinctive characteristics that make it more powerful than most other technologies. Unlike, say, the turbine engine or a shoe manufacturing plant, both of which are centralized technologies controlled by a few people, information communications technology is a distributive technology that empowers large numbers of people. As a productivity tool, the cell phone benefits producer, consumer, and worker.

Information communications technology is also a *disruptive technology*[9] in that it introduces superior features at lower prices and thus reaches new markets, as the personal computer (PC) did when it *disrupted* the minicomputer and mainframe computer business (see Figure I.1). "Poor countries need disruptive technologies," says Quadir, who taught a course called Technology and Economic Development at Harvard's Kennedy School of Government. "It's the only way to shake the narrow interests that are not providing for their people." Indeed the cell phone is a disruptive technology that sometime around the millennium began overtaking fixed-line, or landline, phones around the world.

Figure I.1. Disruptive Technology.

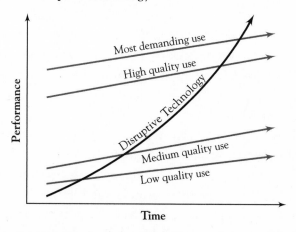

Source: "Disruptive Technology," Wikipedia, 2006, retrieved from http://en .wikipedia.org/wiki/Disruptive_technology.

In the 1980s in India, Sam Pitroda proselytized for communications as "an indispensable aid in meeting basic human needs."[10] This was seen by many as a heretical stance when so many people were lacking adequate food and safe drinking water, basic items on Abraham Maslow's *hierarchy of needs*. But communications, Pitroda noted, are productive and will increase output and income, which will lead to food and water. Nelson Mandela in 1995, a year after assuming the presidency of South Africa and a year after MTN and Vodacom started cellular communications there, also called communications "a basic need." "The desire to be in touch lies deep within all of us," he said.[11] It was recognition of this fact, of course, that led to AT&T's government-approved monopoly in the United States—the quid pro quo was delivery of universal service, no matter how remote the customer.

Because low-cost communications fulfills a basic human need that had been left unaddressed by many governments, cellular technology is now coursing through poor countries. Given that the average telephone penetration rate in much of the developing world is hovering around 12–15 percent, the growth potential for cell phone businesses is huge. At the end of 2005, with new competition from Egypt's Orascom sparking price wars, GrameenPhone signed up a million new customers in six weeks; in the second quarter of 2006, it added another 2 million. India, after a slow start, is adding phones at the rate of 5 million a month. Africa had 8 million phones in 1998; it now has more than 120 million phones. There are now more phones and related services sold every day in Africa than in all North America.

Often, passé products have been "dumped" on the Third World. In the 1980s, for example, when Sam Pitroda returned to India, the country was buying outmoded communications gear from Western companies, dooming itself to a second-rate telecom network. However, information communications technology can be adapted and enhanced through software or SIM (subscriber identity module) cards for a variety of landscapes and markets. By its nature ICT is never passé. Today cell phones are used in developing countries to access the Internet, make financial transactions and cash transfers, search for and advertise jobs, and send medical advice and prescriptions.

Native Entrepreneurs

State-of-the-art information communications technology would not have been imported without native entrepreneurs with implicit knowledge of their countries' cultures and often Byzantine bureaucracies. Today, yes, but not ten years ago. Quadir's relationship with Grameen Bank gave Telenor an inside track on GrameenPhone's license bid (through the clout of the bank and its founder, Muhammad Yunus) and the knowledge to build a universal network that extended beyond the urban elites into the rice paddies, where there is virtually no electricity or other infrastructure. In 2005, having learned the ropes in South Asia from its Bangladesh experiment, Telenor bid for and won a license in Pakistan and signed up 2 million customers in less than a year; in 2006, Telenor bid for (but did not win) a license in Egypt, but won one in Serbia.

Quadir set out to build what would eventually become Grameen-Phone (his initial company was Gonofone, meaning "phones for the masses") with the belief that information communications technology would empower individuals and transform society from the bottom up. As an MBA and venture capitalist trained and working in the United States, he also saw a glittering business opportunity in Bangladesh. He saw an unmet need (communications) and what appeared to be an obvious solution (cell phones), a solution whose cost would decline dramatically and thus open up new markets.

Most, although not all, of the native entrepreneurs who have built big businesses in less-developed countries have been schooled and trained in the West, returning to their homes with new ideas on how to make capital work. The typical pattern had been to make it big in the West, as Pitroda did, and then return to *give back* to one's homeland. But Quadir changed the pattern by truncating his promising and lucrative career in banking to take a shot at business in Bangladesh. Today the accelerated trend is to get an MBA or engineering degree and return home immediately, to take advantage of *market failures* that provide great opportunities for business development.

Foreign Investors

GrameenPhone wouldn't have been started, let alone succeeded, without foreign investors—Norway's Telenor AS and Japan's Marubeni. Quadir wouldn't have been able to cobble together the coalition of Telenor and Grameen Bank were he not supported by angel investor Joshua Mailman, from New York. And Grameen Bank would have struggled to maintain a large minority stake in GrameenPhone without the low-interest loan it received (through its affiliate, Grameen Telecom) from George Soros. The capital markets are just not well developed enough in poor countries to amass hundreds of millions of dollars to start a new business. Only the government has access to that kind of money, and much of it is washed away by corruption. Individuals who strike it rich are more likely to invest their money overseas (so-called flight capital), where capital markets are better developed and there are ready-made vehicles for investment.

Of course such dependence on foreign investors (and native entrepreneurs) is not unique to Bangladesh. Celtel International B.V., headquartered in the Netherlands, which operates in fourteen sub-Saharan African countries, would not have started or acquired stakes in phone companies in Burkina Faso, Chad, Democratic Republic of Congo, Republic of Congo, Gabon, Kenya, Madagascar, Malawi, Niger, Sierra Leone, Sudan, Tanzania, Uganda, and Zambia without $1 billion in debt and private equity from Western investors. "We went to the poorest parts of the world and made it our playground," says Celtel founder and chairman, Mohamed Ibrahim, a Sudanese native who goes by the name of Dr. Mo (or "just Mo"). Celtel was bought by Kuwait's MTC Group in 2005 for $3.4 billion, one of the largest private-equity deals ever in Africa, creating more than fifty millionaires—and paying back its investors an average of 8.5 times their investment. "My head, my heart, and my wallet are aligned with Celtel,"[12] says Dr. Mo, in a poetic reprise of GrameenPhone's "good business is good development" slogan.

Governments That Stymie Growth

Historically, and even today, the three forces of external combustion face equally powerful opposing forces. The primary opposition in Bangladesh and most poor countries is the strength of the government as the dominant economic force. Reasons for the government's predominance vary by country, but the equation typically includes the following mix: socialist and nationalist notions that the state is the best provider (along with burdensome regulations for private business), an aversion to foreign investors (along with import duties that restrict the flow of foreign goods), and large amounts of foreign aid filtered through the government (which inspires first-class corruption at high levels). (Bangladesh is perennially at the bottom of Transparency International Corruption Perceptions Index; in 2005, it was tied for last place with Chad.[13]) These are the forces that impede internal combustion in poor countries and make the external spark necessary.

Throughout South Asia an innate aversion to foreign investors stems from the collective memory of the British East India Company, which used wealth derived from the teas and soft cloths of Bengal to dominate Indian affairs for 200 years.[14] In *Brick Lane*, a 2003 novel by Monica Ali about Bangladeshi expatriates living in London, the father tells his children: "You see, when the English went to our country, they did not go to stay. They went to make money, and the money they made, they took it out of the country. They never left home. Mentally. Just taking money out."[15]

Many of the same forces are at work in large swaths of Africa, where strongman and one-party governments formed neo-Marxist regimes in the postcolonial 1960s, cutting their countries off from world markets while padding their own pockets with huge amounts of foreign aid. *Autarky*—an economy that doesn't trade with the outside world—works only if someone is sending money.

These dominant governments haven't invested that money in business or job creation but have created red-tape bureaucracies that stifle economic growth. This is partly intentional, as it sets up opportunities for graft to cut through the bureaucracy. But turgid economic development also results from a lack of the functional legal and banking institutions that could act as productive intermediaries to formalize contracts and loans. Without money and power, people outside government don't have the leverage to force change. In Bangladesh it now takes thirty-five days to start a business, according to World Bank data; in Kenya, fifty-four days; in Senegal, fifty-seven; in the Democratic Republic of the Congo, sixty-seven. Contrast these data with the numbers in the West. In Canada, it takes three days to start a business; in the U.S., five days; and in France, eight. (See Table I.1.)

Aid is the glue that cements the economic power of governments in poor countries. Bangladesh is certainly not the biggest aid recipient in per capita terms. Israel and Egypt, with far smaller populations and far greater geopolitical importance, eclipse it, as do many African countries. Nonetheless, the name Bangladesh is virtually synonymous with aid (as well as with monsoons and floods). Before Bangladesh won its war of liberation from West Pakistan and became an independent country, George Harrison's 1971 Concert for Bangladesh (held at New York's Madison Square Garden and featuring Bob Dylan, Eric Clapton, Leon Russell, Billy Preston, Ringo Starr, and Ravi Shankar) pled for aid with a clarion call in Harrison's song "Bangladesh." In the thirty-five-plus years since that concert, Bangladesh has absorbed more than $30 billion in aid—not a huge sum in absolute terms but huge relative to the local currency and national income levels.

And to what effect? Robert Novak, a former Pfizer executive who spent thirty years in Bangladesh and other parts of Asia, chronicled

Table I.1. Selected Indicators in Developing Countries.

	GDP 2005 ($US billions)	Per capita GDP ($US)	Per capita GDP (PPP*)	FDI** 2004 ($US millions)	AID 2004 ($US millions)	Main Phones per 1,000 (2004)	Mobile Phones per 1,000 (2004)	% Pop. Less Than $1 a Day	% Pop. Less Than $2 a Day	Days to Start Biz
Bangladesh	$59.9	$415	$1,197	$449	$1,404.1	5.94	31.1	36.03	82.82	35
India	$785.4	$586	$3,485	$5,335	$691.2	40.7	43.8	35.3	81.3	71
Kenya	$17.9	$428	$1,164	$46.1	$635.1	8.94	76.1	22.81	56.08	54
Malawi	$2.1	$154	$667	$26.	$476.1	7.38	17.6	41.66	76.13	35
Nepal	$7.3	$232	$1,528	$14.7	$427.3	15.1	6.7	24.1	65.29	21
Pakistan	$110.1	$595	$2,403	$1,118	$1,420.9	29.6	33.0	16.98	73.58	24
Philippines	$98.3	$1,123	$4,920	$469	$462.7	42.1	403.5	15.5	47.5	48
S. Africa	$240.1	$3,534	$12,346	$584.9	$617.2	105.2	428.5	10.71	34.07	38
Uganda	$8.7	$267	$1,524	$221.9	$1,158.9	2.57	41.8	—	47.48	36

* PPP = purchasing power parity, a technique that adjusts prices in different currencies to determine how many dollars it takes to buy a given basket of goods; **FDI = foreign direct investment.

Source: World Bank, *World Development Indicators 2006* (Washington, D.C.: World Bank, 2006).

the effect of such aid in *Bangladesh: Reflections on the Water:* "Everything in Bangladesh is built with aid: even the hotels and the golf courses, and the swimming pool at the poshest Kurmitolah club were built with Japanese aid. Since the government receives the aid, it controls most of the nation's spending power. And that explains the importance of Dhaka, since Dhaka is the capital. Everything that is not government is proportionately cash-poor to the degree that it is removed from government."[16]

This is the climate in which Quadir was trying to start a private business with foreign money in 1994. He was a capitalist in a poor, quasi-socialist (albeit democratic) country, whose government was significantly sustained by aid. He and Grameen Bank were competing with the government's Bangladesh Telephone and Telegraph Bureau (BTTB), which operated the fixed-line system. BTTB was essentially a monopoly, with the exception of one small, private cellular operator in Dhaka that catered to the elite, but didn't have AT&T's mandate to serve the country. BTTB served primarily the major markets of Dhaka and Chittagong. The job was made more difficult because Quadir and Muhammed Yunus were also looking to implement universal phone service. That essentially meant service everywhere beyond Dhaka, service to the 80 percent of Bangladesh's (then) 120 million people who lived in its 68,000 villages, those "removed from government," those living on less than $1 a day.

Moving Toward Internal Combustion

The twin themes that private enterprise creates wealth and job opportunities and is a quicker route to a poor country's economic development than aid—and that information technology is the best product that foreign money can import—are the key themes of this book. Technology provides income opportunities, and income *is* development. But there are several other closely related themes woven throughout the story.

In the aggregate the poor are wealthy. The idea that poor people have no money to buy products or services they want is wrong, as C. K. Prahalad has shown in great detail in *The Fortune at the Bottom of the Pyramid*.[17] There is more money on the ground than World Bank statistics indicate, given the vast informal (not taxed or statistically tracked) economies and the remittances sent from abroad (up to $300 billion a year is sent to developing countries from rich countries). In addition, where there are abundant foodstuffs, as in Bangladesh, the cost of living is quite low. The poor have no mortgages and no debt, because banks (except for microfinance institutions) don't lend to them. When people are buying very small quantities and sharing goods, $2 a day goes further than seems imaginable from a Western perspective. In the form of local currency, it's typically worth four or five times more in purchasing power than its dollar equivalent.

Inclusive capitalism spreads wealth. Distributing products or services in remote rural areas is not possible—or is at least extremely difficult—without engaging local entrepreneurs. The infrastructure is not in place for Western-style distribution, but locals have the tacit knowledge to cocreate complex supply and distribution chains with foreign investors. This fortuitous reality provides an external and unexpected benefit: as people living on less than $2 per day are slowly connected to one of the world's key grids, hundreds of millions of new income opportunities are simultaneously created.

Income is development. What people in poor countries need is a chance to make money. Humanitarian aid is often needed to recover from disasters, but aid for economic development almost always does at least as much harm as good because it rarely reaches the people it's intended to serve, and the influx of money distorts markets. As the world's population continues to grow, it is becoming increasingly difficult for a sizable minority to live off subsistence agriculture. As cash economies supplant subsistence economies, the poor need a way to generate cash. From the phone ladies in Bangladesh to the *sari sari* shopkeepers and resellers in the Philippines to the phone *top-up* shops in Africa, the cell phone explosion in poor countries has already created more than 1 million (and counting) new income opportunities.

Microfinance and foreign investment are combustible. Microcredit—the extension of very small loans to poor people without collateral—may help an individual or family to survive but will not create scalable businesses that create new jobs. But microcredit combined with foreign investment and technical know-how is a powerful and combustible combination. Microcredit redirects capital to the poor, where its marginal productivity is much higher than that of bank loans to upscale borrowers; in conjunction with outside investment, that productivity ripples through communities.

The digital divide is becoming a digital dividend. In May 2005, the *Economist* ran a cover story titled "The Real Digital Divide,"[18] with an arresting photo of a young African boy holding a mud brick sculpted in the shape of a phone to his ear. Message number one: people everywhere, of all ages, want phones. Message number two: the digital divide has little to do with lack of computers or Internet access, the common perception in the West. Message number three: cell phones are bridging the digital divide (see Figure I.2). Implementation of wireless information communications technology means much more than leapfrogging from a low-order to a high-order technology. It means that hundreds of millions of people are connecting to the world's information communications grid.

The Next Billion

The fact that such a simple tool as the phone, taken for granted in the West for decades, could be creating such widespread change and opportunity in the South is both serendipitous and upsetting. Serendipitous because the confluence of forces set in motion by the declining costs of cellular technology has near magically brought private investment into countries and distributed empowering technology tools, in one fell swoop. But the explosive impact of cell

Figure I.2. Mobile Telephone Subscribers per 100 Inhabitants.

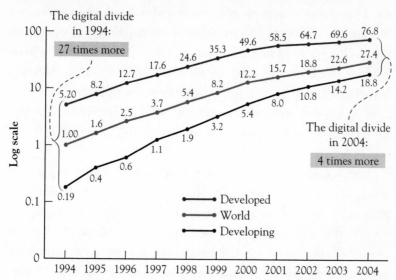

Source: International Telecommunication Union, *ICT Statistics*, 2004, retrieved from http://www.itu.int/ITU-D/ict/statistics/ict/index.html. Reproduced with the kind permission of ITU.

phones is also upsetting, because even with all the brainpower exerted in thinking about how to finance and spark economic growth, all the talk since the 1970s about *appropriate technology,* and all the talk about the digital divide as a lack of PCs and Internet access, no one really could have predicted such a deus ex machina or designed such a smooth-running external combustion engine.

Just as tax-free *export aid zones* promoted by governments were the spark that propelled the *tiger* economies of Asia (South Korea, Taiwan, Malaysia, Thailand) to rapid growth in the 1980s by encouraging the development of garment and electronic exports, and just as the Chinese government's decree in 1978 that Chinese peasants could sell their extra food production freed labor to move to the cities and begin China's explosive industrial growth, the introduction of cell phones into poor countries on a massive scale is igniting long-term economic growth.

Now that the model is being proved—with a major boost from local paradigms such as microloans, shared access, and small-denomination prepaid cards—a new wave of multinationals is moving in to develop new products. The GSM Association's Emerging Market Handset Programme, acting on behalf of operators in Asia, the Middle East, Africa, and Turkey, contracted with Motorola to produce a phone that costs less than $30. When GrameenPhone first started service in 1997, handsets cost around $400, including duties and taxes.

Ripples from this virtuous win-win circle will keep expanding outward. At the end of 2006, there were about 18 million cell phones in Bangladesh; how many will there be in 2010? There are now 2 billion phones in the world for 6 billion people; how many of the next billion phones will land in the developing world? Eighty percent of the world's population is in *cell range*, but only 25 percent has access; how long before 50 percent has access?

If connectivity equals productivity, productivity equals growth, and growth equals poverty reduction—how long will it be before the next billion people are lifted out of poverty? If countries like Bangladesh have been growing at 5 to 6 percent year after year with just a handful of phones per 100 people, imagine what will happen as penetration levels reach 10, 20, 30, or 40 per 100.

Recent econometric research from the London Business School suggests that adding 10 phones per 100 people adds 0.6 percent to the GDP of a developing country.[19] Extrapolating from the UN figures on poverty reduction (1 percent of GDP growth results in a 2 percent poverty reduction), that 0.6 percent growth would cut poverty by roughly by 1.2 percent. Given 4 billion people in poverty, that means that with every 10 new phones per 100 people, 48 million *graduate* from poverty, to borrow a phrase from Muhammad Yunus.

In the West the enduring question in the technology community for the last twenty years has been, "What's the next killer app?" In the South the answer clearly is, "Cellphones!"

In the West free traders triumphantly cry, "The world is flat!" In the South, where many live on bumpy, washed-out roads with no electricity or phones, they might say, "Flatten us!"

In the West the current cry from many rich nations is, "Give them more aid!" In the South the cry from many poor countries is, "Invest in us!"

Bangladesh now attracts around $1 billion a year in foreign direct investment, a huge increase from the $268 million it received in 2003 and $449 million in 2004. At the same time aid is dropping, from nearly $2 billion in 1994 to $1 billion in 2004, from 7 percent of GDP to less than 2 percent of GDP. It is now possible to imagine a time in the near future—if it hasn't happened yet—when private foreign investment overtakes foreign aid—just as the number of subscribers to private company cell phones has long since overtaken the number of subscribers to state-owned company fixed-line phones.

A Reader's Guide

The book is divided into two parts. In Part I, "The GrameenPhone Story," which covers the first six chapters, I tell the story of the formation of GrameenPhone, beginning in Chapter One with Iqbal Quadir's "connectivity is productivity" epiphany in Manhattan. Chapter Two, "Dish-Wallahs of Delhi," takes a step back and examines the foundations of Grameen Bank's microlending, village phones in India, and the dish-wallahs of Delhi (satellite-dish entrepreneurs who distributed video feeds) that were building blocks for Quadir's "phone project." The next four chapters describe the cell phone as cow paradigm for distributing phones, the relentless effort to attract foreign investment, the company's bid for a license, and the buildout of the network.

This case study is emblematic of similar cell phone formation going on in many of the less developed countries of the world, and Quadir is representative of the new class of native entrepreneurs who are striving to build scalable businesses in their native lands by leveraging local resources and foreign investors. I present GrameenPhone as a model case because it was early in the game and set out from the start to provide universal access. In this regard and in its union of for-profit (Telenor) and nonprofit (Grameen Telecom) shareholders, GrameenPhone is unique. Bangladesh, although not unique in its economic and telecommunications poverty, serves as a proxy for poor countries with minimal phone coverage that are being brought into the information age through cell phones. And cell phones, of course, are a proxy for all new and digital technologies.

Part II, "Transformation Through Technology," starts with Chapter Seven, "Wildfire at the Bottom of the Pyramid." Within a year of GrameenPhone's starting service in 1997, cellular licenses were being offered in many other poor countries in Africa and parts of the Middle East and Asia. (The same growth was occurring in Latin America, but in countries with higher levels of income and of phone penetration rates, so the impact was not so dramatic.) By 2000, cell phone sales were going through the roof, and people out of range were building tree houses to pick up a signal. Chapter Eight, "Cell Phone as Wallet," shows that as cell phone use spreads in countries where vast segments of the populations have no access to banks, add-on mobile commerce services are transforming social and economic interactions. Chapter Nine, "Wealth Creation and Rural Income Opportunities," quantifies the wealth creation and distribution of wealth arising from cell phone companies, particularly the economic gains and income opportunities in rural regions, where there are traditionally few jobs in the formal sector.

Chapter Ten, "Beyond Phones: In Search of a New 'Cow'," explores whether and how the model of business-driven wealth creation can be applied to address other unmet human needs and provide local self-employment opportunities. I focus on electricity, examining Quadir's new enterprise, Emergence Bio-Energy, which looks to deliver electricity through generators powered by methane extracted from cow dung—in the process creating a supply chain of micro-entrepreneurs more complex than that of the phone ladies. Finally, Chapter Eleven, "Eyeing the Dhaka Stock Exchange," describes how the explosive growth of cell phones sparked by foreign investment has begun to create new domestic capital markets where private money is invested and traded, enforcing the notion that private parties have the same stake as governments in a country's development and progress.

The story begins in Bangladesh.

For my father,
Gerald J. Sullivan

You Can Hear Me Now

Part I

The GrameenPhone Story

1

Connectivity Is Productivity

Travelers clearing customs at Dhaka International Airport in Bangladesh are greeted by three signs—one for Bangladeshi passport holders, one for foreign passport holders, and one for foreign investors. The first two lines are jammed. There is no third line. Foreign investors aren't exactly swarming one of the poorest and most corrupt countries in the world.

While I waited for my bags, I turned on my cell phone. In a few seconds it displayed the name of a local network operator, GrameenPhone. That was gratifying, because I had come to Bangladesh to visit Iqbal Quadir, who had spearheaded the design and development of GrameenPhone. I had heard so much about this company and its seemingly mystical success in a land that was once virtually phone free, it was reassuring to see how quickly the carrier popped up on my American phone. Reassuring and amazing—that you can travel from the richest country in the world to one of the poorest, from a country with one of the highest telephone penetration rates to one with one of the lowest, and use the same phone.

Arriving in the predawn hours after a long flight from London in January 2005, I made no immediate link between the foreign investors sign and the GrameenPhone network connection, but of course there's a clear one to be made: GrameenPhone would not have been possible without foreign investors.

In 1993, when Quadir first began thinking about the possibility of building a universal cellular network in Bangladesh, more than half of its 120 million people (now nearly 150 million) lived on less than $1 a day. GDP per capita was $220. The adult literacy rate was 37 percent. Foreign direct investment (FDI) totaled a mere $3 million a year.[1] Eighty percent of the country had no electricity. There was no sign welcoming foreign investors at the airport.

With a mere two phones for every 1,000 people, Bangladesh's tele-poverty rivaled that of Nepal. Only Dhaka, the capital and largest city, and Chittagong, the second city, had widespread phone "service," to use the term loosely. But that's not to say people didn't want phones; in 1993, there were more than a million applications for phone service on file. If you knew the right people, you could get a phone in five years; if not, ten was the norm. The completion rate on calls was around 20 percent, about what you'd expect from an Army field telephone in World War I. Taking a rickshaw ride through crowded streets to talk to someone in person, breathing the noxious exhaust of outboard motors powering the three-wheeled *tuk-tuks* (they now run on natural gas), was a much more effective way to communicate. The saw in Dhaka was, "First you get phone service, then you build your house around it." In 2005, a Dhaka newspaper ran the story of a sixty-year-old man who just received a fixed phone line after a twenty-seven-year wait. "I'm not sure why it has taken so long to get my telephone connected," Mohammed Ismail told BBC News. "I suppose it's because I'm an ordinary customer who didn't pay bribes."[2] That is Bangladesh in a nutshell.

There were, and are, positives. Bangladesh is democratic, even though its government is consistently ranked as one of the most corrupt countries in the world by Transparency International. Women are more modern than in any other Muslim country, and the fertility rate dropped from 6.6 in 1975 to 3.1 in 2004. Many work (primarily in the garment industry) and rarely wear traditional burqas (opaque veils). Two women have alternated as prime minister since 1991. (They are mortal enemies and defy each other's efforts to lead, but that is a different problem.) The country has been relatively peaceful, compared to, say, Indonesia or Pakistan, except for occasional political murders and incessant *hartals*, or political strikes. Synchronized bombings across Bangladesh in 2005 and 2006 were a disconcerting signal that Islamic fundamentalists—who want to install Islamic law over the current British common law system—are now operating on the fringes, but they appear to have little traction. The country is rich in natural gas, exports are up to 14 percent of GDP, and the economy has been growing at 5 percent or better for almost ten years.[3] Bangladeshis are incredibly hard working. "How can people work so hard and be so poor?" one of my Bangladeshi guides said to me as we drove through the crowded streets of Dhaka and watched a whirlwind of commerce in wall-to-wall shops at 11 P.M. Good question; one that Quadir has been thinking about for years.

The Liberation War (1971)

Quadir, a Bangladeshi American with a friendly face and piercing eyes, left Bangladesh as a teenager in 1976 to study in the United States, after five years of hell.

When Quadir was a child, Bangladesh was East Pakistan, formerly part of India's Bengal state, until Pakistan was partitioned off in 1947, the year of India's independence from the United Kingdom. In 1971, when Quadir was thirteen, East Pakistan declared itself independent of West Pakistan (today's Pakistan), and took the new name of Bangladesh (meaning "land of Bangla-speaking people"). West Pakistani soldiers invaded and went on a nine-month rampage of killing and rape, attacking especially the intellectual and professional classes. Joan Baez's "Song of Bangladesh"[4] refers to pools of blood, shrieks of terror, and horrific deaths at universities. In the end, somewhere between 1 and 3 million Bangladeshis were killed. "It was like living in Germany for Jews," says Abdul-Muyeed Chowdhury, executive director of Bangladesh Rural Advancement Committee (BRAC), one of the world's largest nongovernmental organizations. BRAC was founded after the war by Fazle Hasan Abed, a Shell Oil executive, to help resettle refugee Bangladeshis who had fled to India. "You didn't know if or when you'd be picked up; we were always living in the shadow of death."

Millions of East Pakistani refugees left towns and cities to escape the butchery, while heavy monsoon rains threatened a humanitarian disaster (and inspired George Harrison's Madison Square Garden concert). As Pakistani soldiers moved along roadways and waterways, Quadir's father moved the family from the small city of Jessore to his own father's house in a tranquil rural corner of the country.

The war ended when the Indian army moved in to stop the killing and drive out the West Pakistani army. Bangladesh was now independent. The next year Quadir's father died in a ferry accident, while saving his daughter. In 1974, devastating floods put most of Bangladesh under water and killed 1.5 million people. The teenage Quadir saw dead bodies floating down the rivers. The resultant famine didn't compare with that of 1943, when up to 9 million died as India's British rulers focused on the Japanese occupation of Burma (now Myanmar), to Bengal's east—but the mere memory of '43 opened wounds in the new country's psyche. In 1975, Sheikh Mujib, who had returned to govern after being released by his Pakistani jailers, was murdered along with his entire family (save his daughter Sheikh Hasina Wajed, who was in Germany at the time, and is now leader of the Awami League, a political party). (Sheikh Hasina was prime minister from 1996 to 2001.) After Mujib's murder, the military took control of the government. Bangladesh was free, but it was also a cauldron of poverty and corruption, with no connection to export markets and no way to earn foreign exchange.

When the war ended, Quadir returned to boarding school in Jessore (where the students played baseball and read copies of *Time* magazine in the library) and finished in the top 10 of the 100,000 Bangladeshi students who had taken the tenth-grade certificate exams. He moved to Dhaka to live with an older sister and enrolled in another high school but found it rough going. "There were a lot of rich kids there, who were a little snobbish toward kids from Jessore. It would be like going from Des Moines to New York," says Quadir. "My grandfather had moved back to his rural roots after college and my father to a small town. In their eras, most people who had attended college in Bangladesh settled in Dhaka, or another urban area. So I had a chip on my shoulder to prove that I was as good as big-city kids." Instead of studying, he mostly spent his time working the bureaucracy to figure out how to leave the country. Most people who left the country for education did so for graduate school; Quadir hadn't even finished high school.

But he was attracted by the foreign mystique. His father had taken him on train trips and told him that the trains were manufactured abroad. His sister's husband was manager of a paper plant, but the German manager who was his perceived equal earned ten times what he did. In Quadir's neighborhood in Jessore, he had seen European managers barking out orders at Bangladeshis. It took weeks, but the seventeen-year-old persuaded the Central Bank to convert his Bangladesh *takas* into U.S. dollars—the country had so little trade there was virtually no foreign exchange in the country—and Quadir mailed in U.S. dollars with his request for an SAT exam.

"Everywhere I went hardened my desire to come abroad. When I went to get permission for fees or something, they always asked me, 'Who is your dad? Why should we help you?' Then I realized that with my dad dead, I could not do well there—everything was dependent on that connection. It made it seem to me that the government was functioning for the privileged and connected. If my father had lived, I might have just moved into Dhaka or Jessore society and taken advantage. I might not have been as driven."

A Teenager Emigrates to the United States

Quadir did well enough on his SATs (including a 770 score in the Physics SAT II Achievement Test) to win a scholarship to Waldorf College, in Iowa, from which he transferred to Gustavus Adolphus, in Minnesota, and then eventually to Swarthmore College, outside Philadelphia. The strong history of education in his family and goals his father had set out for him kept him pushing toward the top. Without the free ride he received at each school, his mother would never have been able to afford the tuition. A widow with ten children, she had packed him off with $1,000.

Quadir chose Swarthmore because of its superior reputation and because it was one of the few liberal arts colleges that offered an engineering degree. He had originally wanted to pursue nuclear physics, until colleges told him that was a graduate course of study. His idealism and desire to do civic good, instilled in him by his father, along with his natural bent for physics, pushed him toward engineering. "I thought that the problem with Bangladesh was that we needed to make more things," says Quadir, remembering the trains and experts that had to be imported. "I learned later that it was more complex than that."

Ending up at a small, high-powered college such as Swarthmore, in such a beautiful setting—part of the campus is a 330-acre arboretum—two years after leaving the chaos and hurt of young Bangladesh, only added to his sense of obligation to give back. He was lucky and he knew it.

Graduating with a degree in engineering, Quadir went straight to the Wharton School of the University of Pennsylvania to get a PhD in decision science, an economics-based discipline focused on managing large, complex systems. In 1983, after finishing a Master's degree, he went to work for the World Bank, having moved past engineering as a solution, now thinking that the massive development institution might be the way to help change the dynamic in a place like Bangladesh. He was somewhat disillusioned by the bank's ineffectiveness, the way its lending seemed to perpetuate statist governments and did little to empower poor citizens, a theme he still happily warms to today when reacting to any sliver of news related to aid or trade. In 2004, for example, he suggested to the *Harvard Business Review* that instead of giving aid to poor countries, the

World Bank should give aid to rich countries like the United States in exchange for an agreement to end agricultural subsidies. The subsequent trade in agricultural goods would do more good for more people than the billions of dollars given to narrow ruling elites.[5]

One of Quadir's two years at the World Bank was spent working with the group that manages the bank's investment capital. Exposed to Wall Street trading practices, he formulated a new perspective on business, one that had been slowly emerging at Swarthmore and then Wharton. What had once seemed straightforward and simplistic, he began to see as a creative intellectual challenge. "I had thought that business and finance was boring and all about making money, probably an idea I got from my father, who was a lawyer," says Quadir. Now, he came to realize, business could provide economic solutions to problems that he had once considered political or technical.

This era was the heyday of junk bonds, corporate raiders, and leveraged buyouts on Wall Street—its greedy titans viciously portrayed as Masters of the Universe by Tom Wolfe in *Bonfire of the Vanities*.[6] But Quadir, who has a gift for seeing white where others see black, learned that an unglamorous thing—a lousy business in distress—could actually be quite an attractive investment. The Wall Street raiders were actually pretty smart and might provide a model. "I came from a poor, unglamorous country in constant distress—so why couldn't it become an attractive investment?" Quadir asks. Buy very low, sell very high. Intellectually, he had moved beyond physics and engineering as the solution to problems, and saw the proper deployment of capital as a possible panacea. In 1985, he enrolled in Wharton again, this time to get an MBA degree.

By 1993, he was working as a venture capitalist in New York. One day when his computer network went down, he flashed back to his grandfather's home in rural Bangladesh, where he had sat out the war. Due to lack of phones, he had once spent a day walking ten kilometers to find medicine for his brother, only to find the pharmacist had left the village to get medicine. What a waste! Quadir was frustrated because he couldn't function for a few hours in his Manhattan office; Bangladesh had been hamstrung by lack of telecommunications since the era of Alexander Graham Bell.

"I realized that connectivity is productivity, whether it's in a modern office or an underdeveloped village," says Quadir. He eschewed the common Western perception that the so-called digital divide was a lack of Internet access and pinpointed the real divide as a lack of basic phone service.

A Perfect Business Opportunity

Whatever social benefits might accrue from spreading telephony, Quadir saw first and foremost a good business opportunity—a low-lying, densely populated nation, perfect for cellular service, with 120 million people and virtually no competition. (Bangladesh has about half the number of people that the United States does, squeezed into an area about the size of Wisconsin.) In 1993, most saw cellular service as a luxury of the rich; Quadir saw it as a tool for the poor. Moore's law stated that data density on an integrated circuit doubles every eighteen months. Accepting Moore's law as a truth, it was reasonable to assume that the price of service would drop proportionately. Despite having no expertise in telecom, Quadir was convinced that a universal, private telecom business could succeed in a country where the government was the primary telecom operator and dominant economic force. In 1994, at age thirty-six, Quadir quit his job in New York and moved to Bangladesh. Many in his family (he has nine siblings) thought he had failed in America and was returning home to start over. Others thought worse.

"I thought, has this man gone crazy?" said Tawfiq-e-Elahi Chowdhury, an economist who was then Bangladesh's secretary of statistics (at other times in his career he served as secretary of food, energy, and planning) when Quadir approached him in 1994 for some background data on the country. " 'This is Bangladesh,' I told him. 'People here don't have enough to eat. What would they do with cell phones?' " Indeed, by the time import duties and taxes were levied, a handset cost about $400 then, nearly twice the average annual income in Bangladesh. That's comparable to a fancy car in the United States that costs $80,000 (roughly twice the U.S. per capita GDP).

Quadir may have been utopian, but he was not crazy. He knew the West had developed organically by allowing businesses to grow and to spread wealth and power throughout society. He had seen more recently how technology had changed the social and economic fabric of the United States (see the box, "The Link Between Technology and Growth"), how nimble companies such as Apple, Microsoft, Dell, Amazon.com, and emerging cell phone companies were changing the rules of business. Finally, having worked a stint at the World Bank, Quadir saw aid as an albatross that Bangladesh needed to get off its neck if its people were ever to flourish economically.

The Link Between Technology and Growth

Take a country with vast labor resources, add capital (that is, machines), and watch production (GDP or output) grow. That was the basic theory (Harrod-Domar model) of economic growth in the 1940s. After the jobless Depression of the 1930s, excess labor was a given. The success of the Marshall Plan in rebuilding war-torn Europe and Japan seemed to confirm this theory.

But there was a key missing ingredient, uncovered by economist Robert Solow. *Solow's surprise,* first published in two papers in 1956 and 1957[7] (and still the dominant theory of economic growth taught in universities today), is that capital plays a relatively minor role in growth. True, a business or country with low levels of machines can grow fast in the short term by adding more machines to catch up with excess labor, but there comes a point of diminishing returns. Workers can operate only so many machines at once. At some point therefore every economy should settle into a long-term steady-state equilibrium where further growth is impossible.

So why, Solow wondered, have countries like the United States continued to grow at a roughly 2 percent a year average decade after decade, long after they, theoretically, should have reached equilibrium? Solow concluded that technological improvement to machines boosted output per machine and thus per worker. The more technical improvement, the more growth you could squeeze out of the same workers and machines. New tractors, for example, clearly harrowed fields quicker. Multiplied a thousand times over, such technical improvements raised production and incomes. Accepting "Solow's surprise" as a truth, it's easy to understand the economic impact of phones in villages that never before had phones.

"It wasn't enough to say that Bangladesh was poor, therefore it's doomed to remain poor," says Quadir. "There was a reason it was poor and the reason was the approach. The bottleneck was at the top of the bottle. Money was being given to the government, and they weren't using it to drive the economy or help the people. If you study why countries have made economic progress, you'll see that entrepreneurs have forced governments to create a climate conducive to business."[8]

Quadir, a contrarian with an upside-down view of the world, points out that in the West companies solve problems. When they don't, nonprofits attempt to fill the gaps. But in developing countries the same types of organizations are called NGOs (nongovernmental organizations). "Why is that?" Quadir asks. "Because in developing countries governments have all the power; they get to try their hands at problems first."

"Nothing good in society ever started out big," says Quadir:

> Everything good, whether it's a company or an institution, starts small and grows and spreads. If the idea is no

good, it doesn't spread, and no harm is done. Even Machiavelli made note of this. He noted that the population is reasonable, because when you have large numbers, the irrationality or arbitrariness of any individual is cancelled out. If an entrepreneur with few resources makes a mistake, it's likely to be small and easily correctable. If a government makes a mistake with its large resources, it's more likely to be a large mistake that is not easily correctable, and it will impact most citizens.

Connecting the Villages

A few days after my arrival Quadir and I were driven in a 4x4 out of Dhaka into the rice-paddy villages that cover the vast delta that is Bangladesh. Snow melt and mud from the Himalayas sluice down the mighty Ganges, Brahmaputra, and Meghna rivers—from India, Nepal, China, and Bhutan. The rivers meet in Bangladesh before spilling into the Bay of Bengal. The mangrove jungle just above the bay is the last wild refuge of the Bengal Tiger.

With more than 2,000 people per square mile, all of Bangladesh is technically urban, but the agrarian countryside has a truly rural feel. The landscape is a soft symphony of greens and yellows. Mustard, rice, wheat, jute, pineapples, and bananas (and in the north, tea and cotton) grow side by side. This country of mud has no rocks; throw almost any seed in the fertile soil and it will sprout within days. With planning, some think it could become the next New Zealand, a huge exporter of food products. As it is, Bangladesh produces a surplus of food, allowing excess labor to move into the cities and work in light industries such as apparel and jewelry.

The air is motionless, hazy and warm, moist and fragrant. At night, without interfering electric lights (and there are none in most places), water, earth, and sky blend into a 360-degree aqueous dome without horizon. In the distance, clumps of land raised above the paddies support small villages, often a family grouping with common grandparents. During the double monsoon, when 120 to 140 inches of rain falls, these clumps are islands accessible only by boat.

On the road out of Dhaka, Quadir pointed to buildings where he had negotiated with landlords to lease space on rooftops for cell towers. Well outside the city, driving through villages with crowded markets, Quadir would excitedly point out bright red signs in Bengali (or Bangla, as the language is increasingly referred to) script heralding a GrameenPhone outlet, a place where you can go to make a call *a la carte*, even though you don't own a phone. We stopped at a few outlets and talked to the phone ladies, who sit at desks with their cell phones, awaiting customers. One had recorded thirty calls by 11:30 in the morning, including several to Saudi Arabia, an indication of why revenue from any one village phone is ten times that of an urban phone.

Another phone lady even complained about competition from a new phone lady entering her market. Quadir loved this! As he sees it, competition, not capital, is the name of the game. It drives prices into the ground; people make more phone calls; the company makes more money, which drives network expansion, which drives more calls. Most capitalists, as he points out, would prefer to be monopolists—like the phone lady, like the government.

Because the village phones are controlled by women—and women who were once poor—the social structure has evolved. Villagers with means, men and women, come as customers to the phone lady. People once cut off from relatives driving cabs in New York or working construction in Saudi Arabia are now connected. Women who previously had no income and lived at the behest of their husbands, now have independence. "When Grameen offered me a cellular phone, it seemed to me like Aladdin's Lamp," says Helena Begum, from the remote rural village of Moukhara in the northwest sector of Bangladesh.[9] "I use income from the phone to buy land. My daughter is now in college and my son in class nine. I myself provided their expenses. The mobile phone of Grameen is a magic lamp." Another phone lady, Delora Begum (no relation), says: "My life is getting better; people consider me a person of honor."[10]

In another village a young boy sits at a table with a cell phone in the middle, held by a plastic purple stand. About thirty business cards sit under glass. Most have a cell phone symbol in the corner, with the village phone number as contact. "None of this existed two years ago," says Quadir. "No one had business cards. No one had a phone." It is amazing—that one phone in a purple plastic holder could generate such enterprise, that a simple business card was a new paradigm in a village without electricity.

Quadir asks the boy how much it would cost to call his mother in the United States. The boy looks shocked at the unusual request, then pulls out a booklet with per minute pricing for overseas calls. (The phone itself records call duration.) Quadir and I help him locate the page and agree on a price. Quadir calls his mother in Boston, wakes up his brother (it's 2 A.M.), and proudly announces that he's calling from a village in Bangladesh. Wide-eyed children look on in amazement.

Bangladesh: Unleashing the Tiger

In 2003, Goldman Sachs researchers identified a group of looming economic powers they called the BRICs—Brazil, Russia, India, and China.[11] These geographically large and populous countries showed solid conditions for growth that would propel them into becoming economic powerhouses by 2025 and 2050.

Goldman Sachs researchers updated this report in December 2005 by examining eleven other countries (the *Next Eleven*) that might have the potential to compete with the BRICs (which to date are performing above original expectations). Of these eleven, they concluded that only South Korea and Mexico will converge to parity with developed countries by 2050. But another one of the eleven countries cited is Bangladesh, which is projected to grow annually by

5 percent or more through 2050 and increase per capita income from $422 in 2005 to $4,501, making Bangladesh the twenty-second largest economy in the world.[12]

I had come to Bangladesh to write about the creation of a successful business in a poor country, but after several harrowing Land Cruiser drives into the villages (trucks, buses, and cars play "chicken" on roads with no rules), I realized that GrameenPhone was more than a successful business. GrameenPhone was a potential countervailing force to the government, perhaps the camel's nose in the tent for a people and a country that had long resisted outside forces. And GrameenPhone was not the second coming of the British East India Company; it was the positive face of globalization.

"The fact that we are where we are is truly amazing," says Tawfiq-e-Elahi Chowdhury, a Harvard-educated (PhD degree in population economics) civil servant and decorated hero of the Liberation War; as a member of the elite civil service of Pakistan, he took up arms on learning about the atrocities committed by the Pakistani Army on its own citizens, and later commanded a group of regulars and guerillas. "Our ruling class, our intellectuals were wiped out thirty-five years ago. We've had to rebuild from dust."

"People used to ask me to compare Bangladesh to the tiger economies of Asia, like South Korea, Thailand, and Malaysia," says Quadir. " 'Is Bangladesh the next tiger?' they'd ask. I'd say, 'Bangladesh is a tiger in a cage, and right now the zookeepers have demonstrated little intention of freeing her. But Bangladesh is the land of the tiger and not a zoo.' "

2

Dish-Wallahs of Delhi
(and Other Early Models)

The cell phone rollout in Bangladesh had a significant prehistory that set the foundation for success. The cornerstone was Grameen Bank (meaning "rural bank" in Bengali), Bangladesh's legendary for-profit microfinance institution that became an independent bank in 1983. Since then, Grameen Bank has lent about $6 billion to 6 million *clients* and realized a 99 percent payback rate (according to Muhammad Yunus, the Bank's founder and managing director and recipient of the 2006 Nobel Peace Prize). Yunus, a former professor and the founder and managing director of Grameen Bank, is now widely regarded as the father of microcredit, or microfinance, even though various nongovernmental organizations and some European banks had been making microloans years before Grameen Bank started. "One day," Yunus says confidently almost every time he delivers a speech, "our grandchildren will go to museums to see what poverty was like."

In 2005, addressing a microfinance summit in Chile, he noted that Chile, with only 3 million people considered poor, had an opportunity to be the first country on the planet to eradicate poverty. "Mr. President," said Yunus, turning to Chilean president Ricardo Lagos, "I have been told that it is especially beautiful in northern Chile. The poverty museum could be built there and you, Mr. President, could lay the cornerstone."[1] Yunus has a beautiful way of expressing large ideas in simple sentences.

When Quadir first started exploring the idea of a nationwide phone network in Bangladesh in 1993, Muhammad Yunus was the most famous person in Bangladesh and was also cementing a global reputation. Bill Clinton, who as governor of Arkansas in 1987 had modeled a microfinance program (the Good Faith Fund, in Pine Bluff, Arkansas) after Grameen Bank, suggested during his 1992 presidential campaign that Yunus be awarded the Nobel Peace Prize (he finally won the Nobel in October, 2006); Jimmy Carter visited Yunus in 1994; and Hillary Clinton would fly with Yunus to the Jessore district to visit a bank branch in 1997. In 2000, President Clinton visited Bangladesh and Yunus and commented about the village phones: "I want people throughout the world to know this story."

In his loose-fitting South Asian tunics, Yunus is as comfortable in Washington, New York, London, or Geneva as he is in Dhaka. He is a charismatic speaker and master marketer. Speaking at one policy-oriented development conference in Europe, he unexpectedly called onto the stage a group of impoverished Bangladeshis. "You always talk about people living on $1 a day," Yunus said to his startled audience. "I thought I'd let you look at them."

From Elegant Professor to Humble Banker

In 1976, Yunus loaned $27 to forty-two landless people to help start a crafts business, and when they quickly repaid it, he started making other small loans out of his own pocket. With no collateral to back a loan, one of the keys was lending to people in groups, which seemed to enforce peer pressure to repay the loan. At the time Yunus was a professor of economics at Chittagong University, in the second largest city in Bangladesh. He had been a Fulbright scholar at Vanderbilt University in Tennessee, where he earned a PhD degree in economics and appeared en route to a successful academic career. But the terrible floods and famine of 1974 shook Yunus to the "core of his being" and changed his world outlook. "I used to feel a thrill at teaching my students elegant economic theories that could supposedly cure societal problems of all types," Yunus wrote in his autobiography, *Banker to the Poor*.[2] "I got carried away by the beauty and elegance of these theories. Now all of a sudden I started having an empty feeling. What good were all these elegant theories when people died of starvation on pavements and on doorsteps? I decided I would become a student all over again, and Jobra [a village outside Chittagong] would be my university. The people of Jobra would be my teachers."[3]

For the next two years Yunus led his graduate students to visit his new teachers in the village of Jobra, where he had his *eureka* moment. Interviewing a woman who made bamboo stools, he learned that she had to borrow 15 takas (Tk) to buy raw bamboo, but after paying back the loan and the middleman, kept only Tk1 (Tk70 roughly equals $1). His graduate students discovered the other forty-one villagers were in the same predicament—they could never make enough to get ahead of their loans and break this vicious lending cycle.

Yunus's mini-experiment in microcredit worked remarkably well, but lending from his own pocket was clearly impractical in the long run. Yunus tried to interest banks in adopting his idea of lending without collateral, but bankers said the poor were not creditworthy. "How do you know they are not creditworthy, if you've never tried?" asked Yunus. Perhaps, he suggested, "the banks are not people-worthy. Saying that the poor cannot be given credit is like saying man cannot fly. You can devise a way to fly, and you can find a way to make credit work."[4]

For three years he and his graduate students continued their experiments with more than 500 borrowers, until in 1979 the Central Bank agreed to operate the "Grameen Project" from seven state-run banks. In 1983, when Grameen had 59,000 clients in eighty-six branches, Yunus left academia and officially launched Grameen Bank to distribute small loans to poor villagers. Starting with preferential loans from the Central Bank and grants from groups such as the Ford Foundation, Grameen Bank became self-reliant with sufficient funds from its own deposits in 1995 and stopped taking donor money. Today Yunus claims that all Grameen Bank assets come from its customers and also that 67 percent of savings deposits are from borrowers. Grameen Bank pays from 8.5 percent to 11 percent interest on savings accounts, more than commercial banks. When a new branch is opened, the manager starts with no money; his (or her) first job is to mobilize savings for lending, and he (or she) has one year to break even.

When once asked why credit was the solution to poverty, Yunus replied: "Some economists have suggested that the solution to the problem of poverty rests in job creation. However, if employment is not designed correctly, it can just perpetuate poverty. A wage-earning job could probably keep a person in poverty forever if his income doesn't generate enough in excess of his basic needs. Thus, you could say that self-employment, supported by credit, has a greater potential to improve the resource base than wage-earning jobs."[5]

As a bank, Grameen Bank is a for-profit corporation, but Yunus often refers to Grameen as a "social business" and as a "business owned by the poor." (Ninety-plus percent of the Bank is owned by the borrowers; the rest is owned by the government.) In 2005, Grameen Bank recorded profits of $15.85 million on deposits of $487 million and loans of $610.5 million.[6] Grameen's internal surveys indicate that 58 percent of its borrowers have already escaped poverty.

Microfinance: Hedging Currency Risk

Because most microfinance lenders operate in poor countries with weak currencies subject to devaluation, Western institutions that lend to or invest in microfinance institutions (MFIs) risk low returns and defaults. Conversely, MFIs risk having to pay back dollar-denominated debts with a devalued currency. Profund, a Latin American investment pool created in 1995 to show that investing in microfinance could be commercially viable, estimated ten years later that its annualized internal rate of return would be 6.61 percent. As the *Economist* notes, "All of Profund's capital was contributed in dollars and then invested in local currency; in every country it operated in, its dollar returns were reduced by local currency depreciations, reflecting the economic chaos in much of Latin America during the decade."[7]

The Growth Guarantees of the Grameen Foundation USA (see box, "Microfinance: An Emerging Asset Class?" later in this chapter) provide a solution to this currency risk by engaging local capital markets. Donor guarantors issue a five-year standby letter of credit (SBLC), backed by assets, to Citigroup. Citigroup in turn issues SBLCs to local banks to support financing for microfinance institutions. (ACCION International first started this practice in Latin America in the 1980s.)

Each dollar provided as a guarantee is projected to be leveraged several times through a variety of structures, such as direct loans, securitizations, and bond issues. For example, a $1 million guarantee to an Indian bank might result in a loan worth $10 million in Indian rupia to an MFI. If the institution defaults on the loan, Citigroup pays $1 million. If the local currency devalues, the MFI is not holding a dollar-denominated debt, but pays back the loan in local currency. The Growth Guarantees thus engage local capital markets *and* hedge currency risk for both the lender and borrower.

Four Types of Loans

Grameen's message and methodology is simple: loan small amounts ($150 or less) to people at relatively affordable interest rates (an initial rate of 20 percent that declines with every payment), let them use the capital to develop small businesses and establish independence and self-esteem, and they will slowly break the bonds of poverty. As for customers, the poorer, the better. Widows and disabled people come first. A borrower agrees to form a group of five, with no family members. Peer pressure and peer support effectively replace collateral. There is no contract but an agreement to abide by the 16 *decisions*, which include such basics as agreeing to send children to school, use contraceptives, and eschew dowries. A woman—96 percent of the borrowers are women, whom Yunus has found to be more responsible toward their families and debts—would buy, say, a cow, produce milk for sale to neighbors, pay off the loan, and own the cow.

Yunus initially wanted half the borrowers to be women, even though women told him, "Give the loan to my husband, I don't know anything about money." After six years of giving half the loans to women, Yunus noticed that women borrowers made more productive use of their money, and began to direct all loans to women.

More recently, Yunus has begun expanding Grameen's loan activities to support mortgages and student loans, both at lower interest rates; larger loan amounts to *graduates* of microloans, so they can buy operating equipment; and loans to beggars (Project Dignity). Housing loans are made at 8 percent interest, student loans at 5 percent, and beggars pay no interest. The only rule for beggars is that they cannot pay back the loan by begging—they have to earn the money. Many have become effective door-to-door salesmen in villages, providing a service to women uncomfortable shopping in the market alone.

Despite Grameen's success Yunus has had periodic struggles in Bangladesh. Religious fundamentalists have suggested that the bank's policies are anti-Islamic; some government officials have described Grameen's lending practices as "usurious." The initial interest rates are high, although not remotely comparable to those of the usurious Kabulaki moneylenders who came out of Afghanistan and the Punjab province of western India to take advantage of starving Bengalis during the 1943 famine. But the simple (noncompounded) interest rate declines as the loan is paid down, providing an incentive to pay it off quickly. For example, even though the initial interest on a Tk1,000 loan is 20 percent, if the borrower makes regular weekly payments for a year, she pays total interest of only Tk100, equivalent to a 10 percent annual interest rate.

Given that Sharia (Islamic law) forbids interest rates at all, which is why there are no mortgages in most Islamic societies, Grameen Bank is owned by its borrowers. Yunus has rulings from Islamic scholars asserting that a bank can charge interest to itself[8]—the borrowers who are the owners—a somewhat legalistic skirting of a potentially flammable cultural issue. Still, women have been told that Grameen Bank will turn them into Christians; torture, tattoo, and sell them into prostitution in the Middle East; and deny them a proper Islamic burial. Others said that Grameen was a new version of the East India Company, looking to recolonize Bangladesh.[9] In the 1980s, rumors spread that Grameen was a front for the Americans' CIA and trying to crush the Bangladeshis' new-found independence. In 1994, a branch of Grameen was burnt down.

Whatever Muslim critics say or do, the concept works in practice now as it did in Jobra more than twenty-five years ago. Capital produces a better return in places where capital is scarce, which means that the aggregate income of a country could rise faster by investing capital in poorer regions than by putting it in richer regions.

Michael Chu, former CEO of ACCION International, a successful global pioneer of commercial microfinance and now a senior lecturer at the Harvard Business School, describes the high marginal productivity of capital where capital is scarce: "When an electric saw is introduced by a carpenter making furniture with a hammer, nails and a handsaw in his one-room dwelling, his productivity increases, not by 20 percent or 30 percent, but by various orders of magnitude. On the contrary, when one more electric saw is introduced in a furniture factory running various production lines fully equipped with electric saws, the increase in productivity may be barely noticeable." That disparity in productivity explains why poor people are willing to pay much higher interest rates than rich people. In addition, notes Chu, the rates are short-term (an effective annual interest rate in excess of 1,000 percent may translate to a $1.50 charge if paid back in two days), there are no transaction costs (in terms of paperwork or trips to the bank), and the money is more readily accessible (meaning it facilitates business transactions that otherwise might be missed).[10]

"With the benefit of hindsight, it seems clear that what prevented banking strategists from seeing the low-income populations with whom they have co-existed for hundreds of years as potential customers was one single insight: the pricing paid by the people at the base of the socio-economic pyramid bears little relation to that paid by the inhabitants at the top," writes Chu.[11]

Some very successful capitalists agree, including Vinod Khosla, founding CEO of Sun Microsystems and a partner at the venture capital firm Kleiner Perkins. Speaking at the conference on Global Business and Global Poverty at the Stanford Graduate School of Business in 2004, Khosla called microfinance "one of the most important economic phenomena since the advent of capitalism and Adam Smith."[12]

Microfinance: An Emerging Asset Class?

The demand for microloans far exceeds the current supply of available funds. Alex Counts, president and CEO of Grameen Foundation USA, a nonprofit dedicated to replicating the Grameen Bank and GrameenPhone models in countries other than Bangladesh, estimates the demand at $300 billion and the current supply at $15 billion. To meet demand, microfinance institutions need an annual injection of $2.5 to $5 billion in portfolio financing. Noncommercial investors such as development banks now disburse about $400 million a year, highlighting the need to engage capital markets. This will be a tall, but not impossible, task. In June 2006, only nineteen of the seventy-eight funds that invested in microfinance institutions showed any return on investment, and the returns didn't top 7 percent.[13]

Despite a weak track record there are signs that microfinance is a fledging asset class that has the potential to attract commercial investors. ProCredit, a German-based enterprise that funds MFIs around the world, with an investment grade rating from Fitch, floated a €45 million bond offering through Deutsche Bank at the end of 2005, the first time a microfinance entity had accessed the European capital markets on such a scale. In Latin America, several microfinance institutions have shown that they can "consistently generate returns superior to banking at the top of the pyramid," says Harvard's Michael Chu, and have successfully issued corporate bonds in local currency, typically offering a slight premium over government treasuries. Mexico's Financiera Compartamos, for example, the largest microfinance institution in Latin America, and Peru's Mibanco, together issued seven bonds between 2002 and 2004, with ratings of AA– or better, and all were oversubscribed (up to 219 percent). The buyers reflected the normal universe of the bond market: pension funds, mutual funds, public entities, insurance companies, and banks. "The purchasers of Compartamos and Mibanco bonds did not show a particular predisposition towards social issues but appear to have made their decision on purely economic grounds," says Chu.[14]

When asked about his strategy for creating Grameen Bank, Yunus underscored the kind of upside-down thinking that would attract Quadir to him.

"I didn't have a strategy," Yunus says. "I just kept doing what was next. But when I look back, my strategy was, whatever banks did, I did the opposite. If banks lent to the rich, I lent to the poor. If banks lent to men, I lent to women. If banks made large loans, I made small ones. If banks required collateral, my loans were collateral free. If banks required a lot of paperwork, my loans were illiterate friendly. If you had to go to the bank, my bank went to the village. Yes, that was my strategy. Whatever banks did, I did the opposite."[15]

Says Quadir, "Someone once asked Yunus what was the difference between the World Bank and Grameen Bank. Yunus said, 'The World Bank has a bird's-eye view of the world, and Grameen Bank has a worm's-eye view.' "

Village Phones in India

Trying to establish a link between telecommunications and economic growth in poor countries, Quadir read an article in the *Harvard Business Review* that confirmed he was on the right track.[16] To start, the author, Sam Pitroda, was not unlike Quadir, even though there were clear differences. Pitroda was Indian, born in 1942 in a small village in one of the poorest areas of rural India, with no electricity or running water. He immigrated to the United States in 1964 after earning a master's degree in physics. Despite his advanced education, at age twenty-one he had never used a telephone. A year later he had earned a master's degree in electrical engineering from the Illinois Institute of Technology and was designing electronic telephone switches. Along the way he also learned how to use a telephone. By 1974, he had thirty patents to his name and was a star designer of digital switching equipment at GTE in Chicago. His father told him he was too young to work for other people, so he quit and founded his own company. "I was also tired of getting a pat on the back and $100," says Pitroda, now in his mid-sixties and CEO of C-SAM, headquartered near Chicago (see Chapter Eight). "I was getting itchy."

Six years and twelve patents later, he sold the company to Rockwell International and pocketed 10 percent ($3.5 million). By 1980, at age thirty-eight, he was a U.S. citizen and a multimillionaire—and feeling guilty that he had "walked out on India." Quadir, thirty-six when he read Pitroda's article, hadn't yet made his millions, but he clearly identified with Pitroda's instincts to give back to his native country.

Pitroda had a three-year consulting contract with Rockwell in the early 1980s, and spent much of that time doing what Quadir would do a decade later—researching the telecom market in developing countries. In 1980, for example, 97 percent of India's 600,000 villages had no phones. In India, as in Bangladesh, which after all was a state carved out of India, phones were considered an often-unreliable urban luxury.

Pitroda saw what Quadir saw more than a decade later—the Japanese, Europeans, and Americans "were beginning to move like information greyhounds,"[17] while India and others were falling further and further behind. India's inability to communicate was more than a modern-day nuisance—it was limiting the country's ability to develop complex goods, pursue scientific study, and participate in international commerce. Pitroda saw modern telecommunications as a way for Indians to create wealth and join the global community; he also saw a telecom industry that could create its own wealth. Validation!

Pitroda decided to look for an entry into Indian telecommunications, a bureaucratic industry with one employee for every ten telephones. When he learned that Prime Minister Indira Gandhi had set up a committee to review telecom development, he met with the committee, recommending that India move away from electromechanical switches to digital systems—and that India build its own digital switches that would work in small rural exchanges for 100 to 200 telephones. "I had been looking for an entry point to come back, and I found one," says Pitroda today, who would end up spending hundreds of thousands of dollars of his own money shuttling between his Chicago-area home and India over the next decade.

Five months later, he was granted an hour-long meeting with the prime minister. He had initially been offered ten minutes, but rejected that offer, saying he couldn't make his case without more time. Finally face to face, he talked; she listened. He rattled off telecom statistics, correlating telephone density to productivity, prosperity, and GDP in about fifty countries. He opined that it was not so much wealth that created telephone density—but telephone density that created wealth. He noted India's unsatisfied demand, poor connectivity, lack of dependability, bureaucracy, bad management, and limited capital. He noted that India was importing obsolete technology and falling further behind. He pulled no punches, and then he laid out a program.

His plan emphasized rural accessibility, digital switching, privatization of far-reaching fax and e-mail networks. He offered two alternatives: make no changes and limp along until failure was assured; or adopt radical new technologies and products, design and build in India with young engineers, and aim for universal service by 2000. Universal service in a country with more than a billion people and at that time only a million phones!

Pitroda suggested issuing bonds to raise massive amounts of capital. He imagined building such a robust manufacturing capacity that India could export digital technology. He was walking the walk and talking the talk of a progressive Westerner who had seen how robust capital markets and unleashed research and development had combined to revolutionize information and communications technology. After living in the United States for so long, Pitroda's "approach to business had become performance oriented," as he wrote in the *Harvard Business Review*. "But every few weeks I left Chicago for Delhi and a set of standards and values that were feudal, hierarchical, and complex beyond belief. From my now thoroughly American point of view, India was in desperate need of modernization."[18]

Gandhi listened and absorbed the data and its conclusions. Within days she asked Pitroda to develop a plan to modernize India's telecom industry. Pitroda saw so much potential for India that he was, he said, "near to drowning in ideas and excitement." In 1984, he connected with Gandhi's son, Rajiv, and together they created the Centre for Development of Telematics (C-DOT), which was funded by Parliament with $36 million over thirty-six months.

In October 1984, Indira Gandhi was assassinated, and Rajiv became prime minister. He hired Pitroda as the principal adviser to C-DOT, at 1 rupee a year. Despite Pitroda's roots, Indians were suspicious of his interest and motives. "At the time, some university students understood what Pitroda was doing," says Mayank Chhaya, whose biography of Sam Pitroda was published in 1990.[19] "Most other people were confused. But now that they have seen the benefits of IT, now that they have seen 1 million village phones, people say, 'Wow, what a change, now I see what he was doing.' "

Pay Phones Operated by Local Entrepreneurs

Three years later C-DOT had delivered an 128-line rural exchange, a small central exchange with a capacity of 512 lines, and was ready to make a trial of a 10,000-line exchange. All were built in India— with 100 other businesses manufacturing ancillary parts.

In 1989, Rajiv appointed Pitroda chairman of the new Telecom Commission. With the power to effect change, he replaced all electromechanical long-distance exchanges with digital exchanges. Two factories were built to manufacture fiber-optic cables that were then laid to connect Bombay (now Mumbai), Delhi, Calcutta (Kolkata), and Madras (Chennai). Throughout the network, digital began replacing mechanical switches, automation replaced operators, and capacity increased considerably. And Pitroda set out to radically increase accessibility to phones by placing them in public places. After all, in a country as poor as India, few would be able to afford private phone service even if it were widely available.

Coin-operated phones were ruled out, due to high manufacturing and installation costs. Instead, C-DOT equipped regular phones with small meters and put them in the hands of entrepreneurs who set them up on tables in bazaars, on street corners, and in cafés and shops. The entrepreneurs, often handicapped people, took in cash for calls and were billed six times a year. A discount of 20 to 25 percent provided their commission and profit. They were, in effect, franchisees of the national phone system who were helping to distribute the service. Hundreds of thousands of yellow signs indicating public telephones sprung up all over India.

Shared Access in Rural Villages

Next on Pitroda's checklist was rural access. Given his roots in a poor, rural village, he was driven to place phones within three or four kilometers of every Indian citizen. That was his metric for universal access (which he admitted might seem ludicrous to an American who had a phone in every other room and who instead of walking to find a phone could leave his house carrying a phone). Years earlier, C-DOT had run a test by installing an automatic digital exchange in a town of 5,000 people. Six months after introduction of the service, bank deposits in the town rose by 80 percent, clearly demonstrating the economic impact of telecommunications.

Pitroda had set the goal of installing one rural exchange a day. By 1993, when he wrote his article for the *Harvard Business Review*, C-DOT was installing twenty-five exchanges every day, and expected 100,000 villages to have telephone service by 1995. He had done what Quadir aspired to do!

Pitroda was by then no longer chairman of the Telecom Commission. When Rajiv was defeated in parliamentary elections in 1990, Pitroda came under political fire, and later that year had a heart attack, undergoing quadruple bypass surgery. (He endured another quadruple bypass in 2005.) Pitroda went back to work but resigned his post in 1991 when Rajiv Gandhi was assassinated. He returned to Chicago, having given up his U.S. citizenship to work for the Indian government, and basically started life over again, at age fifty-three. "I got a tourist visa, but I couldn't work on a tourist visa. I had to wait in line to get my driver's license. I had to open a bank account. It was a very painful experience." And after a decade of pro bono work in India, Pitroda needed to generate income for his children's college education. He started developing the company that became C-SAM, an enterprise that develops financial-transaction software for cell phones (see Chapter Eight).

Pitroda sees the community phone, the village phone, as an instrument of social change, fundamental to democratization and dispersed power. He wrote: "Once exposed, people in rural areas want the village telephone more than they want any other community service. It can raze cultural barriers, overwhelm economic inequalities, even compensate for intellectual disparities. In short, high technology can put unequal human beings on equal footing, and that makes it the most potent democratization tool ever devised. As a great social leveler, information technology ranks second only to death."[20]

Pitroda's perception of information technology as a social leveler derives from his personal experience. He came from a poor family considered low caste (working as carpenters) but found that his association with technology put him on equal footing with world leaders. "I became the 'IT guy.' No one cares what my caste is now," he says, sitting behind his desk in a tall office building with a great view of downtown Chicago.

Dish-Wallahs of Delhi

For Quadir the most compelling model for what he aspired to do was that of the *dish-wallahs* of Delhi (as described by Jeff Greenwald in a 1993 article for *Wired* magazine[21]), rogue entrepreneurs who wired the city with satellite dishes in the early 1990s to pick up global feeds in a country until then dominated by one state-owned TV channel. Dish-wallahs, in turn, were cultural descendants of entrepreneurs who had bought VCRs in the mid-80s, connected their neighbors by stringing cable, and rented movies for a monthly charge.

Wallah is a common Hindi term that translates to "something between 'hack' and 'specialist' "[22]—hence *dish-wallah*. For less than $1,000, you could buy a dish, a few modulators, amplifiers, and hundreds of meters of cable and build a private cable TV network! You could buy the gear—signal splitters, dishes, transistors, LED displays—at the Lajpat-Rai market in Delhi, where turbaned shopkeepers hung cords of cable over paintings of Hindu gods—kind of a paean to the past.

Deepak Vishnui, for example, whom Greenwald profiled in *Wired,* was a thirty-one-year-old New Delhi electrician who borrowed 60,000 rupees (about $2,000) from his brother and eventually wired sixty apartments to his rooftop dish. In addition to making money, Vishnui's particular incentive (and marketing pitch) was to broadcast the World Cup cricket games, which the government TV network was largely ignoring. He charged each subscriber 300 rupees (about $10) for installation, and 100 rupees a month for service. To a country that three years earlier had been dependent on Indian National Television, the dish-wallahs brought in the outside world. Greenwald figured there were 200 to 300 such dish-wallahs in Delhi, with anywhere from 50 to 1,500 subscribers each, and 20,000 such networks across India.

The dish-wallahs hit pay dirt in 1990 when the United States invaded Iraq in the first Gulf War. Anyone with a twelve-foot dish could pick up CNN and news anchor Bernard Shaw and watch war—live! Kilometers of SAT cable snaked through the cities of Delhi, Bombay, and Calcutta, over trees and across roads. Rooftops were cluttered with dishes.

A year later, Star TV, broadcast out of Hong Kong, replaced CNN as the network of choice, bringing BBC Asia, MTV, Prime Sports, and Western soaps into Hindu households. In six months the number of Hindu households receiving Star jumped from 720,000 to 1.6 million. The cat was out of the bag, the slow-moving government had no clue how to regulate the revolution, and a lot of enterprising people were in business. Today Star TV is still big in Bangladesh and India—and you can watch cricket all day during the season.

Quadir loved this story for a number of reasons. It showed people's hunger for technology and indicated how technology could change the political landscape by engaging people in commerce. And it showed how you could circumvent logistical and bureaucratic hurdles by letting individuals disperse the technology. The government didn't start satellite networks, and never would have, because it had no incentive to spend money to challenge its own monopoly. Once started the networks had grown like kudzu and effectively challenged the monopoly, exactly what Quadir felt was needed to unleash the Bangladeshi tiger.

"New technologies are disruptive and change the rules of the game, and vested interests don't see it coming," says Quadir. "This happened in the U.S. with Apple Computer and America Online. Monopolies underestimate the potential impact of ICT [information communications technology] because they don't understand it, in part because they've never had competition." This would prove to be true in spades for BTTB.

Much about the dish-wallah phenomenon and Pitroda's village phone success provided a template for Quadir's project and fueled his enthusiasm. And there was something intriguing about Grameen Bank's group lending. Shared access and shared responsibility were not highly valued concepts in the capitalist West but clearly had traction in South Asia. A dish, of course, wouldn't route phone calls—you needed a central switching station for that. And unlike Pitroda, Quadir didn't have an inside track with the prime minister and the national phone system—although Yunus and Grameen Bank had innumerable political connections. Nor did Bangladesh have the engineering talent that India did. But if nothing else, the stories proved that poor people would use technology if given the chance, they would pay enough to generate cash flow for a business, and they were willing to share. The anecdotal evidence proved that Quadir was within reach of a business model.

3

Cell Phone as Cow

A New Paradigm in Search of Investors

I qbal Quadir began to dream that a profitable company could be organized to provide telecom services in Bangladesh, and it was clear that Grameen Bank would be key. The Yunus philosophy— "handouts take away initiative and help maintain poverty"—fit his own notion that cell phones weren't a luxury but a necessary productivity tool. Muhammad Yunus was not in the telecommunications business, but he had implemented a radical idea once— why not entertain another? Yunus and Grameen Bank were icons in Bangladesh, and their credibility would be important in landing a license from the government—especially if Grameen could be induced to invest. Grameen would be a perfect first customer. Most important, Grameen Bank had a rural branch operation already in place.

One of the fundamental problems in development is that it's hard to build new systems when basic systems aren't in place. The Internet took off in America only after PCs, modems, and digital phone lines were widespread commodities. In Bangladesh the state-owned Bangladesh Telephone and Telegraph Bureau (BTTB), even if it had been convinced of the positive economics of rural telephony (which it wasn't), might well have skipped rural areas due to the difficulties of sending people to live and work there. There aren't enough roads to move about freely, banks to loan and collect, or schools for children—and 80 percent of the country had no electricity. Who would leave the city to live in darkness with the poor and commit their children to an inferior education? (Today, 70 percent of Bangladesh's 148 million people still live without access to regular electricity, which opens up business possibilities for those who see the underserved rural poor as eager consumers.)

Grameen Bank had somehow broken the back of the infrastructure dilemma and was providing banking services throughout most of the country. Yunus had challenged the fundamental premise of bank lending, which held that only literate property owners could be expected to pay back a loan, and had seen his idea take hold in the most remote villages. Grameen Bank operated 1,000 branches, with 12,000 employees serving nearly 34,000 villages. (Today it operates 2,185 branches with 20,000 employees serving 69,000 villages.[1]) In a country with shoddy infrastructure, this was an amazing accomplishment. Few companies would be able to employ 12,000 people without a telephone system to connect them. More amazing, each week every Grameen borrower is in contact, theoretically, with a Grameen loan officer; the operation is very high-touch. Beyond that, Grameen is a bank, which means collecting and dispersing money is its business, and a phone company too would need to collect fees on a regular basis.

Grameen is not a bricks-and-mortar bank in the conventional Western sense. Its Dhaka headquarters is an impressive twenty-story glass building, the focal point of a complex that also houses Yunus's modest two-bedroom apartment. But its branch offices are typically small buildings or huts with filing cabinets, stacks of hand-written ledgers (which were recently computerized), and drawers filled with money—staffed by one manager and eight loan officers. Grameen doesn't bill for loan repayment; borrowers are expected to assemble weekly in a hut built for this purpose and pay cash to the loan officer, who makes a mark on a pre-printed collection sheet with installment amounts for each borrower. This sophisticated distribution network would be virtually impossible for another company to duplicate—unless, of course, it allied with BRAC, whose network was on par with Grameen's.

Quadir Meets Yunus

Iqbal Quadir had met Muhammad Yunus a few times (the first encounter was at Oberlin College in May 1993 when Yunus was receiving an honorary degree and Quadir was picking up his younger brother Kamal after his freshman year; the second was in Dhaka in October 1993), but the first time Quadir tried to interest Yunus in the possibility of connecting all Grameen's branches by phone was in Washington, D.C., at a December 1993 meeting.

"At that point, I didn't have any plan but just a general idea and somewhat sheepishly asked Yunus if he might have any interest in connecting his branches by phone," says Quadir. In a country dominated by the government, which was happy with its Dhaka-centric phone system, Grameen was the best-known institution outside the government. Grameen had a great distribution system, and Quadir, like many in the West, was an admirer of Yunus for his success in serving the poor. Quadir would later tell Yunus that the International Telecommunications Union (ITU) had produced a study showing that each new phone in a country with low income, such as Bangladesh, would add to the national GDP three times as much as the installation cost (which was $2,000 for a fixed-line phone in 1993). If you had resources and really wanted to develop a country, phones were a good way to achieve your goal—and get a good return on investment. People didn't think the poor could afford phones, but Quadir saw them as a productivity tool that could raise incomes. Perhaps drawing from Pitroda, Quadir had developed counterpoints to anyone who said the poor couldn't afford cell phones (see Table 3.1).

But at this first meeting, Quadir's idea was so unformed and tentatively presented that it made little impact. Today, Yunus doesn't even remember the conversation. At any rate, he had already built a very decentralized business that was operating smoothly. Despite

Table 3.1. Debunking Myths About Cell Phones and the Poor.

Myth	Fact
The poor can't afford phones.	Costs of communications are declining, and shared access reduces cash outlays.
Phones for the poor need to be subsidized.	The poor already pay a high price for communications by traveling long distances to reach a phone or customer.
Phones follow wealth.	Wealth follows phones.
One should aid the poor, not profit from them.	Phones are profitable and thus useful, whether used by rich or poor.
The poor need to meet primary needs (food and shelter) first.	If the poor are empowered through phones, they can assert their own needs and better meet them.

Source: GrameenPhone Annual Report, 1998, p. 35.

its green-eyeshade feel, the system worked. Why rock the boat by connecting it? Besides, Yunus was already on the world stage, and Quadir was a backstage understudy with grandiose dreams. They agreed to study the issue further.

To Quadir, Grameen Bank was a brick upon which to lay another brick. Quadir is always looking for bricks, a metaphor for solidity and strength anywhere but particularly in a muddy country with no stones and little infrastructure that happens to make tons of bricks. During the dry season, when the flood waters recede, Bangladesh's alluvial delta flats are turned into brick factories, with workers hauling mud toward tall brick chimneys for firing. The smoke mixes with bus fumes in an unpleasant way, but the by-product is solidity.

Encouraged by his meeting with Yunus even though it was inconclusive, Quadir asked one of his three younger brothers,

Khalid, to visit Bangladesh and study Grameen Bank further. (At this point six of Quadir's nine siblings and his mother were living in the United States.) A month later Iqbal and Khalid concluded that minute-to-minute communications were not of critical importance to the management of Grameen Bank, so it would not be a likely first customer.

"Iqbal was trying to convince me that cellular could be a money-making business," says Yunus. "I was asking if it is possible to provide telephone service in the rural areas, can it be made cheap enough for the poor to use it? Only when he convinced me on both counts did I become interested in applying for a license."

The truth of the matter is that Quadir himself was not fully persuaded of the project's viability. He was at the same time toying with the idea of an energy business, basing it on the fact that Bangladesh had huge, untapped reserves of natural gas, the vast majority of the country was not electrified, and electricity is necessary to power a phone network. But phones had Moore's law propelling them forward, making them a more alluring business proposition.

Connectivity and Credit

Despite its indifferent response, Grameen had so many attractive attributes as a partner that Quadir could not let go. Grameen's credibility and clout would attract outside investors and would help to win a license from the government, and its human network would help reach potential customers.

Quadir saw connectivity as a sibling of microcredit. Despite obvious differences, connectivity and credit could both empower the individual and play a large role in development. Just as credit allows a woman access to a capital-based economy, connectivity could give her access to new markets in that economy, allowing a one-person business to grow and eventually provide jobs. Like capital where capital is scarce, connectivity produces high returns where communications are scarce. Credit and connectivity empower all people, even the poor and illiterate—a key point in a country with a high rate of illiteracy. And both connectivity and credit meet basic human needs.

Stripping Grameen's credit program to its fundamental elements, Quadir probed to find a single clear link his connectivity-is-productivity notion might share with it. In 1994, walking to work one cold February morning in New York, nearly a year to the day that he first started looking into tele-density statistics, Quadir had his *eureka* moment. "Why cannot a cellular phone be like a cow?" he asked himself. Suddenly, the pieces fit together. Grameen was a perfect telecom partner!

In extending credit that allowed a poor woman to make a living by raising a cow, Grameen was essentially promoting self-employment and entrepreneurship. Why couldn't a poor woman with a credit history borrow money from Grameen Bank to buy a handset and subscribe to cellular service, then rent the phone to villagers? She would be in business. The Grameen Bank borrowers could be phone-wallahs! Even better, her business would bring a phone to a village and make it accessible to people who couldn't afford their own phones. Bangladeshi villagers could share cell phones as Indian villagers were sharing fixed-line phones.

The phone was a productivity tool that would do as much to pull people out of poverty as a loan. Rather than walk to the next village looking for a doctor, people could call ahead. Rather than sell produce at any price, farmers could shop around. In fact the phone would likely produce more revenues than a cow, which could produce only so much milk. The phone could produce as much air-time as there are minutes in the day. Poor countries don't have as many resources as rich countries, but they both have the same number of minutes in a day. Bottom line: the cell phone would promote self-employment and complement Grameen's socially responsible development ideology. Like most new paradigms it was so obvious, so clear, in retrospect.

Quadir quickly wrote up a plan to provide cellular coverage for the whole of Bangladesh by leveraging Grameen Bank's network and customers. Imagine a graphic showing loan money going from the bank to a woman who buys a cow and sells milk to repay the loan (see Figure 3.1). Replace the cow with a phone (see Figure 3.2), and repeat, tens of thousands of times over.

Quadir sent the plan to Yunus and then visited him in Dhaka in March 1994. On hearing of the opportunity to apply for a cellular license to operate a phone company in Bangladesh, and the idea of taking cell phones into the villages, Yunus wrote in his autobiography, "It sounded like an exciting idea."[2] Quadir, talking to *The WorldPaper* in 1998, remembers it like this: "In March 1994, Yunus informally gave me a challenge. 'If you think it's doable, come and do it.'"[3]

Figure 3.1. Cow as Income Source.

Source: Iqbal Quadir.

Figure 3.2. Cell Phone as Cow.

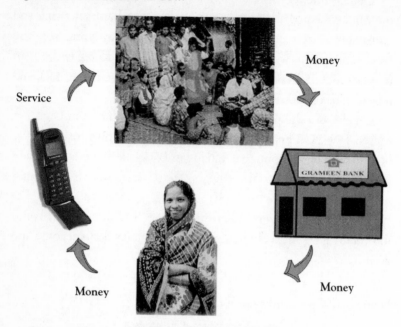

Source: Iqbal Quadir.

Yunus liked the idea, but neither he nor Quadir knew how to implement it. Their combined knowledge of telecommunications could have fit on the head of a pin. But with Grameen's tentative blessing, Quadir had a brick in place—a cornerstone brick. Now he needed money—and know-how.

The Hunt for Foreign Investors

The positive message from Grameen Bank was encouraging, but the burden of proof still lay with Quadir. Grameen, for example, was not about to put up money. However, money was one brick Quadir might be able to supply as he was a financier of sorts at the time. He was vice president of Atrium Capital Corp., a venture capital firm in New York City (since relocated to Menlo Park, California). Although Atrium's projects were of no particular relevance to this project, Quadir at least had some idea of how to raise money.

Of course raising venture money in the United States is a far cry from raising it in or for Bangladesh. Most of the money flowing into Bangladesh around 1994 came from the World Bank or other international financial institutions or from the more than 2 million Bengalis working in the Middle East and elsewhere who sent money home. Bangladesh was not exactly on the radar screen for foreign investors at that time. "We would not go to Bangladesh," said an executive at a U.S. cellular operator when Quadir approached him about a partnership. "We are not the Red Cross."

At this point Quadir's heart and soul were totally committed to his phone project, to the extent that he was ready to quit his New York job and devote himself full time to it. The cow paradigm had convinced Quadir that the phone business was viable and a better business proposition than energy. Temporarily giving up on cellular operators as investors or partners, he turned toward individuals for angel support. Through his brother Khalid (who has recently started a wireless networking company in Bangladesh; see Chapter Eleven), Quadir had earlier met Joshua (Josh) Mailman (both Khalid Quadir and Mailman are graduates of Middlebury College). Mailman is the founder of the Social Venture Network, a network of entrepreneurs promoting social ventures around the world, and had been an early investor in Global TeleSystems (GTS), the first private telecommunications firm in Russia, in which George Soros was a big investor.

Mailman had initially pledged $250,000 to pursue Quadir's energy project, but he liked the phone idea better, given his experience in Russia. If Quadir would devote two years to the project, Mailman would put up $125,000, a small but effective start for a dream that would eventually attract and absorb hundreds of millions of dollars. Together, they would own Gonofone Development Corp. In Bengali, *gonofone* means "phones for the masses." Quadir added *development* to the name to underscore the company's ultimate goal. The company was registered in New York in May 1994.

Quadir quit his job in New York and moved to Bangladesh, ready to dive into the project. He had no background in telecommunications and a limited background in development, and he hadn't lived in Bangladesh for nearly twenty years. But he had been building a core philosophy about the role of business in development, and this was as good an opportunity to test his ideas as he was likely to see. If you wanted to measure the impact of phones on society, the rural areas of Bangladesh were a tabula rasa.

Cellular operators were making good money everywhere, so Quadir figured he would eventually convince one to take a shot at Bangladesh. The digital revolution was in full swing, with Moore's law probably as well known to American teenagers as the Pythagorean theorem. The number of transistors, and thus the data density, on a microchip were doubling every eighteen months. That was a given. So was Quadir's theory that connectivity is productivity. Pitroda had proved it in India. The flow was going in his direction.

Not that Quadir was strictly analytical about the opportunity. He was also feeling a strong emotional pull back to his native land. After all, in 1994 the American economy was beginning to rev up for its longest and largest expansion since World War II, and Quadir was in venture capital in New York. If he had been strictly analytical, he would have stayed put, made his nut, and *then* experimented in Bangladesh. That's what Pitroda had done; that was the style for émigrés.

"Some people, maybe some of my family, thought maybe I had failed in the U.S. and was returning home. But I had an idea I couldn't let go of," says Quadir, assessing what had been an unusually bold move. "I had made $257,000 the year before through a windfall deal, had a green card, and had fulfilled my residency requirements. So I had some money and knew I would be eligible for U.S. citizenship in two years. In all, the opportunity cost was not too high. Had I been a partner, say, at Goldman Sachs, it's hard to speculate what I would have done."

Building a Case for Bangladesh

The young nation of Bangladesh had lived intermittently under martial law from the time of the murder of Sheikh Mujibur Rahman in 1975 (a year before Quadir left for college in the States) until 1991, when the widow of General Zia, who had succeeded Mujib, was elected prime minister. The political situation was still somewhat tumultuous, with numerous *hartals* (strikes) organized by opposition parties to shut down commerce. In the years since Quadir had left, the country had exploded in size, from 75 million to 120 million, and Dhaka had grown from 1 million to 9 million.

Organizing a new life in Dhaka was somewhat painstaking and required cultural readaptation. Quadir had friends in Dhaka, but virtually all of his immediate family (except two sisters) had emigrated to the United States. One of his Dhaka friends was a Wharton classmate whose female cousin Quadir had met several times on previous visits. Within two months they were married. "We don't go for long courtship like people do in the States; we have arranged marriages in Bangladesh. But in my case, I arranged the marriage," says Quadir, who has a peevish sense of humor. "I feel more comfortable in America, but I never really assimilated. I'm still Bangladeshi."

Quadir bought an apartment, car, and computer and applied for a telephone. A year later, thanks to high-level contacts he had cultivated at BTTB, he would get his phone installed. Less-connected customers often waited five to ten years for service.

Moving from meeting to meeting throughout the day, he used his car as his office. Even in Dhaka, there was little telephone culture. If you wanted to see people, you slogged through traffic, a cacophonous mélange of animals, people, rickshaws, cars, buses, and three-wheeled tuk-tuks (so-called because of the sound their two-stroke engines made). Then you waited outside the office of the person you wished to see, drank tea, and took your chances. "Getting anything done was almost impossible," says Quadir, who had arrived with the same go-go American mentality that Pitroda had brought to India. "The only people who used phones were the top managers, and they'd sit in their office reading the newspaper while assistants dialed and dialed before announcing a connection."

Driving through traffic, inhaling black smoke, avoiding eye contact with crippled beggars, Quadir imagined how modern telecommunications might unleash the energy of his native land. Bangladeshis were incredibly hard-working. The streets were lined with shops, and the shops were filled with customers. Dhaka was growing, with barefoot workers pouring concrete slabs everywhere. The poor communications in the country as a whole were largely responsible for the extremely high real-estate prices in Dhaka, which mirrored those in Boston; if you wanted to talk to people you had to live near them. In the West, broadband Internet communications were taking off, creating wealth upon wealth, not to mention connectivity that was driving economies. For Quadir, who was used to an office in midtown Manhattan, it was this gap between the two cultures and economies that kept propelling him forward.

And he was propelled. Within a few months of arriving in Bangladesh, Quadir started firing off memo after memo to Grameen Bank officers, hammering home point after point, building a case. Here, for example, is one titled "Some Thoughts on Grameen Telecom":

> I believe that Grameen will be able to prove that the rural market is attractive. First, the rural market is not competitive. Second, it represents 80% of Bangladesh, which is not made up of only "poor" people. "Rich" farmers also live there. Cities of Dhaka (9 million) and Chittagong (4 million) are a recent phenomenon. The urban population has immediate roots in the rural areas. Most workers and food supplies in the cities come from the rural areas.

Note that rural people already pay more for communications than the urban people in Bangladesh. We will spend only Tk3 from Mirpur to make a phone call to Karwan Bazaar to check the price of rice or to Stadium Market to check the price of a refrigerator. A village person will spend considerably more time and money to obtain a correspondingly important piece of information for him. Thus, just as Grameen found it necessary to charge 20% for a loan to the poor when the rich borrow at 10%, it may not be necessary to make telecom service cheaper in the rural areas than in the urban areas.[4]

Who was this American who had landed in Dhaka? Yunus took notice and offered Quadir the use of Grameen's computer center and phone (although Quadir was responsible for paying for what would be hundreds of international phone calls). Yunus also introduced Quadir to Khalid Shams, who as deputy managing director was known as the "number-two man" at Grameen Bank.

Shams, who holds one master's degree in political science from Dhaka University and another in economic development from Harvard, had an excellent record in public service. In 1964, he finished number one on the competitive Pakistani public service examination (his friends still marvel at this today). A calm but impassioned professional, Shams quickly became a believer in the project, and over time his ability to solve complex problems and his government contacts proved to be invaluable. (Shams is now managing director of Grameen Telecom and was chairman of GrameenPhone from 1998 to 2006.)

Finding Gold in the Mud

To bolster his argument for a telecom partner, Quadir continued researching the country's economy and tracking signs of a government tender for cellular licenses. En route he found a Coopers &

Lybrand study on telecommunications in Bangladesh, commissioned by the World Bank and completed in 1992. One piece of information jumped off the page: Bangladesh Railway (BR) had laid a fiber-optic cable along its tracks.

The railroad had installed the cable to upgrade its own dilapidated phone system connecting 300 stations, as it had historically found it difficult to run a railroad without good communications. What a surprise! How vast areas of the country functioned without telephones was a miracle. Now, to amortize maintenance costs, BR was looking to lease the fiber. What a find! For a telecom operator, fiber was gold.

In the mid-1980s, BR had applied for help from international development agencies, and the Norwegian Agency for Development and Cooperation (NORAD) had responded. NORAD's proposal was to lay a copper cable along the tracks, but Mokkaram Yahya, BR's telecommunications director, pleaded for fiber optic. That was exceptionally farsighted; at the time fiber-optic cables were new even in developed countries. In fact the organization that was to become Qwest Communications in the United States, which later bought US WEST and bid to buy MCI in 2005, got its start at about the same time by laying fiber along the Southern Pacific and other railroad right-of-ways and used that as its springboard to wealth. Yahya argued that the slightly more expensive fiber-optic cables would open up unlimited possibilities in the future. NORAD bought the argument, and by 1990 had laid 1,800 kilometers of fiber at a cost of $30 million. Four years later that cable lay virtually dormant under the mud and silt.

Quadir was fired up (he fires up easily) and went to see Yahya (who is now director of fiber-optics for GrameenPhone). Quadir was surprised to learn that Yahya had tried several times to lease the fiber-optic cable to BTTB, but the railway and telephone arms of the government could not cut a deal. Given that impasse, there was a great opportunity for a private party to lease the fiber. Like others, Quadir saw the fiber as another potential brick for the rural network.

Although it was certainly possible to operate a network without fiber-optic cable (you could install microwave receivers or bounce signals off satellites), fiber made connecting a call between two points, say, 250 kilometers apart, much more efficient. Sending a call 22,000 miles up to a satellite and then 22,000 miles down to its intended target was expensive and slow. Bouncing a call from microwave tower to microwave tower, with the range between towers affected by the curvature of the earth and the interference of buildings, is not nearly as reliable as sending a call underground along a fiber-optic cable. Fiber is faster, cheaper, and more reliable than satellite or microwave—and it already was lying in the soft earth of Bangladesh.

This was a great piece of new information to bring to a foreign investor. The need for a foreign investor was clear, as the only player in Bangladesh that might have stepped up was the player that held all the cards, BTTB. Making a handsome, monopolistic profit off the current phone system, which existed almost exclusively in the two main cities of Dhaka (70 percent) and Chittagong (20 percent), BTTB had little reason to expand. Its long-distance rates were exorbitantly high, partly because of low capacity and partly because of no competition. Having labeled cellular as a marginal business in a poor country, much as Western investors had, BTTB didn't much care that the government was proposing to hand over cellular communications to private parties.

Initial efforts to land a U.S. cellular operator had proved fruitless. That made sense, as cellular was a much bigger business in Europe and Asia than in the United States, where the fixed network was so extensive and efficient. Through Atrium Capital, Quadir had met George Lindemann, who regularly appears on the Forbes 400 Richest Americans list.[5] He had started the Metro Mobile cell phone company, which he sold to Bell Atlantic in 1992 for $2.6 billion, and had a penchant for spotting investment opportunities in new areas before the crowd. Lindemann was encouraging, but he couldn't assess the viability of a project far from New

York, both literally and figuratively. Plus there was still so much opportunity in the United States, why look for trouble on the frontier? But Quadir learned a lot about the cellular business from his discussions with Lindemann.

Bangladesh was clearly a special case that would require a special investor. Quadir trained his sights on Scandinavia, where cellular telephony had first taken off in the early 1990s, and which had already produced money to lay fiber. When in doubt, follow the money trail.

4

On the Money Trail in Scandinavia

Because cellular operations were most successful in Scandinavian countries, Iqbal Quadir reasoned, Nordic telephone companies might provide the best know-how and have the confidence to take a risk. They had jointly planned and put into operation the very first international cellular system, Nordic Mobile Telephone (NMT) in 1981 (450 MHz), followed by a 900 MHz service in 1986, and then GSM in 1992. In 1995, 22 percent of Norwegians used a cellular phone, the highest cellular penetration in the world. Today, the percentage of residents with mobile phone numbers is higher in the European Union than in the United States.

Given their countries' relatively small populations, Scandinavian companies were active in new markets. Following their successful expansion into Eastern Europe, Scandinavians were more comfortable than Americans when dealing with weak infrastructure, low purchasing power, and bureaucratic governments—which would *begin* to describe Bangladesh. In the United States, cellular operations were urbancentric; in Scandinavia, coverage was universal, which is what Quadir envisioned for Bangladesh. Finally, telephone companies in Nordic countries were largely state run, and the Nordic states were particularly sensitive to the development needs of Bangladesh, as evidenced by the early investment in fiber made by the Norwegian Agency for Development and Cooperation

(NORAD). These were the kind of points that marked Quadir's memos; much like a lawyer arguing to a jury, he liked to build a case with a preponderance of evidence.

Through a Swedish lawyer friend, Bertil Nordin in New York (who had registered Gonofone), Quadir set up a meeting with Yjro Sirkeinen, the managing director of Telecon, a telecommunications consulting firm owned by Finnish Telecom. Quadir was eager to make inroads in Finland, home to Nokia, the global leader in cellular phones. Sirkeinen agreed to do a feasibility study in Bangladesh, if Quadir could find funding. Quadir hoped to use the study to approach Finnish Telecom.

Quadir persuaded Muhammad Yunus to write a letter acknowledging Grameen Bank's interest in the "Gonofone Project," which Quadir took to Helsinki in July 1994. But Sirkeinen had bad news: Finnish Telecom had no interest in Bangladesh. He suggested Finnet, another Finnish company. Gunnulf Martenson, managing director of Finnet International, was not encouraging, but he gave Quadir more names. Quadir sat in a hotel lobby desperately making phone calls all over Scandinavia from a pay phone. Bo Magnusson, manager of business development at Telia International, the international project company of the state-run telephone operator in Sweden, agreed to a meeting. Quadir flew to Stockholm.

Magnusson was intrigued. A country of 120 million people with no phones and no competition—what's not to like? The fact that Bangladesh was poor was perfect—it would scare away competitors. Like Quadir, Magnusson saw the price of handsets declining to the point that broad market acceptance was around the corner. He didn't have time to discuss the project further but asked Quadir to come back in three weeks.

On Quadir's return Magnusson gave him a formal letter indicating a high level of interest. It was the first time a credible telephone company had recognized the value of deploying cellular technology across all of Bangladesh. Telia, however, did not want to go it alone; it wanted to partner with Telenor (at that time called

Norwegian Televerket), the national telephone company in Norway, with which Telia had invested in Italy and Hungary. Nonetheless, Quadir was boosted by the vote of confidence from such a major player.

Letter in hand, Quadir returned to Dhaka to learn that the Ministry of Posts and Telecommunications was preparing to float a tender for a cellular license. The announcement was made on the fifth anniversary of the issuance of the first cellular license in Bangladesh, to a company called Pacific Bangladesh Telecom United (PBTL). PBTL had been offered a five-year window of exclusivity, which it had used to market the high-cost CityCell service to elite business customers in Dhaka. (CityCell remains a small player in today's increasingly competitive Bangladeshi telecom market.) Tender documents would be issued by August 15, 1994, with bids due September 30. It was now August 1! The race was on, and Gonofone was not close to the starting gate. Then, after a period of confusion, the deadline was extended until November 30.

Quadir purchased tender documents and delivered them to Sweden in mid-August, when most Scandinavians were on vacation, enjoying nearly twenty-four hours of daylight. "They like their fjords," says Quadir, "and once in them they don't come out." But the trip was not entirely useless. He managed to persuade Telia to send a representative to Bangladesh to begin work on the proposal. In early September, Amir Zai Sangin, a native of Afghanistan with a good reputation as a radio engineer, arrived.

The day after he arrived the political opposition party, Awami League, called for a *hartal* in Dhaka. With the city shut down by rock-throwers, Quadir and Sangin walked the eight kilometers from the Dhaka Sheraton, where Sangin was staying, to Grameen Bank and arrived in Yunus's office drenched in sweat. With the appearance of Sangin, however unsightly, Yunus and Khalid Shams began to envision how the project might ultimately unfold. Quadir was just glad Sangin was an Afghani and not a Swede who might have been less tolerant of the insane politics and brutal heat.

Treaties to Protect Foreign Investors

International law does not protect investors in foreign countries. If a government seizes assets of a foreign national, there is no dependable legal recourse. To compensate for the lack of international legal protections for foreign investors, more than 2,200 bilateral investment treaties (BITs) between developed and developing countries have now been signed. More than 1,500 of them have been signed in the last decade as foreign investment has increased around the world. These treaties protect foreign investors by giving them the same rights as national investors against expropriation of funds without fair and immediate recompense. A World Bank arbitration tribunal adjudicates any claims. The United States has signed more than 30 BITs (including one with Bangladesh that was ratified in 1989) and has increasingly inserted investment protection language into trade treaties (starting with NAFTA, the North American Free Trade Agreement). And while most BITs are between a developed and developing nation, in the last decade more than 800 "South-South" BITs have been signed between developing countries, with China being the leading signatory.[1] Norway does not have a BIT with Bangladesh.

Telia sent two more people to Bangladesh in early October, and then Quadir went back to Sweden to finalize the proposal. He returned to Dhaka a few days before the November 30 deadline. But at the last minute the tender process was put on hold by an injunction from the Bangladesh Supreme Court. PBTL had complained that it had not in fact been given a full five-year window, as the government had not immediately given it interconnection with the fixed network owned by the Bangladesh Telephone and Telegraph Bureau (BTTB). Whether this was true or whether PBTL was merely using its government connections to extend its monopoly on cellular operations, Quadir didn't care. He would use the extra time to prepare a stronger proposal—if he could keep his coalition together. And he made a mental note about interconnection difficulties with BTTB.

The owner of CityCell, who came from the same village as Yunus, was also encouraging Grameen to buy a majority or minority stake in CityCell. But Yunus told him he was looking to persuade American or European investors to apply for a new license and didn't want to buy into an existing company.

Grameen's Due Diligence

Extra time cuts both ways. You have more time to marshal forces and prepare. People can also lose focus and interest—or begin to think twice about what had once seemed to be a done deal. In the next six months, time indeed cut both ways on the Gonofone project.

Right after the injunction halting the tender was issued, Sam Pitroda visited Bangladesh, at Yunus's invitation, for a conference organized by Grameen Bank. Following his success in implementing rural networks, Pitroda was on the verge of becoming the first CEO of WorldTel, a World Bank–style institution intended to bring telephony to poor countries. Pitroda confirmed for Yunus that despite Grameen's lack of experience in telecommunications, it could play a meaningful role. "I told Yunus the days of fixed lines were over—if he wanted to go into the villages like I had done in India, cellular was the way to go," says Pitroda.

Pitroda, of course, was talking as an engineer who had worked with the prime minister of India. Despite his rural roots, Pitroda was a top-down guy; Yunus was a bottom-up guy. Nonetheless, Pitroda's reputation as a brilliant telecommunications engineer in America and implementer of networks in India made his affirmation extremely powerful. While Pitroda was in Bangladesh, Yunus had him meet with government officials to lobby on Grameen's behalf.

Grameen also asked NORAD to fund a consultant to assess the feasibility of Grameen's entrée into communications. "There was a fear factor for both me and Yunus, because neither of us really knew anything about telecommunications," says Quadir.

NORAD hired Teleplan, a Norwegian consulting firm, to advise Grameen Bank. After two weeks of study, Teleplan concurred that telecommunications was a perfect addition to Grameen's portfolio, given telecom's important role in development. However, GSM (Global System for Mobile Communications), according to Teleplan, was not the right technology. GSM was new and included a large number of sophisticated functions that poor people would never use. GSM was the "Mercedes of cellular technology"; Bangladesh needed a Volkswagen. This was, on a technical level, the equivalent of saying that cell phones were a luxury poor people didn't need.

This view was a serious challenge to the project, as Telia knew and believed in GSM, despite experience with other technologies. Telia and Telenor, in fact, were two of the players which specified the original GSM design, first commercially implemented in Finland in 1991. Telia had organized its business to develop and deploy GSM and certainly had no interest in retooling for Bangladesh. Whether it was the perfect solution or not was immaterial. Equally important, the government's allocated frequencies were in the GSM band. That meant GSM was a virtual necessity for the proposal.

Quadir moved quickly to put the issue to rest, before Grameen had a chance to buy into the consultant's argument. His simple logic was as follows. Digital cellular phones are mostly microchips and software. The reproduction cost of a copy of a microchip and software is close to zero, irrespective of complexity. It costs the same for Microsoft to make a copy of Microsoft *Word* whether it has 100 special functions or 1,000. This is not true for cars. The cost to the manufacturer of copying (reproducing) a Mercedes is much higher than the cost of copying a Volkswagen. So much for the car analogy.

As to whether first-time phone users would need all the conceivable functions of a GSM phone, does the average person use all the functions of Microsoft *Word*? No, and he or she does not suffer one iota, in expense or difficulty, for not fully using everything the technology offers.

Making GSM even more appealing to Quadir, it is by design an open system. That means any manufacturer can produce GSM components, and components from different manufacturers should work together. This would lead to competition and rapid price declines, just as the cost of IBM PC clones dropped through the floor in the mid-1980s. In the end, there was just no reason to turn away from GSM. Today, 70 percent of all phones in the world use GSM technology, which facilitates international roaming.

Scandinavia, Round Two

That tempest tamed, Quadir returned to Stockholm in January 1995 to feel Telia's pulse. It was beating somewhat more slowly, partly because of uncertainties around the tender date. But Telia was also bidding for cellular licenses in India, where there were no delays. India's open-door policy for attracting foreign investors, started in 1991, was speeding up the pace of business there. It was becoming clear that Telia was losing interest; Magnusson, out of sympathy, sent Quadir to Norway to see Telenor's Odd Synvis, a gracious man who described the idea of introducing cell phones to Bangladeshi villages as "beautiful." He had been to the villages and had fallen in love with the whole idea, as many do who visit rural Bangladesh.

Synvis had seen people working the paddies in small groups, plowing the wet ones to prepare for planting in the dry ones, uprooting seedlings from the green to replant in the brown. He had seen women in the villages drying and husking harvested rice on cement or dirt by spreading it thin and flat, before building it into mounds and then scooping it into baskets. He'd seen men and women along the road carrying huge baskets and rolled wheat bales on their heads. He'd seen children playing cricket in the paddies. And he imagined them carrying cell phones.

Synvis's boss, Knut Digured, indicated that Telenor was also bidding in India. There's a natural rivalry between Bangladesh and India. Its root is the Muslim-Hindu antagonism, but it has been exacerbated by what Bangladesh perceives as India's unfair trading practices—that is, India sells to, but does not buy from, Bangladesh. (However, the huge Indian conglomerate Tata Group recently pledged to invest $3 billion in Bangladesh, by far the biggest investment ever in that country; see more in Chapter Eleven.) At any rate, hearing about India as a preferred target for the second time in two days put Quadir in full prosecutor mode—relentlessly laying out one point after another. If questioned on one of his assertions, he would respond, "Let me respond to your point with this point," or, "Yes, that's a good point, let me make another point." Then he'd later swoop back to specifically address the other person's point.

Arguing the Case for Bangladesh Versus India

Quadir argued that Bangladesh had a slightly lower per capita GDP than India ($250 to $300) but that income was actually slightly higher in Bangladesh ($1,650 to $1,500) if one considered the prices of goods in the two countries. Quadir was using the PPP (purchasing power parity) methodology that economists use to compare countries with widely different currency and price valuations; it estimates what it would cost to buy a given *basket of goods*. According to World Bank data—Quadir was now pulling from the voluminous research he had conducted while waiting for the tender offer—the income distribution (the percentages of the population falling into given income bands) and nonagricultural activities were virtually the same in Bangladesh and India. Digerud nodded gracefully, as if enjoying the lecture.

In terms of telecommunication investments—drum roll!—Bangladesh was clearly the better bet. Yes, India was a far bigger country. With approximately 15 percent of the world's population, it was a good-sized market. But the area under any one licensee was not going to be bigger than Bangladesh in area or population. The telephone penetration in Bangladesh was presently one-fourth that of India (this was one of the first facts Quadir had stumbled on in his early research), meaning a much lower saturation of the market. Bangladesh wanted foreign investors and allowed majority (up to 100 percent) ownership by foreigners—India did not. And, Quadir assured Digured, foreign remittances from abroad were much higher in Bangladesh on a per capita basis, and this money could be expected to contribute to the telecom sector. Not only that, the huge number of expatriate Bengalis created a natural "network effect," as almost every family knew someone overseas to talk to. Finally, the rest of the world's absolutely terrible perception of Bangladesh had kept and would keep the AT&Ts, BTs (British Telecom), and NTTs (Nippon Telegraph and Telecom) away, far away. In short, if you liked India, you should love Bangladesh. It was a telecom investor's dream—low saturation, no hills, no competition. Digured nodded somewhat nervously.

Quadir took that as a sign to continue. He waxed poetic about the beauty of poverty. Bangladesh had faced massive humanitarian problems after wars and floods. That had forced a government with limited capacity to allow NGOs to flourish in order to provide necessary services. Where there was no economic incentive, the government would cede power to others. This in turn had led to a dispersion of power that somewhat mitigated the power of the centralized government bureaucracies that typically plague other poor countries.

Quadir used this complex logical train as a springboard to his next point: Thanks to the many successful NGOs, the earning power of the lowest-income group was demonstrably rising. Grameen Bank was the most prominent but certainly not the only NGO success story. The Bangladesh Rural Advancement Committee (BRAC), for example, had started in 1972 and was providing financial, health, education, and job training services in virtually all of Bangladesh's villages. National income would continue to rise thanks to the new export orientation sparked by the apparel industry and the rise of a new class of entrepreneurs. Bangladesh now had nearly 2,000 garment factories (in 1994), five times as many as a decade before. The tiger economies of Thailand and Malaysia had been sparked by their garment-based export orientation. And partly because the garment industry employed more than a million women, the population growth rate had slowed from 3 percent to 2 percent. In Pakistan (another Bangladesh rival), the rate was stuck at 3 percent. Bangladesh was creating a modern Muslim woman, one who worked, wore cosmetics, carried a purse—and didn't wear a burqa.

Grasping at Straws

Digerud listened but said Telenor would not go in without Telia. Perhaps he had filled in the blanks that Quadir had left out: Bangladesh was a poor, agrarian country—nearly 80 percent of the population was rural and officially classified as poor by the World Bank, and 60 percent of the economy was agrarian—not exactly the target market for a cell phone operator used to catering to well-heeled Norwegians. Perhaps he had read a 1995 investment report by UBS Global Research, which was tracking the hot Asian markets. The report concluded: "As one of the world's most esoteric emerging markets, Bangladesh is not really featuring heavily on most investor's radar screens at the moment. However, one day, emerging markets will come back to fashion and then good money will be made in Bangladesh."[2] An esoteric emerging market out of fashion? Not encouraging.

A month later, in February 1995, Telia officially dropped out. Telia had won two licenses in India and had no more appetite for South Asia. In addition, in the increasingly deregulated markets of Scandinavia, Telia and Telenor were becoming more competitors than partners. With Telia out, Telenor's resolve continued to weaken. Quadir kept calling and writing Synvis, essentially recapitulating the litany of reasons why Bangladesh made sense for Telenor. The correspondence was increasingly one way. Quadir didn't immediately give Yunus and Shams the hard truth, waiting for good news to cancel the bad.

Two months after Telia dropped out, Synvis (who was to die prematurely shortly thereafter) called to say that if Grameen could secure the railroad fiber-optic cable, Telenor would go to Bangladesh. That was positive news, but leasing the fiber was a tall order. A transaction of that magnitude would certainly be a long and arduous bureaucratic process. Beyond that, without a telecom partner, Grameen would have no credibility as a potential lessor. So Gonofone faced a chicken-or-egg dilemma.

Quadir also faced a more direct personal problem in that his wife was expecting their first child and he had spent his savings plus most of the $125,000 from Josh Mailman. To keep going, he sold a small stake he had earned in a biotech firm through his work with Atrium, cashing out and forsaking the opportunity for a much bigger payday down the road. The firm at the time was making great progress in developing cancer treatments. Shams was worried about Quadir's ability to made ends meet, and offered him a consulting job at Grameen Fund, a newly formed venture capital unit that funded entrepreneurs in rural areas. Quadir worked one day a week as an adviser to the manager of the fund, drawing a monthly salary of Tk10,000 ($250), which happened to be the average annual per capita income of the country.

A New Push for Investors

With progress stalled Quadir pursued a third-party study. He met with a firm in London, hoping that independent confirmation of the project's feasibility would sway Telenor. But he didn't have the money for the study, and Grameen wouldn't put it up. Yunus suggested approaching NORAD, where Grameen had an admirer of the project, Mette Jorstad. She quickly got approval to fund half of a $100,000 study, with the contingency that the consulting firm be Norwegian.

While looking for a consulting firm (he certainly didn't want to get Teleplan engaged again), Quadir started a new search for investment partners. He met with Marco Huberts, a Dutchman who ran the Singapore office for Alcatel, a French company that was helping BTTB establish 150,000 new digital phone lines in Bangladesh. Huberts liked the Gonofone idea, and connected Quadir to a telecom company in Thailand, named UCOM. Herbie Gladhill of UCOM came to visit with Yunus and Shams, and liked the Gonofone idea. But Gladhill didn't like the idea that Grameen Bank was not investing in the project. That was a deal breaker.

Quadir used that rejection as an opportunity to persuade Grameen to invest. To that end, he wrote several concept documents portraying a putative Grameen Telecom as a "people-based" company (playing off the Gonofone name), with both cellular and data networks reaching into villages. Clearly, Grameen's "skin in the game" would be attractive to a foreign investor. Domestic investment sends the strongest possible signal to a foreigner that there's some reason to join the party. If domestic capital flees (*flight capital*) or remains on the sidelines, there must be a reason for it. Insiders should know better than outsiders what's really going on inside a country, especially a country that ranked near the bottom of the barrel in transparency.

If the Gonofone Project ever got off the ground, Quadir argued, Grameen's development agenda might be in jeopardy if the bank didn't have a clear stake in the business. Telia had once promised a 15 percent share as "free" equity to Grameen Bank, just for the use of Grameen's good name and distribution system. But Grameen needed more than equity—it needed enough clout to control and protect its development agenda. Grameen's recalcitrance created another chicken-or-egg dilemma—who was going to be first in? At this point only one wealthy New Yorker had had the guts to put his money on the table.

Quadir fired off another memo to Grameen: "To Invest or Not to Invest?"

> Now that Grameen has decided to get involved in a cel-
> lular project, it faces an important decision. Should it

invest in the consortium company which would be owning a license to operate and the necessary hardware?
Before we answer this question, there are two issues to
be settled:

1. What is Grameen's real goal with regards to this
project? Its real goal is to provide cost-effective telecommunications in rural areas. Grameen has decided on this
goal because it finds telecommunications to be a natural
next step in its evolution. Information is like credit.
Both credit and communications empower without
reducing choice. A hallmark in Grameen's credit program is that borrowers themselves choose in which businesses they apply the money they borrow. Similarly,
telecommunications will allow them to communicate
without dictating the content of communication. Thus,
if credit constitutes the heart of Grameen, telecommunications has the potential to be its lungs.

2. Should Grameen decide to invest in this project
depending on whether funds are available? The answer is
NO. The right question to ask: Is the above goal (of providing effective telecommunications) furthered by investing? We should not confuse this question with Grameen's
ability, or the lack of ability, to invest. Grameen should
decide to invest if (a) it furthers its goal described in
(1) and (b) it is prudent to invest in the project from a
financial standpoint, without considering the availabil-
ity of funds. Once a decision is made on the merits of the
investment, we can always channel our energy and cre-
ativity in finding funds. In short, we should first decide
whether it is a good idea to invest in the first place.

The project has almost a perfect match with Grameen's
purpose, outlook and strengths. The only area of mis-
match is that we compete with greedy speedy capitalists
and we risk being outmaneuvered by them.[3]

Despite the difficulty of attracting an investor, Quadir did feel a sense of urgency. "The opportunity was so great, it wouldn't sit there forever," he says. "Already, I'd heard rumblings about our 'NGO status,' that we were not a serious business. We needed to act fast."

Persistence (Finally) Pays

On July 1, 1995, Quadir's wife, Samina, delivered their first child, a daughter. "It was one of the happiest days of my life, when I was at one of the lowest points of my career," says Quadir. "I had very little money."

Shortly thereafter, the Supreme Court allowed the government to go ahead with the tender. Quadir notified Telia and Telenor. By this point (August 1995), Grameen Bank had registered Grameen Telecom as a nonprofit entity (see Chapter Five) and purchased the tender documents, a sign that it was getting more serious about investing. But the clock was ticking.

Quadir had no money to travel to Oslo for another pitch to Telenor. He did have an old return ticket to New York via London, but he didn't have the courage to ask Mailman for more money. Grameen finally put up travel expenses, and Quadir went to Oslo. When he told Synvis about the NORAD consulting deal, Synvis's eyes brightened. Telenor International had a consulting arm called Telenor Consult, which had worked with NORAD. He got approval to spend $25,000 the next day, and Yunus agreed to match that so Gonofone had the necessary $100,000. (In the end, NORAD picked up 75 percent of the fee, absolving Grameen's responsibility.) This was a better pace, more American.

With the feasibility study under way, Quadir took the overnight train from Oslo to Stockholm to talk to Telia one more time. You never know. Magnusson was out of town, but Quadir met with one of his more junior colleagues. He said Telia was working on a proposal for Nepal. Nepal? Quadir was nonplussed. Nepal had a lower per capita income than Bangladesh, probably the worst terrain in the world for cellular coverage, no railway and no fiber, a miniscule population, and an economy one-fifth the size of Bangladesh's. How could a company reject Bangladesh and look toward Nepal? Quadir figured the negative image of Bangladesh was so deep and ingrained that otherwise rational people could not see what they were looking at. Quadir left Scandinavia to visit Mailman in New York.

Deus Ex Machina

A few days after he arrived in New York, Quadir got a call from Gunnstein Fidjestol in Norway. Fidjestol had been assigned by Telenor Consult to visit Bangladesh for three weeks, but he saw little point in going. He already knew the country, having once tried to land a consulting project with Bangladesh Railway. Fidjestol figured that the chances of completing the study in time for Telenor to make an actionable decision were nil. Quadir fired back: "If I'm hanging from a cliff by one hand, do you want me to let go without trying to climb back up with the other hand?" The phone went silent for what seemed a minute. Then Fidjestol said he'd be flying with a colleague from Olso via London tomorrow, and asked if Quadir could meet them at Heathrow Airport. Quadir agreed to do so, then encouraged Fidjestol to stay in the game. The way things had gone before, the government could suddenly postpone the bid submission deadline and open a new window of time.

It was now September 1995, two months before the bid was due. At Heathrow Airport, in the British Airways departure lounge for flights to Delhi and Dhaka, Quadir spotted two tall blonde men pacing about. Scandinavians were not hard to spot on a flight to Bangladesh. They were indeed Fidjestol and his colleague, Inge Skaar (pronounced "Score"). Fidjestol had corralled Skaar because he had participated in preparing a bid for Telenor's GSM license in Hungary, with a consortium that included Telia. Fidjestol was six-tyish; Skaar was in his early-to-mid forties and six feet four. They were on their way to Bangladesh after all—Fidjestol had just been testing Quadir's reserves.

"I thought we might have a few interesting weeks in Bangladesh, and then go home," says Fidjestol today. "After a week, I changed my mind."

The three jumped into a debate at Heathrow about how the village phones were going to work. What if a call came for someone who lived a five-minute walk away? Would the caller call twice, once to give a message and once to actually converse? Quadir could see some good coming of these guys.

On the long plane ride to Dhaka and then holed up in the Dhaka Sheraton, they slammed out their feasibility study. Skaar was a problem solver, not a consultant who walks away and bills. He drew on his experience in Hungary. He understood the value of Grameen, and appreciated Quadir's tireless efforts over the past two years. After four intense weeks, Skaar produced a computer model for the project. Where had this guy been hiding?

Modeling Phone Coverage

Actually, Skaar already had a model on his PC. He had developed it for his work in another country. "The model linked investment, operating costs, markets, and revenues," says Skaar. "Based on limited inputs, it provided the basis for detailed planning."

The model resolved two outstanding issues. The first involved developing a way to charge the Grameen borrowers who would be retailing services in the rural areas, those who would be operating the so-called *village pay phones* (VPPs). Because Grameen had said it would purchase airtime minutes in bulk, figuring the proper discount was the next step. Until Skaar arrived with his PC model, there was no way of telling whether the project would be viable at a price level that was affordable to the villagers. Yunus had been pushing Quadir on the price issue, wondering if the call tariff could be made affordable for villagers.

The second issue involved coverage. How would the new phone company decide which urban and rural areas to cover? If two cities far apart were covered separately, the government would require that they be linked by the state-run BTTB—another revenue source for the government. As it was, BTTB didn't have enough transmission capacity for its own needs. At the same time, the tender documents allowed continuous coverage to be independent of the state-run operator's links. Considering this, the need to provide rural coverage, and the prospect of obtaining a lease of BR's fiber-optic network, Skaar proposed intensive coverage of major urban areas combined with thin but continuous coverage along the railway tracks. This solution solved three problems in one swoop. It produced continuous coverage, and thus independence from state-run BTTB's moribund network; it created necessary rural coverage; and it minimized transmission costs by keeping the network close to the railroad tracks.

This solution hinged on obtaining the fiber-optic cable lease from Bangladesh Railway, which would certainly not happen in the next month. Thus, with encouragement from Yunus, Skaar's coverage maps showed shaded areas along the tracks without explaining why. The benefit of leaving fiber out of the equation was that the bid evaluators, who were sympathetic to BTTB and less receptive to Bangladesh Railway, could have put up major roadblocks to gaining the lease. If questioned about the arc of coverage by suspicious government investigators, Grameen could have claimed the map was following the population density, which is what the railroad did.

Yunus Agrees to Invest

Skaar and Fidjestol were preparing to ask Yunus to invest $2 million in the new (and as yet unformed) company. The Norwegians had persuaded themselves that Telenor should go in, and they wanted a tangible partner to take back to headquarters in Norway. "We were both old enough to remember when everyone in Norway had to use a pay phone to talk," says Fidjestol, "so the idea of shared village phones made perfect sense." Says Skaar: "In a country of 120 million, I knew there had to be several millions who could afford a telephone."

To their surprise and Quadir's, Yunus wanted to buy a majority of the company, as much as 75 percent. "When Yunus said he was willing to put up $7 million or $8 million, Inge [Skaar] was so shocked he needed a smoke," says Fidjestol. "Khalid Shams raised his eyebrows to indicate that no one smoked on the Grameen campus. But Yunus walked over to a bookshelf, pulled back a few books and produced an ashtray for Inge. After that, it was fine."

"No one within Grameen had ever talked about a rural phone system before Quadir arrived, so you have to give Yunus credit for grasping the idea and recognizing its potential and deciding to invest," says Muzammel Huq, former general manager, who worked at Grameen Bank for more than twenty years, until his retirement in 2003.

The news that Grameen was finally ready to invest was fantastic. Unfortunately, Telenor wanted to be the majority shareholder. If it were going into Bangladesh, where no Western telecom company had dared venture, it certainly wanted control.

Emerging Markets Aren't as Risky as You Think

Analyzing investments in emerging markets, the consulting firm McKinsey & Company has concluded that analysts overestimate the risk premium and grossly inflate assumptions about the cost of capital, often pegging it at more than twice the level of similar projects in developed economies.[4] McKinsey finds that even though the risk in any individual emerging market may be higher than the risk in a developed market, and even though the cost of capital in any emerging market is higher than the cost in Europe or the United States, the actual risks and costs are not nearly as high as perceived by investors.

In fact, according to McKinsey's analysis of annual returns over fifteen years, a wide portfolio of emerging-market index investments has not been more risky than an investment in a single blue-chip corporation in the United States or Europe. Because there is a low correlation between individual risks in different countries, the overall performance of an emerging market portfolio can be quite stable if investments are spread over several countries.

At the same time, Quadir tried to persuade Skaar that he should become Telenor's "man in Dhaka." Quadir felt that Telenor might be reluctant to enter a country without executives they knew and trusted. It would be a stretch for Skaar, who had lived his entire life in the small Norwegian village of Varhaug, with the exception of a stint in Hungary. But Quadir hoped that Skaar's natural inclination to solve problems would be more than satisfied in Bangladesh. Skaar and Fidjestol attended a prebid conference on September 28, where they joined other bidders in asking for an extension, then they returned to Norway.

About a week later Skaar called to announce that Telenor had tentatively approved preparation of a bid. Tormod Hermansen, CEO of Telenor, had accepted Fidjestol's and Skaar's recommendation, and given Skaar approval to set up shop in Bangaldesh if the license were won. "They came back from their fact-finding mission full of enthusiasm," says Hermansen. "They liked Yunus and Shams, found them to be good, intelligent people." Hermansen had also been lobbied by Norway's ambassador to Bangladesh, an old friend of Hermansen's who had come to know of the project through NORAD's involvement and thought highly of Grameen Bank. "In addition, it was clear to me that Western Europe was too crowded and competitive, and that Telenor would be better off playing in emerging markets," says Hermansen, who served as CEO of Telenor until 2002. At the time he approved the bid, he had never been to Bangladesh. When he did visit some time later, Shams and Yunus took him by speedboat to Bogra to showcase fish farms as a symbol of the country's overall potential. "No where else in the world was anyone selling phones to the rural poor," says Shams. "Telenor didn't believe it was possible. We had to convince Hermansen." Says Hermansen: "GrameenPhone would not have been possible without Yunus and Shams, and their personal and political clout in sponsoring the license proposal."

Quadir was elated. After nearly three years the path ahead seemed less rocky. The next day Yunus decided on a name for the company that would operate the network—GrameenPhone. As Grameen means "rural," Yunus felt it important to connect the two words so that people would understand GrameenPhone as a brand, not as a term meaning "rural phone." Although Quadir feared that this name might lead people to think the company was providing only rural phones, or that Grameen had generated the idea for the new company—rather than tiny Gonofone—he was happy to see Grameen putting its name and money on the line. The bid deadline had been moved out again, to November 6, 1995.

5

Building a Company

Grameen Bank, for all practical purposes, knew everything about rural Bangladesh and virtually nothing about telecommunications. Telenor, the Norwegian state-owned telephone company (which was partly privatized in 2000), for its part, knew everything about telecommunications and nothing about rural Bangladesh. Further, Grameen Bank was a microfinance institution looking to eradicate poverty, and the Scandinavians were in it for the money (with a side order of development). The combination of these two unlikely entities in a major commercial business enterprise has proved to be a path-setting model for doing business in poor countries.

Back when Sweden's Telia was still in the mix, Grameen's Muhammad Yunus recommended forming two organizations registered in Bangladesh. One would be a nonprofit company called Grameen Telecom. This entity would purchase minutes in bulk (at a 50 percent discount) from the network operator and resell those minutes to rural women who, in turn, would retail them to end users. It was important to Yunus that Grameen Bank not be financially involved with GrameenPhone; because the government owns part of Grameen Bank and appoints several board members including the chairman, such a structure might have given the government undue influence in the phone company. In addition, Yunus felt that Grameen Telecom's shareholding would provide a mechanism to eventually transfer GrameenPhone shares to Grameen Bank borrowers (and shareholders) when the company went public.

The network operator, GrameenPhone, would be collectively owned by Telenor, Grameen Telecom, and Gonofone. GrameenPhone would own the license, build the network, and market the service. "We needed to design an institution that served the needs of two interest groups—businesspeople and development people," says Khalid Shams, managing director of Grameen Telecom and former chairman of GrameenPhone.

GrameenPhone didn't need to know how to market to or collect from rural customers, who had no checks or credit cards to pay with. Grameen Telecom would handle rural marketing and sales through the Grameen Bank network of loan officers, using "cell phone as cow" as an operating principle. Meanwhile GrameenPhone could market to urban customers, Western style.

That much had been agreed upon. But before the bid could be submitted the various parties had to work out share allocations. Clearly, the two key parties were Telenor and Grameen Telecom, both of which wanted majority control. Because Telenor was the network operator with communications know-how, and because Bangladesh was an "unattractive" market, Telenor certainly held the bargaining chips. On the other hand, Yunus felt that he was offering up the "Grameen" name for free, which would be a huge marketing asset.

There were two minority parties, one being Gonofone as represented by Iqbal Quadir and Josh Mailman (they were later joined by Ben Cohen of Ben & Jerry's Ice Cream; Arnold Hiatt, former CEO of Stride Rite; Phil Villers, the founder of Computervision; and several other investors). The other was Marubeni Corporation, a large Japanese trading company, with revenues in the arena of $150 billion at the time, that had showed strong interest as a passive investor.

Marubeni had been doing business in Bangladesh since the 1950s, so it knew the country well. It had also been involved with Nippon Telegraph and Telephone in Japan to market the Personal

Handy-Phone System (PHS), a form of wireless phone well suited to densely populated areas. Marubeni had held a reception in Dhaka early in 1995, indicating its interest in entering the telecom business. Here was an unsolicited foreign investor! But that interest had not yet translated into a commitment.

On the control issue it was quickly decided that Telenor needed a 51 percent share to maintain majority control, that Grameen would take 44.5 percent, and Gonofone 4.5 percent. As it was, Telenor's Tormod Hermansen was having difficulty persuading his board to invest—"many knew nothing about Bangladesh, except that it flooded a lot," says Hermansen—so anything less than a majority stake would have been difficult to swallow. To make this more palatable to Yunus, Telenor signed its "intention" to cede majority control ("less than 35 percent") within six years; in fact, ten years later, Telenor has increased its stake.

Telenor was opposed to Marubeni's involvement, according to Yunus, or at least to reducing its 51 percent stake to make it possible. If Marubeni wanted to come in, Yunus agreed to reduce Grameen Telecom's stake to 35 percent, giving Marubeni 9.5 percent. On the issue of board seats, Telenor would take three, Grameen Telecom two, and Marubeni one—there would be none for Gonofone. If Marubeni didn't come in, Telenor and Grameen would each have three seats. Quadir, who had lobbied for a 10 percent stake for Gonofone along with a board seat, was less than pleased with this outcome but rationalized that it was better than having the whole deal collapse. However, Telenor appointed Quadir, who was already on the startup Steering Committee, to be one of its three representatives on the board from 1996 to 1998.

Filing the License Bid

The day before the bid was due, Marubeni was neither in nor out. A *memorandum of understanding*, which became the basis of the GrameenPhone Consortium, was signed at 1 A.M. on November 6 by Skaar, Shams, and Quadir at their current headquarters—Room 1001 on the top floor of the Dhaka Sheraton. The understanding authorized $13.33 million in start-up capital, to be drawn when requested by the board. Within the year, the formal Shareholders Agreement increased the initial capitalization to $17.5 million. Telenor, Grameen Telecom, and Gonofone each received $600,000 credit for work to date, which by a prior reckoning translated into a 4.5 percent shareholding. For Quadir, being treated on par with the "giants" somewhat compensated for Gonofone's lack of a board seat.

The company was not capitalized at that point and would not be until a license was won, but the shareholders' agreement noted that GrameenPhone could make capital calls for shareholders to buy shares pro rata, according to their interests. The license itself was free! The government didn't seek a fee because it probably didn't think the business would amount to much and didn't want to deter foreign investors. It may also have been giving a free ride to other license winners who had political connections. Ten years later, when it had been well proved that providing technology to poor or distressed countries was good business, Telenor would pay $1.7 billion for a license in Serbia.

Outside loan financing would also be sought at a premium, but if it was not secured, the partners would be required to find additional monies according to their allocated interests. Shams and Quadir had already started talking with the Asian Development Bank; the International Finance Corporation, a private-sector investment arm of the World Bank; and the Commonwealth Development Corporation (CDC), the venerable British government development lender.

The executive summary of the comprehensive proposal, replete with maps and technical specifications, laid out the GrameenPhone case quite clearly:

> GrameenPhone proposes to provide customer-friendly, low-price and high-quality GSM cellular telephone services for the whole of Bangladesh. It is proposing to

start offering services within four months after license award . . . [covering] nearly half the population of Bangladesh in the first 18 months after license award, and 98 percent of the geographical area of the country in six years.

GrameenPhone plans to offer services to the people of all walks of life. For the urban areas, it proposes to offer very customer-friendly and cost-effective services. For the rural areas, on top of these qualities of service, GrameenPhone plans to introduce an innovative program which would provide self-employment opportunity for many while at the same time enabling a rapid rollout of coverage. Through this program, poor individuals will be able to borrow money from Grameen Bank to purchase handsets and enter into the business of providing telephone services from their respective villages.

Grameen Bank considers it important to play a meaningful role in bringing communication services to the doorsteps of all Bangladeshis, including the villagers, be they poor or distant. . . . By making rural people accessible, GrameenPhone would not just be serving the rural people as a market for itself but the Government and businesses as well, which would work more efficiently if they could access rural people who constitute 80 percent of the country's population.[1]

Marubeni was not part of the deal but was mentioned as a potential investor over the next year. A letter of intent from Marubeni was an appendix to the proposal, as was a letter from the World Bank's International Finance Corporation, expressing interest in financing through debt and equity up to 25 percent of the phone project's cost.

At 4 A.M. on the morning of November 6, 1995, Skaar put the bid in a secure Samsonite suitcase (he was worried about some last-minute *hartal* disaster on the streets) and had Quadir take it to his apartment, which was a block from where the bid would be submitted. Masud Isa, a high-ranking Grameen Bank officer who was to become the first managing director of Grameen Telecom, also came to Quadir's apartment. Every precaution was taken to ensure a safe delivery.

Quadir and Isa arrived at the building designated by the Ministry of Posts and Telecommunications at 8:30, a half hour early, and found Skaar waiting. (The building is opposite the giant Dhaka Parliament Building designed by Louis Kahn, an American architect.) But communications union members opposed to private companies entering the business had formed a barricade outside the building. Quadir remembered Sam Pitroda's tales of fighting the entrenched unionists in India—and Bangladesh was little different.

Twelve other bidders had shown up! Gonofone and Grameen had not been working in isolation. Rather than force bidders to crash the barricades, the ministry announced that it would accept the bids at another office, eight kilometers away. Quadir and Isa jumped in Quadir's car and raced to submit the bid. The bidders wouldn't get their answer for a year.

Upping the Ante

With the bid filed and little clue as to when a decision would be made, Quadir, Skaar, Shams, and Gunnstein Fidjestol began operating on multiple fronts. Before the bid was filed the general understanding had been that the initial capitalization of GrameenPhone would be $17.5 million, with shares bought according to interest allocation. Right after the filing Quadir began campaigning for a much larger investment, more on the order of $100 million. Quadir wanted to out-do potential competitors, achieve economies of scale, make a distinction in the minds of consumers with a "revolutionary" product and company, and essentially grab what would become known in Internet parlance as *first-mover advantage*.

"I thought we were quite vulnerable with a small investment, and also might have to compromise on nationwide coverage," says Quadir. "Even if we won a license, two others would get licenses as well. Some of the other groups already perceived us as an NGO-type organization, and I could envision them investing heavily at the outset to cripple us. If we really wanted to build a countrywide network, it was going to take money."

Yunus responded to Quadir's estimate of $100 million in investment with enthusiasm. "I agree on aggressive nationwide rollout strategy," he wrote in a memo to Quadir. "If that means $100 million, we should go for it. We'll have to make sure that the competitor cannot get any foothold in Dhaka and its neighborhood. Our 18-month rollout in the rural areas can still be maintained with saturation coverage in Dhaka and Chittagong—if we go for a $100 million business plan. Let's go for it."[2]

Skaar at that point was agnostic on the investment issue, as he was more of a technical problem solver and implementer who would work with whatever he was given. Telenor corporate, it turned out, was not yet fully sold on the Grameen project, despite its CEO's support of the bid. "I used the S-curve argument over and over—that GrameenPhone would start slowly, ramp quickly, then settle into a long-term cash cow," says former CEO Hermansen. (This was the era when U.S. venture capitalists were using *hockey-stick* graphs to show a business starting slowly and then skyrocketing up—without ever curving downward.) Hermansen also told his board he'd "keep things simple," as Norwegians always did, using the same technology, suppliers, and engineering as Telenor used elsewhere. Finally, he took Skaar's argument that "in a country of 120 million, several millions could afford phone service" a step further by stating that "5 to 10 million Bangladeshis have the same income as Norway's per capita income." With Norway's population at less than 5 million, he sold the notion that within Bangladesh there was a hidden Norway! A brilliant argument. At any rate, actual investment would have to wait until a license was won.

Attention Turns to Fiber-Optic Cable

Bangladesh Railway's fiber-optic cable would speed development of
the network and the speed with which economies of scale could be
achieved. The existence of this fiber in a country with such poor
infrastructure was almost unbelievable. Even in the United States
there was a Gold Rush mentality to lay and access fiber. Wayne
Perry, a cofounder of McCaw Cellular Communications, a cellular
company bought by AT&T in 1993, said at the time: "Fiber is a
great equalizer."

The railway's fiber would allow GrameenPhone to connect geographically disparate cells to one another through a reliable, high-
speed connector. New technology installed at terminal points would
allow GrameenPhone to drastically increase the carrying capacity
of the fiber, from the current 128 channels (allowing 128 calls at
one time) to 30,000 or more. Quadir also saw the right-of-way that
would come with a fiber lease as another headache resolved.
GrameenPhone could use the railroad stations or the land along the
tracks for putting up cell towers, without having to lease land or
buildings.

The 1,800-kilometer fiber starts at Chittagong, in the southern
part of Bangladesh, just west of the Myanmar border and the tribal
regions of the Chittagong Hills and east of the watery delta that
spills into the Bay of Bengal. It follows the tracks north to Dhaka,
then further north to Bogra, above the center of the country, and
then heads southwest before looping back down south all the way
to Khulna. The shape is a messy upside-down U, with the two end
points remaining unconnected because of the delta.

GrameenPhone would have to install microwave to complete
the loop, sending calls over the heads of the few remaining Bengal
tigers. The U-shape itself would be effective, but a loop was far superior. It would open up whole new sections of the country and provide insurance against a failure in any part of the system. A call
could just reverse itself and move the other way around the loop.

A clause in the government's license tender mandated that to connect any noncontiguous cells, the cell company would have to pass calls through the government network. It had set the allowable size of an urban cell at seven kilometers, and that of a rural cell at seventeen kilometers. You couldn't use a microwave tower or fiber or a satellite to send a call from Tower A to Tower B unless those towers were in contiguous cells; if not, you had to use the government network to connect the call. "BTTB had a restrictive attitude toward competition," says Fidjestol, in an understatement. Says Quadir: "This was a clever way to force more fees from the cellular providers. The government had no idea we'd actually try to build a contiguous network throughout. Who would string seventeen-kilometer cells together across the country?"

Modeling a True Cellular Network

Skaar's shaded map showed that GrameenPhone would provide cellular service over a very large area divided into many cells, like a beehive—or a clump of caviar, as Quadir prefers to describe it—with a background system handing over calls from one cell to another as customers moved freely among cells. Because handing over calls from one cell to another in a seamless, *molecular* way is the very essence of a cellular system, continuous coverage is the most faithful adoption of cellular technology. But that doesn't mean it's easy or practical to build, as many current-day users of cell phones know from dropped calls. And cell towers require electricity, which was hard to find in most rural areas, except along the railroad.

What the fiber meant, in practical terms, was that Grameen-Phone could rapidly build a contiguous network of cells along the railroad and use the fiber to deliver the signals back to the central switching station in Dhaka. GrameenPhone would be able to connect callers in the north to people in the south, without using the government-owned fixed network. Fidjestol and Skaar were back and forth between Norway and Bangladesh, laying the groundwork for a network by soliciting bids from suppliers such as Ericsson, Alcatel, Siemens, Nokia, and Motorola. If they were to provide service within four months of winning a license, as promised, they had to hit the ground running.

Cultivating Relationships with BR

Since 1994, Quadir had stayed in touch with Mokkaram Yahya, the railroad man who had, essentially, staked his reputation on the fiber when he convinced NORAD and the government to install it over copper back in the 1980s. The fiber was being used for BR's own network, with a phone at each of 300 stations. It had served the railway's basic needs but had not done anything more than a copper line could have achieved. The $30 million fiber was clearly underused. "This was like driving nothing but a couple of motorcycles on an expressway," says Fidjestol. And BR employed 500 people to maintain a phone system for 300 phones. What would Pitroda think?

BTTB had several times rejected a proposal that it should lease the fiber, saying that the quality was not good enough for its needs. Quadir and others perceived this as standard operating procedure in Bangladesh and took it to mean BTTB wanted government money to build its own network. Another group, Bangladesh Rural Telecom Authority (BRTA), had tried to lease the fiber, but BR had rejected them. BRTA, despite its statist-sounding name, was a private telephone company with a license for the northern part of the country, but it had done virtually nothing with that license.

It was early 1996. The fiber had been in place for nearly a decade, the same fiber that was disrupting the telecommunications industry in the United States, and Yahya, the visionary who had staked his career on fiber over copper (Shams calls him the "father of fiber" in Bangladesh), had little to show for his pet project except an internal phone system between railroad stations. If Yahya had made the same play in America, he'd have been a titan.

When the first tender (designed to identify qualified bidders) came out in March 1996, it allotted extra points to those who planned to build a universal service covering all rural areas. Certainly no one but GrameenPhone was thinking about universal service. GrameenPhone's fiber-lease proposal was essentially a carbon of its cellular license proposal—but it also made a large point of the fact that leasing fiber meant foreign exchange would not leave the country in order to import microwave stations.

Sitting down with Skaar and Fidjestol to file a fiber bid, Quadir urged an aggressive approach. Based on months of conversations with BR, which had been begging GrameenPhone to license the fiber, he had a good idea what would catch the railroad's attention. Quadir suggested hiring the 500 railroad workers to maintain the fiber, thus relieving the railroad of payroll. He suggested throwing in cell phones for all railroad workers, which would certainly jump-start Grameen-Phone but would also be attractive to the railroad. Finally, he proposed a huge up-front bonus payment of $3 million—equivalent to the total foreign direct investment in Bangladesh in 1994!

The Waiting Game

It was March 1996. The GrameenPhone consortium had filed two bids. Time, which had been racing, slowed to a crawl. Quadir was working with the development banks and generally "snooping around" trying to figure out how to prod the authorities. That July, Marubeni, which had made winning the fiber a condition of investment, finally joined the consortium. No money had yet changed hands. Still, it was exciting that Japanese, Norwegian, and American investors—bricks rated AAA—were ready to place a big bet on forlorn Bangladesh.

Response to the license bid was slowed by a government crisis in the new democracy, which had elected its first civilian leader in 1991. The president dissolved parliament in November 1995 and called new elections for February 1996. He asked Prime Minister

Khaleda Zia—the widow of General Zia, the strongman leader who had been assassinated in 1981—to stay in office until a successor was chosen. The Awami League opposition party vowed to not to take part in the elections while Zia remained in office, claiming the elections had been rigged to ensure the ruling Bangladesh National Party a landslide victory. The Awami League staged a series of crippling *hartals*, trying to transfer power to a neutral caretaker government. In February the newly elected parliament did so, and then *it* was dissolved. (Yunus served in the cabinet of the caretaker government.) Finally, in June, the opposition Awami League won the elections and Sheikh Hasina Wajed was sworn in as prime minister. She is the daughter of Mujibur Rahman, the first leader of independent Bangladesh, who had declared one-party rule and then was assassinated in 1975.

National politics is a blood sport in Bangladesh and clearly more engaging than cellular licenses. However, the government was still functioning, as evidenced by a letter from BTTB sent in January 1996 asking for detailed information from all bidders on the solvency of their partners and their experience in building cellular networks. "BTTB didn't like the idea that a private company was being offered a license, and particularly one that was connected to Grameen," says Shams. "A committee set up to evaluate the merits and demerits of the international bids reputedly observed that Telenor had no experience in developing countries, and wouldn't be able to operate in Bangladesh." Shams solicited an opinion from the in-country World Bank representative (Pierre Landel Mills) on what constituted a *developing country* and learned that any country that took loans from the World Bank was considered to be *developing*. Those countries included Russia and Hungary—countries where Telenor was already operating. Shams persistently followed up with BTTB, stressing Telenor's technical capabilities and success in multiple developing countries.

In April, having heard nothing, Shams, who speaks in a soft, calm, matter-of-fact voice, wrote again to BTTB, with an increased sense of urgency: "At this very moment, several people in Norway, Japan and Bangladesh are employed fulltime organizing and planning for the project. We have kept our personnel on their toes so that they can hit the ground as soon as you approve our proposal. Any added costs due to delays would ultimately be passed on to the consumers. Furthermore, we lose the confidence of the equipment suppliers due to unexpected delays."[3]

Most of this was true, although GrameenPhone was very clear about being the low-cost provider, not "passing on costs." The idea was not just to make the service affordable in a poor country but to introduce competition and then squash it—American style. But personnel were, in fact, on their toes. Fidjestol and Skaar, besides soliciting bids from suppliers, were also beginning to train local engineers in mobile telephone technology, as well as preparing to place base stations and build a salesforce.

In his memo Shams evaluates how well the GrameenPhone proposal matches the technical framework provided by the government and scores it at 90 of 100. Top that. None of the other bidders possibly could. "We hope that in the end you pick those proposers which will further competition in telecommunication, bring the latest technologies and services, and deliver them most cost effectively, so that this nation is not held back for a lack of good communication facilities, a critical piece of development in any country."[4]

Given Grameen Bank's track record, *development* was a trump card Grameen continually played. "We are not here to make money," Muhammad Yunus had told the Dhaka *Daily Star* (purveyor of "Journalism Without Fear or Favour") about the new phone concept the year before, in an interview on his being named 1995 Man of the Year in Bangladesh. "We are here to make sure that poor people make money out of this. It is not what the company makes. It is what the borrowers of Grameen make."[5]

This was a fine and lofty ideal, but by July BTTB was requesting specific pricing information and proposed connection fees—that is, what was in it for the government? This, of course, was a sign that final negotiations were about to commence. On pricing, Grameen-Phone figured its tariffs would average Tk3 per minute—one-third what little CityCell was then charging. GrameenPhone also proposed sharing more than 3 percent of its revenues (on average over ten years) with the government for calls from GrameenPhone that connected to the BTTB network. GrameenPhone clearly needed connection to BTTB phones—otherwise its customers would initially have few people to call. But Quadir had thought for some time that this technical conundrum could be GrameenPhone's Achilles' heel. He had witnessed the immense difficulties upstart MCI had had connecting to AT&T's once monopolistic network in the United States in the 1980s. And he remembered CityCell's legal complaint.

Even though things were looking up, Shams and Yunus heard from their close government contacts that Sheikh Hasina's newly elected government was thinking of scrapping the tender process and starting over from scratch. Needless to say, that would have been the end of GrameenPhone and its fragile consortium. Yunus put his personal power and prestige on the line in a one-on-one meeting with Hasina, who had already selected two licensees, leaving out GrameenPhone. Hasina had been told that the country could not support three new companies. Yunus argued that if that were true, the two companies would be in no rush to build out a network, but that adding a third would create a more competitive environment that would be better for the country. He also argued for the all-encompassing benefits of providing universal phone service, stretching into the most remote reaches of Bangladesh, which no other company could possibly imagine doing. His performance won the day.

GrameenPhone Wins a License

Finally, in August 1996, at a big meeting with representatives from fourteen bidders, GrameenPhone was called out as one of the winners. The others were Aktel (with foreign partner Telekom Malaysia) and Sheba Telecom (with foreign partner Celcom, also Malaysian). "When the bid was read out, there was a huge uproar," says Shams. "People were saying, 'Yunus and Grameen, with all their contacts, they're taking us on a ride, they can't provide low-cost calls all over the country.' " Negotiations continued for another three months, before the final agreement was signed on November 28, 1996. More than a year had passed since the initial filing—and about four years since Quadir's "connectivity is productivity" epiphany in midtown Manhattan.

The newly incorporated GrameenPhone was ready to rev, operating out of borrowed space in Marubeni's Dhaka office. About ten Norwegians and Bangladeshis were crammed into the office—with two desks and one phone. "Looking out the window, we could see people rafting to their flooded shacks, using the same faucet for showering and drinking," says Fidjestol of the sprawling shanty towns that continue to grow on the perimeter of Dhaka. "They did not look like potential GrameenPhone customers."

Skaar, the imposing consultant from the small Norwegian village of Varhaug, who was a get-things-done guy, was named CEO. Quadir's initial role was to act as an intermediary between Norwegian executives and Bangladeshi bureaucrats, but that quickly morphed into director of finance. At a dinner hosted by the Norwegian ambassador to celebrate Yunus's signing of the license, Yunus asked Skaar to target March 26, 1997—National Independence Day of Bangladesh, the day East Pakistan had declared independence from West Pakistan—as opening day for the network. Nearly a year earlier, Skaar had indicated that he could make it happen—even though the date was just four months away.

Crazy! Ericsson, the main switch supplier, said a network had not been built that fast anywhere in the world. And Bangladesh had a few asterisks by its name, calling attention to such things as poor infrastructure and a consistently high ranking on Transparency International's Corruption Perceptions Index. Everything had to be imported by air, including eight tons of lead batteries to run the main switch, because electricity was so undependable. God knows how many bribes would be required to move that cargo from the airport. As for BR's fiber-optic cable, who knew if it was anything more than a fantasy. But Skaar didn't care. He'd fly in a few microwave towers and set them up himself. Now that they had the license, any mixed feelings were tossed to the wind. He wanted GrameenPhone to be number one. He was Telenor's man in Dhaka. He was Inge Skaar, CEO, GrameenPhone Ltd, Dhaka.

6

Building a Network

In January 1997, during the Islamic festival of Eid (which marks the end of the Ramadan fast), when business virtually stops, Iqbal Quadir rode out to Dhaka International Airport to accept a shipment of switches and batteries. Inge Skaar and Gunnstein Fidjestol had negotiated an initial $5 million contract with Ericsson for switching equipment—using a low bid from Alcatel to bid down Ericsson—which was being shipped in on British Airways flights when there was room in the cargo belly. The three forces of external combustion—information technology imported by native entrepreneurs backed by foreign investors—had finally arrived in the same spot at the same time.

The Ericsson shipment was the beginning of what was to become a major fixed investment in Bangladesh that now totals nearly $1 billion from GrameenPhone alone, not to mention the competitors who are now pouring in millions to eat into Grameen-Phone's market share. Egypt's Orascom, for example, which bought Sheba Telecom for $50 million in 2005 (and rebranded it as Banglalink), immediately invested $250 million and landed a million new subscribers. Back in 1997, of course, investors didn't drop $5 million in Bangladesh at the drop of a hat, as GrameenPhone was doing.

That equipment was arriving five weeks after the signing of the license was remarkable. "We had done a lot of groundwork, and things would begin to happen very quickly, and much on our own terms," says Skaar, who had settled in nicely in Bangladesh. When he had first arrived, with a return ticket four weeks out, he was in a frenzy to leave. "My first impression of Bangladesh is impossible to describe," he says. Quadir had coaxed him through the rough early days with this comforting maxim: "They say you cry twice in Bangladesh: once when you arrive and want to leave, once when you have to leave and want to stay." This proved to be prophetic in Skaar's case, as Telenor brought in a new managing director after Skaar's first year on the job, in early 1998.

GrameenPhone needed offices, and also housing for Ericsson's central switching equipment that would route calls from one caller to another. Quadir found three floors at the top of a new twenty-story office building; one of the tallest in Dhaka, it made a perfect host for microwave towers. Building was booming in Dhaka; in fact the central business district, which was once in the vicinity of the Dhaka Sheraton, has since migrated two miles to the north—as has the GrameenPhone building, which is now a gleaming modern office building.

"Starting in the 1980s, Bangladesh has experienced rapid urbanization; with more mechanization of agriculture, surplus labor began moving to the cities," says Khalid Shams, who peppers his language with economics terms. "Now the country is filled with shops and factories, people making things, people going places. The agrarian lifestyle of the country is changing. Walk into a bazaar in the rural areas or a shopping plaza in Dhaka and 30 percent of the shops sell electronic goods and cellular phones."

The emergency generator in the basement of GrameenPhone's first office building provided backup for the switching equipment during the daily power cuts. The rooftop was an excellent spot for cell towers (base stations) and antennas. In keeping with the license requirements that urban cells measure seven kilometers, cell towers and antennas needed to be placed throughout the city. In Hungary placing such equipment had been a problem for Telenor, as the government wanted to protect the look of the skyline by hiding any antennas. In Bangladesh, where growth is helter-skelter, there was no need for government permission to build antennas or place equipment on rooftops, and most landlords were accommodating, happy to take a windfall rent. "In a country with few rules and regulations, anything is possible if you act first and ask questions later," says Skaar, who quickly developed a reputation for charging ahead like a bull. "The initial phase of operation was a marvelous time where we operated very much on our own terms."

Except for issues with Bangladesh Telephone and Telegraph. GrameenPhone needed links at the BTTB building, to connect calls from the cellular network to the fixed network. However, it was pretty clear that BTTB was in no rush to help the company prosper. GrameenPhone temporarily improved communications with BTTB by hiring several engineers and other personnel from BTTB.

GrameenPhone's engineers were an odd mixture of Norwegians and Bangladeshis. "Many of the Norwegians were not well educated but had practical technical skills and experience," says Fidjestol. "The Bangladeshis were highly educated, but had no experience. This combination caused some tension, but there had to be some way to transfer knowledge and they worked through it." Indeed, this is a clear example of one of the perceived benefits of foreign direct investment into developing countries—beyond the money itself is the knowledge transfer that increases a country's human capital.

As promised, GrameenPhone moved quickly to implement a network that covered the major areas of Dhaka. A few weeks before the network opened, all GrameenPhone employees were equipped with phones to test the network. Dhaka's flotilla of drivers—many people use personal drivers—found the phones invaluable, as Dhaka traffic had become so bad it was difficult to meet people at the right time without some communication.

The ceremonial first call took place on schedule in the office of Prime Minister Sheikh Hasina, who called the prime minister of

Norway. "This was not an engineer's idea," says Fidjestol, who had tested reception the day before. "Her office was far from all base stations and had thick concrete walls." Indeed, the prime minister had very poor reception.

"Telenor engineers were in total panic," says Yunus. "They had two prime ministers on the line and the CEO of Telenor was in attendance. Finally a miracle happened." The prime minister, who had been seated, rose and picked up a few signal bars. In a choreographed conversation she spoke to Prime Minister Thorbjorn Jagland about the weather. It was –30°C in Finnmark, Norway, and 30°C in Dhaka, making for a natural topic. The two countries were strangely synched.

The next call was to Laily Begum, a villager who had been the first Grameen Bank borrower and was to become the first *phone lady*. This was in keeping with the plan to lend to borrowers with a strong credit history. The day before, Fidjestol had also been in her village, eight kilometers outside Dhaka, to test the system. He asked the villagers if they knew anyone in Dhaka who had a phone so GrameenPhone could try a test call. One woman said her aunt in Dhaka had a phone. She called her aunt, but there was almost no conversation. When Fidjestol asked her why, she said, "My aunt says she doesn't like it when people make fun of her and she knows there are no phones in my village." "Her aunt hung up!" Fidjestol says. The next day, village children were assembled in front of CNN cameras for the ceremonial first call to the prime minister. The day after that violent thunderstorms knocked out all the transmitters, but it didn't really matter. No one owned a phone yet.

Despite the snafus, GrameenPhone's accomplishment was extraordinary. Its network opened as planned, four months after it received a license; the other two license winners, Aktel and Sheba Telecom, wouldn't launch service for well over a year. GrameenPhone had seized first-mover advantage.

Winning the Fiber Lease

The week before the network opened, Bangladesh Railway had notified GrameenPhone that it had been selected as the most qualified bidder to lease the fiber-optic cable. BTTB, however, resisted any bid to lease out the fiber. "Like a giant awakening from slumber, it simply said that the fiber network could not be leased out because it would be used for telecommunications, which was within the jurisdiction of BTTB," says Shams. The Ministry of Posts and Telecommunications (MOPT) sided with BTTB, saying the fiber was vital to the country and couldn't be controlled by a private company. The railroad argued that it had been trying to lease the fiber to BTTB for years, without success.

Quadir had hoped that GrameenPhone would be able to activate the fiber with the opening of the network, but this news was almost as good. However, MOPT asked for additional time to review the matter, to see whether the lease conflicted with any provision in the cellular license—specifically the requirement for "contiguous coverage"—or with other interests of MOPT. Three months later, MOPT approved the lease *and* GrameenPhone's plans to use the fiber to connect distant towns. The contract (the seventeenth iteration) was finally signed in September 1997—$3 million up front, with millions to follow in rent, and a return of 30 percent to Bangladesh Railway on any sublease agreements.

"We showed up at railroad headquarters half an hour late to sign the contract, due to traffic, and the director was quite impatient. He pushed the contract in front of us and told us to sign immediately and left the room," remembers Fidjestol. "I thought it was odd to proceed without ceremony. When the director returned, he said the Minister of Communications had arrived to stop the signing, and he had rushed outside to stall him while we signed." One of the many ironies about Bangladesh is that in a country perceived to be among the world leaders in corruption, contracts are honored and upheld. It may take time to agree to terms and sign the contracts, but the contracts hold up in a society that by and large respects the rule of law.

GrameenPhone now had first-mover advantage *plus* infrastructure that would cost a competitor at least $100 million and several years to install—if it could arrange alternative rights-of-way with landowners. Despite this coup the ten-year-old fiber was "getting ready to deteriorate," says Fidjestol, and needed repair. In addition, the company wanted to upgrade the carrying capacity of the cable, to account for growth and leave extra capacity to sublease. GrameenPhone invested in redundant links to ensure that the fiber was available during repairs that might cause breaks in the cable, and immediately hired Bangladesh Railroad personnel to maintain the fiber. Three months and $6 million later, Grameen-Phone had completed the upgrades, giving Bangladesh a state-of-the art telecom backbone.

During this six-month period Quadir had been working with the engineers to install base stations on the roads leading out of Dhaka along the railway, in accordance with Skaar's plan. As the engineers moved physically from cell to cell, creating a honeycomb of cells (or "clump of caviar") that started along the railroad tracks and then moved into the countryside, one of Quadir's jobs was to negotiate leases with landlords to erect stations and antennas on their rooftops. "All I needed was a lawyer and an engineer," says Quadir. "With such people, which at the beginning we didn't have, we could do three or four towers a day." Still, the work went slowly. Just 102 towers were *planted* in 1997, many of them in Dhaka.

The Village Pay Phones

As the company's money and energy were initially invested in fiber and in urban areas, only thirty-two village phones were installed in 1997. They were originally called *village pay phones*, as the owner would charge others to use the phone—just as entrepreneurs in India had set up shop in villages with fixed-line phones in the 1980s and 1990s.

Nevertheless, the few village phones in use proved the concept. Average airtime was more than double that of urban business phones (today, average airtime for rural phones is ten times that of urban phones) and it was clearly a profitable business for both the phone ladies and GrameenPhone—even though it was selling minutes to Grameen Telecom at a 50 percent discount. By the end of 1998, a mere 221 village phones were in operation but were attracting international attention. The combination of microloans and cell phones in remote rural villages—set within the context of surging Internet growth in the West—was universally perceived as a harbinger of hope. World press clippings read like rave movie reviews:[1]

"Grameen Bank's rural game plan sets the company apart."
—*Far Eastern Economic Review*

"The scheme—to create a rural communications network by equipping one woman in each village with a cell phone—is the most imaginative of several new efforts to address one of the world's most basic technology gaps."
—*Los Angeles Times*

"GrameenPhone wants to seed villages with as few as one cellular phone per village, encouraging agents in each one to sell phone time."
—*BusinessWeek*

"Public telephones are an important communications link in Bangladesh where there is one phone for every 500 people."
—*International Herald Tribune*

"The system works as both development and business."

—*The New Statesman*

"Indeed, the impact of these mobile 'pay phones' on village life may be as significant to these peasants as the country's fabled typhoons and floods."

—*The WorldPaper*

The main reason for GrameenPhone's early success with village phones was that each of the phone ladies was a Grameen Bank borrower who had already paid back at least two loans. Grameen Telecom preferred women who lived in or near the center of a village and who knew English letters or numbers (or had a household member who did). The women were so well selected that they only needed one day of training to set up shop.

But why weren't the phones spreading faster? If the world wanted village phones and if airtime was double that of urban phones, why were there only 221? Once you got the hang of it, how hard was it to install a cell tower and a pod of batteries to power it?

In GrameenPhone's 1998 annual report (as GrameenPhone was a subsidiary of a larger public company it was not required to issue such a document) the company was up front about its progress:

> Despite [early] success, GrameenPhone is pursuing its rural program on a small scale during the initial stage. This leaves room for fine tuning the service after a learning period through pilot programs. In addition, a commercial operation must concentrate on securing its position in the competitive urban markets. Grameen-Phone has no special concessions from the Government for its development agenda and can only serve the rural

areas well after securing profitable urban businesses. Moreover, rural callers' real needs are to connect to cities, highlighting the need for a well-established urban network to serve the rural areas.[2]

Interconnection Difficulties

All this was true, but the report also masked a problem that Quadir had foreseen years before: interconnection with BTTB. In 1998, GrameenPhone started with 330 voice channels from BTTB. That July another 360 channels were approved, but by the end of the year only 180 of those 360 had been made available, 90 of them for Chittagong. The good news was the contiguous cell chain was complete along the railway from Dhaka to Chittagong, where service was just opening. The bad news was that in Dhaka channels increased only from 330 to 420 during 1998, not nearly enough capacity for a city of 10 million that housed the central switching station.

The congestion was horrible. To successfully manage with so few channels, GrameenPhone imposed charges on incoming calls originating from BTTB. Until then GrameenPhone had billed on the European model, which typically doesn't charge for incoming calls (as U.S. carriers do). But because BTTB charged per call and not by the minute, callers from BTTB to GrameenPhone had no incentive to keep the call short. This clogged the GrameenPhone network and led to numerous customer complaints about dropped calls or busy signals; by charging for incoming calls GrameenPhone forced its customers to limit the length of the calls.

Because BTTB had refused to share any revenue from calls made to GrameenPhone subscribers, GrameenPhone was essentially building out BTTB's network to end users at no cost to the government. As a result, while GrameenPhone was garnering garlands and roses from the world press, its own customers felt as though they were being shafted by a foreign-owned company (shades of the East India Company), playing right into BTTB's playbook (when in doubt, resort to xenophobia). On top of this indignity, outgoing calls to BTTB's fixed network often either didn't get through or were dropped; BTTB just didn't have the capacity or the quality to keep up with a state-of-the-art digital phone system.

"GrameenPhone just moved too fast for Bangladesh," said Mahbubul Alam, editor of *The Independent,* a Dhaka daily, at the time. "I am the loser and I am the one paying. Isn't the customer always right? But to say the Grameen name or image has been tarnished is too strong. Let's say that before where there was no question about Grameen, now there is in people's minds."[3]

"BTTB didn't believe there was a market; therefore it made no investments to build up its network and channel capacity," says Trond Moe now, who had replaced Skaar as GrameenPhone's CEO.

GrameenPhone, in contrast, was investing and building to deliver on its promise of universal coverage. With the Dhaka-Chittagong route and then the Dhaka-Khulna route complete with contiguous cells, GrameenPhone began installing a microwave link between Khulna and Chittagong. These are the two end points of the railway, the ends of the upside-down U along which the fiber ran, in between which lay the Bengal tiger delta, peopled by small fishing and farming communities. The microwave link, when completed the following year, brought telephones to poor rural areas and completed the circular structure of the transmission system that GrameenPhone needed so that traffic could reverse itself if any part of the system was down for repair.

GrameenPhone used the existing electrical grid where it could, but because the grid was unstable it also installed twelve-hour battery backup for all base stations. "We had to modify the equipment with insulators to protect against surges from low to high voltage," says Moe. Where GrameenPhone built outside the grid, power was supplied by diesel generators.

With the relentless investment and congestion, GrameenPhone was eating cash along with complaints. The shareholders were well on their way to executing the $100 million investment plan—but they didn't have $100 million. Finally, three years after the initial discussions, in August 1998, the boards of the World Bank's International Finance Corporation (IFC), the Asian Development Bank (ADB), and the Commonwealth Development Corporation (CDC) approved a debt-and-equity package of $55 million. This marked the first joint venture by the three prestigious development institutions and the first private-sector investment in Bangladesh by the Asian Development Bank. Along with the loan, each institution was to buy a 3 percent equity stake in the company in the form of nonvoting preferred shares. However, the money was contingent on reaching several benchmarks, the major one being 35,000 subscribers. By the end of 1998, GrameenPhone had only 31,000 subscribers. The interconnection problem had slowed sales and so had the monstrous floods during that year's monsoon (July through September), which had affected 30 million people. The $55 million wouldn't come through until the end of 1999.

But the response to the floods, when call volume doubled on cell phones and the government was able to prevent massive loss of property through better communications and logistics, showed that the country was on a new development path. Moe had sent emergency generators on boats to keep the cell network functioning. Business in Bangladesh was clearly not business as usual.

A Bold Move: Bypassing the Fixed-Line Network

The extra channels from BTTB had helped marginally, but GrameenPhone still had a large underutilized capacity. It had put up hundreds of cell towers and the fiber was live, but sales were not keeping pace. In the middle of the 1998 monsoon Yunus and the board pushed for and approved a radical tactical move: GrameenPhone (GP) would stop marketing subscriptions with access to BTTB and would pioneer a new, all-mobile service, called GP-GP. Subscribers would not be able to connect to the fixed-line network, which still represented the vast majority of telephones in the country (there were 450,000 fixed phones and less than 50,000 mobile phones at that time), but only to other cellular subscribers (which would eventually include subscribers to GrameenPhone's competitors). Initially, customers were upset and confused, but with the spread of GrameenPhone subscribers and the quality of the service, more and more subscribers signed up for GP-GP. At the same time, marketing efforts focused more on small businesses than big companies. By the end of 1998, nearly a quarter of GrameenPhone's 31,000 subscribers were buying service that couldn't connect to the nation's main phone system. In short order the three other cellular providers offered a similar service.

"This was a bold decision, which many said would never work," Moe said at the time. "However, we believed that the inherent demand was so big there would indeed be scope to build up an alternative network. Our analysis shows an immediate unmet demand of a minimum of 5–6 million subscribers. The challenge for GrameenPhone for the future is surely to meet the demand."[4] So much for a business predicated on 250,000 subscribers, which was the ceiling that analysts predicted for mobile telephony in Bangladesh. As the investment tally had mounted, so had the prospects for growth. Today Yunus and Moe both say that even Telenor didn't believe GP-GP would work.

Nowhere else in the world did a cellular system operate independently of the fixed-line network. There had been no need to do so, and it reduced the number of people a subscriber could call. The so-called network effect, which says that a network becomes more powerful and valuable as its size increases (witness Microsoft), was being turned upside down in Bangladesh. Restricting the size of the network in order to better control the quality of service for its customers was GrameenPhone's new strategy to reach millions of customers. The strategy was certainly bold and reflected on the brilliance of Quadir and Skaar's original model to route contiguous cells along the railroad and bet on the fiber. If push came to shove, as it had, GrameenPhone could operate without BTTB.

"Interconnection was our Achilles' heel," says Quadir. "I knew they could kill us. What was *their* Achilles' heel? Bad quality, high prices, and negligible long-distance service. By offering good service and low prices, especially on long-distance calls, we made quick gains. Thus, the nationwide coverage was not just to transform the rural areas, but an essential survival strategy. It was the practical means to overcome the otherwise deadly interconnection problem."

Today, throughout the developing world and especially in Africa, independent mobile networks are a given. Operators start from scratch with no intention of connecting to fixed-line networks. After the village-phone "scheme," Yunus touts the mobile-to-mobile network as GrameenPhone's most important contribution to telecom business models in developing countries.

Cash Flow Problems

Neither brilliance nor boldness is necessarily rewarded by bottom-line profits. GrameenPhone lost $13 million in 1998, on top of a $7 million loss in 1997. Twenty million in the hole and unable to draw on the IFC, ADB, and CDC credit line caused acute cash flow problems; on top of that, a $10 million loan from NORAD (the Norwegian agency that had installed the fiber cable a decade earlier) was held up due to technicalities.

Telenor had seen enough long-term potential in GrameenPhone to up its investment, as a bridge until the outside financing came through. Telenor increased its commitment from $15 million to $26 million. If Grameen Telecom wanted to maintain its 35 percent stake, it needed to up its stake to $18 million. Marubeni had no problem keeping up, but Gonofone needed new investors to maintain its 4.5 percent stake. "My best roll, aside from putting in money at the beginning, was pressing the idea that we needed to maintain our stake and keep putting more money in," says Josh Mailman, who eventually invested about $1 million. Quadir, meanwhile, to stay on a par with Mailman kept upping his stake by selling the initial shares he had received as sweat equity to new investors at a premium and then reinvesting in Gonofone.

For its initial stake, Grameen Telecom had pulled together a $7 million loan from a consortium of Bangladeshi banks. But Yunus had a better option for the second round. Not long before, George Soros's Open Society Institute invited Yunus to speak to a select group of investment executives, NGO leaders, and social activists in New York. Soros invited Yunus to join him for lunch at his apartment the next day. After a wide-ranging discussion on the future of Grameen Bank, Soros offered Yunus any support he might need to expand microcredit. Yunus quickly asked for money to increase Grameen's equity in GrameenPhone.

The Soros Economic Development Fund (SEDF) eventually loaned Grameen Telecom $10.6 million (which has since been paid back). The man who lent small sums to the poor at above-market rates took out a massive loan at a concessional rate (5 percent) from one of the world's richest men. Just as the prime ministers of Bangladesh and Norway were strangely synched, so were these two global icons. Their common ground was the village phone idea.

"It was an amazing case of quick decision making by a philanthropic investor," says Yunus. "He had no idea if the project would succeed. But he liked the idea of bringing cell phones to the poor women in Bangladesh, put his trust in me, and acted decisively."

"There was a lot of anxiety at the time because we were borrowing in dollars, and we'd ultimately have to pay back in dollars," says Shams. "It would be tough for Grameen Telecom since we'd have to convert takas, which were depreciating vis-à-vis the dollar, into dollars. If things didn't work out, how would we pay back the loan?"

Settling into Growth Mode

In all the start-up frenzy was subsiding. The village phone "scheme," as many reports labeled it, was still small but effective. The GP-GP mobile-to-mobile network was accepted by consumers, helped along by its radically low pricing. Using this network upped the marketing cost per subscriber, but the extra call volume meant the costs were recouped within a month. The main cities of Dhaka, Chittagong, and Khulna were nearly connected, awaiting only completion of the microwave link between Chittagong and Khulna. GrameenPhone had outspent and outplayed its weak competitors, had temporarily finessed the BTTB interconnection issue, had money in the bank and more coming from the loans, and had a grasp of cellular's huge market potential.

In 1999, GrameenPhone consolidated its gains and added to them while continuing to innovate. Its main new product was the EASY prepay card, which allowed customers to control their usage and fit it within their budgets. (New cell phone operators that started later in other developing countries had the advantage of starting service with prepaid cards, which radically simplified the billing and collecting process—and also created another set of income opportunities for entrepreneurs; see Chapters Eight and Nine.) International roaming agreements were signed with operators in Singapore, Denmark, Norway, Hong Kong, the United Kingdom, Switzerland, Taiwan, India, and Sweden. Voice mail and SMS (short message service, or text messaging) also went online in 1999.

By June 2000, nearly a year beyond the postlicense period referred to in the bid proposal as the "initial phase," GrameenPhone had invested $80 million out of the $125 million under its control, making it one of the largest private sector investors in the country that year. The number of cell towers increased to 200, village phones to 1,100, and overall subscribers to 60,000. This marked a twofold increase in each year, and the plan was to double the base again in the next year. The company even signed up its first sublease customer for the fiber. Overall revenues in 1999 increased 137 percent and margins by 158 percent, and the net loss dropped to $8 million. The major operational expense, of nearly $4 million, was to BTTB for interconnection—even though half GrameenPhone's customers had signed up for GP-GP. In 1999, actual earnings before interest, taxes, depreciations, and amortization (EBITDA) were positive for the first time! In its annual report GrameenPhone continued a section that Quadir had introduced the year before, "Yearly Government Revenues from GrameenPhone." This was part of an ongoing campaign, which had started with the initial license bid, to show the government the value of private investment and that GrameenPhone's success was accompanied by multiple "externalities" that were of benefit to the government. Payments to the Ministry of Posts and Telecommunications, the National Board of Revenues, the Bangladesh Railway, and BTTB and other fees, such as customs duties on handsets from retailers, amounted to Tk865 million (about $20 million) in 1999.

Working on that annual report would prove to be one of Quadir's last acts with GrameenPhone. He left the company in July 1999 to move back to the United States, where he would eventually end up lecturing at Harvard's Kennedy School of Government. (He has since started another business in Bangladesh; see Chapter Ten.) He had spent more than six years on the design, fundraising, and implementation of what was now a fully functioning cellular network in one of the world's poorest countries. But, like many entrepreneurs who lose control when their business ideas finally flourish, Quadir had lost his appointment to the board (it was not his seat, of course, but Telenor's) and felt his influence in the company was waning. At the same time, what had been his dream was becoming a reality—information communications technology was taking hold in Bangaldesh.

That same annual report included a short essay from Yunus, titled "IT Can Be Bangladesh's Road to Prosperity." Yunus urged the government to privatize communications and set up an independent regulatory agency. "If we can connect the fiber optic backbone network along the railway tracks to the fiber optic submarine cable, I feel strongly that Bangladesh can be a world-class player in the IT sector very soon. We must make the telecom infrastructure truly a superhighway to take us to the future without any stoplights or sharp turns."[5] Yunus was calling the right shots. In 2002, the Bangladesh Telecom Regulatory Authority was set up as an "independent" body to oversee what is now full-fledged privatization of the fixed-line network, and in the spring of 2006, Bangladesh finally connected its domestic fiber cable to the international submarine cable running through the Bay of Bengal.

Trond Moe, in his year-end letter to shareholders, predicted that "the total number of mobile subscribers will surely soon surpass the total number of fixed-line subscribers." He was right—it was about to happen in Bangladesh, as well as in developing countries around the world. Cell phone sales in developing countries were about to explode.

Part II

Transformation Through Technology

7

Wildfire at the Bottom of the Pyramid

If you had taken a satellite image of tele-density in the world in the 1990s, Bangladesh and a few of its neighbors, such as Nepal, Pakistan, India, and Myanmar, would have radiated "dangerously low." Except for a few rich or lucky people, no one had phones. The only other part of the world that competed with South Asia for paucity of phones was sub-Saharan Africa.

But about the time Iqbal Quadir had his "connectivity is productivity" epiphany in New York, a group in South Africa was already fighting the government there for a cellular license. M-Net, which had started pay TV service in South Africa in 1986 (one of only two such services in the world outside the United States), had conceived a "cellular project" in 1990, the year Nelson Mandela was released from prison.

M-Net's project (the company is now called MTN, an acronym for Mobile Telephone Networks), which took four years to get off the ground, marked the beginning of the opening of the African continent to widespread telephony, and has even led, more recently, to replications of GrameenPhone's village phone scheme in Uganda, Rwanda, and Nigeria. By the year 2000, combined with activity in South Asia and elsewhere, information communications technology was spreading across least developed countries like wildfire.

MTN proposed to state-owned Telkom in 1991 that they jointly develop GSM service for South Africa. As recounted in *MTN*:

10 Years of Cellular Freedom,[1] published in honor of MTN's tenth anniversary in 2004, Telkom gave that a flat no, forecasting that only 18,000 people in South Africa would *ever* need cell phones, and saying that if this forecast changed, Telkom would provide the service itself.

A year later, Coopers & Lybrand, commissioned by South Africa's Department of Posts and Telecommunications, recommended that the country's telecom sector be restructured and that two digital cellular licenses be offered, Telkom getting the first. M-Net pounced on the study and again approached Telkom to partner on the first license. It was no go—Telkom said it was now actively planning its own network.

In 1993, in the midst of the political upheaval after Mandela's release from prison and the emergence of the African National Congress (ANC) as a serious threat to President de Klerk's hold on power (de Klerk had released Mandela from prison and lifted the ban on the ANC), the government confirmed that it would grant two licenses to provide a "national cellular radio telephony service," with applications due June 1. In South Africa the first fully democratic elections were less than a year away.

It would be a mistake to equate democracy with liberalization, privatization, or deregulation, for certainly there are enough examples in recent history of nondemocratic regimes and "benevolent" dictatorships that have achieved economic success with free-market systems—China being Exhibit A. But democratization clearly implies devolution of power from the top of a hierarchical government with narrow interests down to the general population. In South Africa's case the dramatic shift in the balance of power meant power devolving from a white minority toward the black majority, in Bangladesh's case power devolved from a military "strongman" rule to a parliamentary democracy—and such political mind-shifts can certainly be equated with pressure to reform the monopolistic control of sectors that serve the public interest and common good.

MTN's Battle for a License

But that's a theory, and theories often hit the ground hard and get up slowly, if at all. In South Africa right after Mandela was freed, the "liberation" movement that would lead to his election was not sure that two cellular licenses would best serve the interests of the people. Weren't cell phones for the elite? How would they help poor blacks, who had never had phones, who could not afford them if they were available?

In addition, many South African black leaders saw nationalization, not deregulation and privatization, as the best socioeconomic option. A newly enlightened state should control and distribute resources evenly across the population, without outside influence. A similar xenophobic impulse had coursed through newly independent Bangladesh in 1971. In South Africa these issues were hotly debated during the political negotiations for a new constitution.[2]

Cyril Ramaphosa, who as secretary general of the ANC was a chief negotiator for the government of liberation, had heard the claims that cell phones were an "indulgence." But he saw vast potential for affordable communications for a broad base of people. Ramaphosa, now chairman of MTN, refers to the early days in *MTN: 10 Years of Cellular Freedom:* "However, in my mind, no lily-white company was going to succeed in the new South Africa. I thought this bunch of white businessmen and engineers would have to change and face the reality of their operating market."[3] That is to say, what were the chances that a new black government would tender a cellular license to a white-owned TV group?

Enter Nthato Motlana, personal physician to Nelson Mandela and chairman of NAIL (New Africa Investments Limited), the first black-empowerment group ever listed on the Johannesburg Stock Exchange. Motlana spent nine months lobbying the ANC for a second license to be granted. He won the battle, MTN won the license,

NAIL took a 20 percent stake in the company, and Motlana became MTN's first chairman. The fledgling company was 30 percent black owned (the South African Black Taxi Association and the SA Clothing and Textile Workers Union each owned 5 percent), a true pioneer in the new South Africa and a harbinger of a new multi-racial power structure.

Today the Black Economic Empowerment Act of 2003 mandates that to win government contracts companies must be either "black empowered" (more than 25 percent black ownership) or "black owned" (more than 50 percent black ownership), with different requirements by industry. And today, all Motlana's grandchildren have cell phones. "Cell phones are no longer a statement of wealth," he says. "They are a part of life."[4]

Fast and Furious Buildout

Once awarded the contract, MTN built a network with the same ferocity as GrameenPhone would build out Bangladesh a few years later. With logistics planned by Cable & Wireless, out of London, engineers fanned out across the country to quickly build what would for many years be the largest geographical cellular network in the world, larger than the area of France and Germany combined. Service started in April of 1994, a month ahead of Mandela's swearing in as South Africa's first black president. MTN henceforth became synonymous with the black-empowerment movement and the new push toward a more inclusive capitalism, as full enfranchisement replaced the apartheid system.

Telkom (whose cellular subsidiary, Vodacom, is 35 percent owned by Britain's Vodafone Ltd.) had a minor head start, but within six months MTN had matched Vodacom's number of subscribers and then quickly surpassed it. Forecasts for 18,000 subscribers in June 1994 changed to 58,000 by December 1994. When MTN rolled into a new town or village, people excitedly gathered to see the new towers go up. MTN quickly realized the importance of first-mover advantage in any virgin territory, which meant locking up 80 percent of the subscribers.[5]

When MTN was listed on the Johannesburg Stock Exchange in 1995, Nelson Mandela gave a speech in which he noted the need for Africa to expand its communications and information network: "The desire to be in touch lies deep within all of us. It is a basic need."[6] A *basic need*—it is reminiscent of Pitroda's comment that "as a great social leveler, information technology ranks second only to death." But this statement came from the president of a sovereign state, a revolutionary leader who was publicly equating information communications technology with progress and development.

At the time, less than 1 percent of Africans had access to a fixed-line phone, and there were fewer than 1 million mobile phones for Africa's 800 million people. Tele-density was about the same as in Bangladesh; clearly, African governments were not providing this "basic need." And it would be some time before other African governments heard Mandela's cry.

Showdown with Mugabe in Zimbabwe

A more typical African story was unfolding in Zimbabwe (the former Rhodesia), where President Robert Mugabe at one point outlawed cell phones. Like Mandela, Mugabe was the first black leader to take control of his country after wresting power from white-run governments. But Mugabe is no Mandela.

Strive Masiyiwa, a Rhodesian-born black who had studied in Scotland and Wales (focusing on engineering) and returned to the new Zimbabwe in 1980 when the white government was overthrown, had proposed in 1993 a joint cellular venture with the state-owned Posts and Telecommunications Corporation (PTC), much as MTN had proposed to Telkom. Masiyiwa had worked for PTC during the 1980s and then started his own engineering firm, for which he was named Businessman of the Year in Zimbabwe in 1990, when he was twenty-nine.

PTC first insisted it had a monopoly and no interest in a joint venture, but Masiyiwa took that to court—and won. PTC had no right to a monopoly if it had no intention of providing the service. According to the *Economist*,[7] Mugabe's government suspected that cell phones might be used for "spying," and forced the Zimbabwe Supreme Court to overturn the decision. Masiyiwa then argued that the telecom monopoly violated the constitutional right of Zimbabweans to free speech. To everyone's surprise, the Supreme Court ruled in his favor. Masiyiwa, with help from Ericsson, started putting up cell towers around Harare, the capital of Zimbabwe. Mugabe outlawed cell phones and instituted a two-year jail term for offenders. That drove Ericsson out of the country.

Masiyiwa, who had a rebel streak, appeared unfazed. A devout Christian, he was opposed to paying bribes, which is why he had turned to the courts. After he graduated from high school in Scotland in 1978, he had come to what was then still Rhodesia to join the freedom fighters. However, a senior rebel officer said to him, "Look, we're about to win anyway, and what we really need is people like you to help rebuild the country."[8] That sent Masiyiwa back to study engineering at the University of Wales.

Now, essentially going one on one with Mugabe, Masiyiwa again appealed to the Supreme Court—which ruled Mugabe's decree unconstitutional and ordered a tender for a private cell phone license. By this time, PTC had started its own cell company, NetOne. (After ten years of operation, NetOne had signed up only 200,000 subscribers.) The new license was awarded to Telecel, a politically connected group that included Leo Mugabe, the president's nephew. Masiyiwa sued to see Telecel's bid and found it didn't meet the tender specifications. The license was revoked, then reinstated, then canceled again. In December 1997, Masiyiwa was given the license.

Masiyiwa had sold his engineering firm in 1994 and used the money to begin a cell operation in Botswana, so he was ready to roll. In the first week his Econet signed up 10,000 customers, and within two months it had a 45 percent market share. At thirty-seven, Masiyiwa was named one of the Ten Most Outstanding Young Persons of the World in 1999, by the Junior Chamber International. By 2002, when Econet was operating in eight countries with revenues of $300 million, Masiyiwa had moved Econet headquarters to South Africa and had been named a Global Influential by *Time* magazine.[9]

If MTN and Vodacom had changed the dynamic in South Africa, both in terms of distributing the *common good* of communications and, in MTN's case, by persuading the government to deregulate the telecom sector, Econet had certainly made it clear that even in a very corrupt country, the courts were willing to back private entrepreneurs promising to deliver telecommunications. By 1997, other nations in Africa started opening up their government-run telecom markets to private cellular investors, and MTN expanded into Uganda, Rwanda, and Swaziland. But MTN didn't have the continent to itself. The gold rush was on, and new prospectors moved in.

Sudan's Dr. Mo Returns to Africa

As governments saw the opportunity to attract foreign investment, license tenders went out all over the continent. And that brought in some exciting new players, most notably Mohamed Ibrahim. Dr. Mo, as he is fondly known (or "just Mo" as he refers to himself), is Sudanese by birth, of Nubian origin, studied electrical engineering in Egypt (University of Alexandria), and earned a PhD degree in engineering in England (University of Birmingham). He then worked as a technical director with British Telecom's Cellnet, one of the world's first mobile networks. His basic story is not unlike that of Sam Pitroda, who left India to get his engineering doctorate in the United States and then logged multiple patents at GTE. Dr. Mo is a native entrepreneur who became a world-class success and reinvested foreign money into his homeland and home continent to create a fantastic business, with annual revenues now in excess of $1 billion.

After his early success with Cellnet, Dr. Mo had taken a few British Telecom engineers and started a consulting firm, Mobile Systems International (MSI), to help new cellular license winners design their mobile systems. As multiple mobile licenses began to be issued in the Western world, it was clear that the winners had either money or the inside track but not much telecom know-how. MSI designed a software package, *Planet*, that optimized the design of networks.

By 1998, MSI was a very successful, global consulting firm and software house, with revenues of $130 million, 800 consultants (400 in the United States), seventeen offices worldwide, and stakes in fast-growing cell phone companies in Hong Kong, Africa, and India. (Dr. Mo was a founding board member of Bharti Mobile, now the number one cell phone operator in India.) "We were in many cases given a small share of the equity as our contribution for helping to win the license," says Dr. Mo. "But we had to find an opportunity to become a major operator in our own right."

Dr. Mo, a pipe-smoking "former Marxist" who calls himself a "reluctant entrepreneur," was ready to return to Africa. He knew the cellular business and could read the lay of the land:

> Licenses were affordable there, unlike in the developed world. The big operators were afraid to go there; they thought that business in Africa meant dealing with corruption, wars, and famines. On every continent and almost every country, cell phones were taking off, but even the South African operators MTN and Vodacom were not touching sub-Saharan Africa. It was lack of understanding and the African fright factor—fear of bad governance, lack of law, war, poverty. I am African, and many of the other executives are either African or have extensive experience in emerging markets. This gives us

a unique insight into the continent. In particular, we
were keenly aware that Africa is not a country.

No, Africa comprises fifty-two countries, stretching from the
North African Saharan nations to the landlocked and tropical
nations in the center to bountiful South Africa at the tip; from Eng-
lish-speaking East Africa to French-speaking West Africa; from
autocratic monarchies to kleptocratic dictator-presidents to full-
fledged parliamentary democracies. The Democratic Republic of the
Congo itself is almost half the size of the United States; and fifteen
of the United Nations' thirty-one *landlocked developing nations* are
in Africa.

From a business perspective it *is* tempting to view Africa as a
mass of humanity—more than 850 million people, one seventh of
the world—that almost rivals the populations of China (1.3 billion)
and India (1.1 billion). That's a huge market, which just happens
to be divided into many parts. Once you get in and begin to understand the intricacies of doing business in potentially dangerous and
corrupt countries, you can begin to cover the checkerboard quickly.
Not that it's easy to do—from a telecom perspective, Africa would
be divided into *at least* 52 separate licenses (in actuality, more than
100), just as India was divided into multiple cellular licenses covering different regions (one of Quadir's selling points for the beauty
of a single license that covered all of Bangladesh).

Tapping $1 Billion in Investment

In 1998, almost two years after GrameenPhone had won its license,
MSI-Cellular Investments (now called Celtel International BV)
began operations in Africa. With $11 million in assets acquired
through MSI, Dr. Mo set out to raise money, and had a far easier
time of it than GrameenPhone had had three or four years prior. For
one thing, Dr. Mo was both a proven entrepreneur and a knowl-
edgeable telecom engineer. For another, by 1998 even squeamish
Westerners could see the opportunity in distant and dangerous lands,

especially if the business had any connection to technology and especially if native guides were available. In the United States, venture capitalists were funding business plans on napkins, as long as the word *tech* was scrawled somewhere! Finally, the recent emergence of prepaid phone cards made the idea of selling service to poor people without bank accounts or credit cards much more feasible.

In all, Celtel raised more than $1 billion in debt and equity, from a combination of development lenders such as Britain's CDC Capital Partners, Holland's Netherlands Development Finance Company (FMO), the World Bank's IFC—and U.S.-based venture capitalists, such as Bessemer Venture Partners, Emerging Markets Partnership, Zephyr Asset Management, and Citigroup Venture Capital International. Often the presence of development finance institutions (DFIs), who are driven more by development success than profits, scares away private money looking for the big, quick return. But not in this case—there was comfort in knowing that the DFIs might bring a steady hand to what could be a wild bet and certainly a wild ride.

The money didn't come in all at once, of course. In the first year, Celtel raised $16 million and acquired GSM licenses in Malawi, Zambia, Sierra Leone, and Republic of the Congo (also known as Congo-Brazzaville), plus a minority stake in Egypt. In 1999, Celtel raised another $35 million and acquired licenses in Gabon, Chad, the Democratic Republic of the Congo, and Guinea. This was by and large new territory for U.S. venture capital investors, but the early returns were positive. The first day Celtel offered service in Gabon, the doors to its offices were literally knocked off their hinges. That kind of pent-up demand quickly translated into paid subscribers.

Even if Celtel was burning cash, it was gaining customers and driving revenues (unlike most Internet companies of that era), and that attracted more cash. In 2000, Celtel raised $63 million to purchase interests in Burkina Faso, Niger, and Sudan, then raised another $153 million in 2001 to acquire 35 percent of Tanzania's fixed-line network—and to build out its cross-continental holdings. Along with the share of the fixed-line network, Celtel bought a new cellular license in Tanzania. At every turn of the wheel, Dr. Mo invested his own money; MSI had been sold in 2000, giving him liquidity.

But Celtel still had a voracious need for cash, and the banks were slowing down lending for telecom. "During the global slowdown between 2000 and 2002, $2 trillion of value in telecom companies was wiped out," says Dr. Mo. "Banks were overexposed, having lent tens of billions for licenses." When it came time to bid for a license in Nigeria at a cost of $285 million, Celtel could only muster $250 million, and had to drop out of the bidding in Africa's most populous country. Nonetheless, Celtel survived and prospered. (In May 2006, Celtel bought a controlling stake in Nigeria's VCom for more than $1 billion.)

"Everyone thinks Africa is full of starving people and pretty lions," says Dr. Mo. "They don't realize it's also full of normal people who want to do normal things, like make a telephone call." The three forces of external combustion—information technology imported by native entrepreneurs backed by foreign investors—were affecting sub-Saharan Africa as they had affected South Asia.

Difficult Local Conditions

Africa, of course, has its own special problems of corruption, drought, famine, and war (Bangladesh, in contrast, has only corruption and floods). Celtel took care of the corruption issue by adamantly refusing to pay any bribes, even if it cost the company business. "I was determined to bring a Western style of business to a non-Western environment," says Dr. Mo, who also notes that Celtel has been to court five times to enforce contracts and has won each case. "Over time, we are changing the way business is conducted. We do not do business using brown envelopes." He also condemns the hypocrisy of bribery in Africa, saying bribery "is a crime committed by two consenting adults," and that it is "usually less the idea of the African than the Westerner," one who is often frustrated at the slow pace of business and trying to speed things up.

As for doing business in conflict zones, such as Sierra Leone, Celtel has prospered. Revenues increase, because both rebels and government supporters need to communicate. (The same has proved true for cell operators in Iraq.) In remote areas Celtel pays villagers to guard cell towers twenty-four hours a day, although there has been almost no vandalism, as cell towers are perceived as a communal benefit. Marauders used to steal copper cables from landlines; so few people had phones there was no incentive to protect the network.

Another major problem is the terrain. Unlike Bangladesh, which is flat and densely populated, perfect natural conditions for a cellular network, much of Africa is hilly and mountainous, with impassable roads and raging rivers and thinly spread populations. Building a network in the Democratic Republic of the Congo, for example, Vodacom reports its trucks getting stuck in the mud, requiring fifteen to twenty men to haul cell towers into place with ropes.[10] And because Africa's highest-density populations are in the highland regions, such as Ethiopia and Rwanda, where rainfall is more reliable and the soils are better,[11] villagers build fifty-foot-high tree houses to catch signals from distant towers.[12]

"We got a call once that people in rural areas were breaking their arms falling out of trees and it was our fault," says Dr. Mo. "I said, 'How can that be our fault?' It turns out they were climbing trees to get better reception."

While Celtel was buying up licenses as if it were collecting travel posters, MTN was primarily focusing on its South Africa franchise, where it was and is locked in fierce competition with Vodacom and a new entrant, Cell C, a black-owned company. In November 2001, Cell C signed up more than 100,000 customers in its first twelve hours! (In June 2006, Cell C was rebranded as Virgin Mobile, through a 50-50 joint venture with Britain's Virgin Group.) MTN did, however, start operations in Cameroon in 2000 and Nigeria in 2001, where it bought the license coveted by Celtel for $285 million.

By 2002, there were seventy licensed mobile networks in Africa, and some governments were hitting pay dirt: Morocco earned $1.1 billion with a license sale in 2000; Nigeria raised $850 million selling three cellular licenses in 2001.[13] With four cellular companies (and a state-owned landline company that is losing money), the number of phones in Nigeria skyrocketed from 700,000 in 2000 to 12 million in 2005; in addition to license fees, $2 billion has been invested in the telecom infrastructure. (Vodacom has been trying to buy a stake in a Nigerian mobile firm since 2003, to compete with archrival MTN.)

Egypt's Orascom: A New Global Player Emerges

Sensing a feeding frenzy, Egypt's Orascom Telecom Holding (OTH) decided to test the waters. OTH is African, even though North Africa is a different world from the rest of Africa, and it had money. It is part of the Orascom Group, a business empire owned by the Sawiris family. The Orascom Group also has holdings in hotels, technology, tourism, and construction and was worth $12 billion in 2005.[14]

Naguib Sawiris, the eldest of three brothers who run the empire created by their father (Onsi Sawiris), made his first telecom foray in 1998, buying a share in Egypt's MobiNil, and then expanding into Jordan, Yemen, Syria, and Pakistan. By 2000, OTH reached more than 2.5 million subscribers in twenty countries, having gone on an African shopping binge, buying licenses in Zimbabwe, Uganda, Togo, Ivory Coast, Gabon, Zambia, Benin, Republic of the Congo, Burundi, Chad, Burkina Faso, and Niger. With an uptick in revenues, Orascom was getting heady, not unlike Internet players in the United States, and was already talking about developing a "third-world Internet" strategy to interface with its GSM operations through its LINKdotNET Internet subsidiary in Egypt.

But as Celtel had learned, operating in multiple sub-Saharan countries consumed inordinate amounts of cash. Each country posed new problems and required new relationships. In 2002, reeling with debt during the global telecom slowdown, OTH sold ten of its sub-Saharan African properties (as well as its Jordanian operation) in order to restructure its debt and focus on countries closer to home, such as Algeria and Tunisia. In 2003, OTH sold its Kuwaiti operation to MTC (a Kuwait-based MTC Group had a market capitalization of $13 billion at the beginning of 2006) and sold out of Syriatel. While it recouped, OTH turned its sights eastward with the goal of becoming number one in the Middle East, North Africa, and Pakistan.

Today, OTH has more than 30 million subscribers in Egypt, Algeria, Tunisia, Zimbabwe, Pakistan, and more recently, Iraq and Bangladesh. In 2005, Orascom bought bereft Sheba Telecom in Bangladesh, which had won a license along with GrameenPhone in 1996 but which had only 60,000 subscribers. This is a quick reminder that even though it may seem that a cell license is a license to print money, you do have to use guts and guile to deploy capital if you are in a competitive market. That's something Sawiris knows how to do. In less than a year, Orascom invested $250 million in Sheba, started a pricing war with GrameenPhone, and added 1 million new customers. Orascom also lost license bids in Iran, Saudi Arabia, and Nigeria.

OTH owns 100 percent of Iraqna, the first mobile provider in Iraq. Security costs for two years reached $30 million, but 2005 revenues exceeded $300 million, with 1.5 million subscribers and an EBITDA of 66 percent. "Wherever the risk is high, the profits are also high," Sawiris told the *New York Times*. "We know that calm will come one day and Iraq will be a second Saudi Arabia. We believe that Iraq harbors large potential for growth and remains a very attractive market for Orascom Telecom."[15] No doubt he's right. If Africa is any precedent, insurgents might blow up oil fields, but they wouldn't dare touch a cell tower.

OTH expects to reach 50 million subscribers globally by 2007 and 100 million by 2010.

Cell Phones in India: After a Slow Start, 5 Million a Month

Despite the frenzy to buy cell phone licenses in India in the mid-1990s—fourteen private operators (including Sweden's Telia) rushed in—distribution and subscriptions lagged behind other parts of Asia and Africa. Much of this was due to license regulations that led to high call tariffs. One operator (Reliance, now one of the leaders in the Indian market) famously said that mobile telephony would work in India only if phone calls became cheaper than postcards.

By 1999, regulations were eased and call tariffs dropped, but it wasn't until the launch of CDMA (Code Division Multiple Access) services in 2003 to compete with GSM that prices dropped sufficiently to spark a boom in sales. In January 2003, there were 10 million cell phone subscribers, a penetration of less than 1 per 100 people. (In June 2003, Telia, which owned 26 percent of Bharti Mobile, India's largest operator, and which had decided not to enter Bangladesh in part because of its Indian initiative, sold its stake.) By early 2004, the number of subscribers had tripled to 30 million. It wasn't until the end of 2004 that mobile overtook fixed lines, somewhat later than in other developing countries, due to India's more advanced fixed-line network. Nonetheless, "rural India was not brought into the fold," says Madanmohan Rao, coeditor of *Asia Unplugged*.[16] Indeed, there were reports in 2006 that Indian villagers on the northwestern Bangladesh border were using GrameenPhone accounts to make calls. This is ironic given that Quadir was inspired in part by accounts of Sam Pitroda's efforts to introduce fixed-line village phones in India in the early 1990s.

In August 2006, India surpassed the 100 million subscriber mark (with GSM phones comprising nearly 80 percent of these phones), and it is now one of fastest growing markets in the world, adding about 5 million subscribers a month. Including its 80 million fixed-line connections, India is approaching 20 percent penetration of phone service.

The Tipping Point

In developing countries, 2000 marked the beginning of a tipping point that has become a deluge. While the West was lamenting the pop of the dot-com bubble, it was clear that cell phones in the South were selling at exponential rates and that an information communications revolution was under way. By 2001, cell phones in many poor countries outnumbered fixed-line phones (see Figure 7.1), which contributed to a worldwide lead for mobiles in 2002. Amazingly, the adoption curves on each country's chart seemed to cross at about the same time. The rapid spread of cell phones is reminiscent of the unstoppable action of the magical broom in the tale of the sorcerer's apprentice, in which the broom splits in two and fetches water faster and faster until there is water everywhere.

In Uganda, thanks to MTN Uganda's early start, the tipping point was reached earlier: between 1997 and 1999, the number of

Figure 7.1. The Tipping Point: Telephone Subscribers per 100 Inhabitants, Africa, 1995–2004.

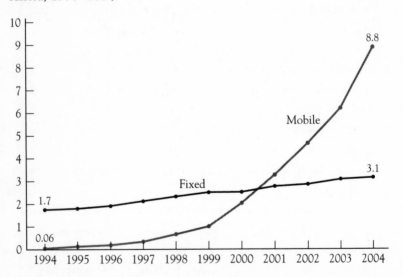

Source: International Telecommunication Union, "Africa Fixed Line Comparison," in ICT Statistics, 2004, retrieved from http://www.itu.int/ITU-D/ict/statistics/ict/index.html. Reproduced with the kind permission of ITU.

mobiles exploded from 7,000 to 87,000, whereas the number of fixed-line phones inched up from 54,000 to 59,000. In the Philippines the story was the same. Between Globe Telecom, a private company, and Smart Communications, a wholly owned subsidiary of the state-run PTLD, mobiles overtook fixed-line phones sometime in 2002; by 2004, mobiles outnumbered fixed-line phones four to one.

Past the tipping point, companies in developing countries routinely have doubled their number of subscribers every year and have used their soaring revenues to expand the network, add services, and generate more revenues. The most recent forecast is that Bangladesh will have 20 million mobile phones by the end of 2007. That's one for every 8 people (12 percent), compared to one landline phone for every 500 people in 1993. By 2006, there were 100 million phones in Africa (also a tele-density of 12 percent), and 75 percent of those were mobile (see Figure 7.2). By the middle of 2005, MTN and Vodacom each had close to 25 million subscribers;

Figure 7.2. Average Annual Growth Rate in Mobile Subscribers, 1999–2004.

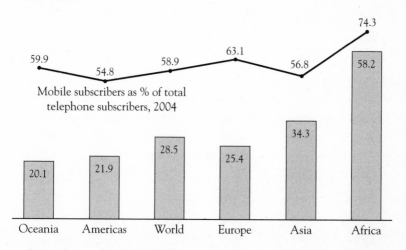

Source: International Telecommunication Union, "Global Mobile Comparison," in *ICT Statistics*, 2004, retrieved from http://www.itu.int/ITU-D/ict/statistics/ict/index.html. Reproduced with the kind permission of ITU.

Celtel, despite its huge footprint in fourteen countries, was third in Africa, with about 8 million subscribers. (In 2005, MTN bid $2.7 billion to buy Celtel but was swamped by MTC's $3.4 billion offer.)

Noting the spoils that await the bold in emerging markets, the *Financial Times* (in its Lex Column) in late 2004 singled out Africa: "Special rewards were on offer for those willing to bet on growth of mobile telephones in sub-Saharan Africa. The key appeal of African telecom operators remains that these risks are largely uncorrelated with global economic trends."[17]

Azmi Mikati, CEO of Investcom Holding, with mobile operations in Afghanistan, Benin, Yemen, Sudan, and Syria, told the *New York Times:* "Those countries have more resources than you read, because of the gray economy and the cash economy. They are not as poor or as dangerous as they are portrayed."[18] Michael Joseph, CEO of Safaricom (60 percent owned by Kenya Telecom, 40 percent by Britain's Vodafone Ltd.) says, "We all misread the market."[19]

The same satellite imagery that would have shown 1 percent tele-density across much of South Asia and Africa in the 1990s would today show relentless new phone adoption. Africa is now the fastest-growing region in the world in terms of mobile phones. There are more new mobile customers every week in Africa than in North America. In Bangladesh there are now six cellular operators, including Orascom's Banglalink (formerly Sheba); BTTB's 2004 entry, Teletalk; and Warid Telecom, based in the United Arab Emirates, which bought a license in 2005 (after buying one in Pakistan in 2004). "I'm not sure Bangladesh can support six independent operators," says Erik Aas, CEO of GrameenPhone. "I would not be surprised if we see some consolidation over the next few years."

With cell penetration rates still so low—around 12 percent—there's almost no barrier to stop this growth. The poor, the rebels, the sixty-year-old men who have been waiting for twenty-seven years—everyone wants a phone. Somehow they can afford it or share it. The cell phone is becoming a bank, a credit card, and a computer—in many cases for people who have never had any such services or tools.

8

Cell Phone as Wallet

The cell phone in the developing world, as in the developed world, has quickly fast-forwarded into a mini-PC with Internet and transaction capability. But the social and economic impact of this technology is much more dramatic and disruptive in the developing world, where many people have never had phones before, let alone computers or Internet connections—or bank accounts (see, for example, Figure 8.1).

The cell phone is not only bridging the digital divide but is changing the way people who have never had bank accounts or credit cards deal with money. In Zambia, Coca-Cola distributors *text* payments to truck drivers, and consumers text payments to gas stations, dry cleaners, and other shops.[1] In Rwanda, local craftspeople without electricity or telephone lines can take credit card payments through their cell phones.[2] In the Philippines, people buy soap and pizza by phone; in the Philippines and India, villagers receive remittances from overseas by phone. In Bangladesh, bank customers can check their accounts by phone. *As a great social leveler, information technology is second only to death.*

The key stepping-stone to mobile banking is prepaid SIM (subscriber identity module) cards for cell phone subscribers. In places such as the Philippines and Africa, almost everyone is a prepaid subscriber, with rates between 95 percent to 98 percent. In Bangladesh the prepaid subscriber rate was initially lower,

Figure 8.1. You Don't Have to Be Rich, But It Helps: Prevalence of Bank Accounts at Different Income Levels.

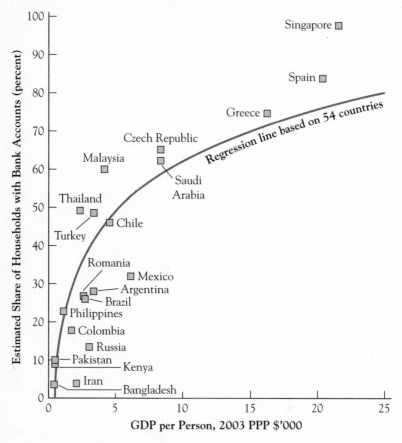

because GrameenPhone started before prepaid cards were available, but it has now essentially caught up with other developing regions. Once you have loaded prepaid minutes (*value*) into your phone, no matter how small the amount of time you have purchased, your cell phone becomes your wallet. Before you know it, money's flowing in and out. For many poor people the upside is that they are for the first time connected to a banking grid, which over the long term improves their chances for saving and establishing credit—and for moving from an informal cash culture to a formal credit-and-debit culture.

Mobile banking in developing countries is just the beginning of an expected avalanche of services and applications that collectively will constitute mobile commerce (*m-commerce*). After voice communications (and text messaging, or *texting*, in some cultures), connection to financial services is the first big "killer app" for cell phones, initially manifested in three ways:

- Storing money in the phone and using it as a virtual automatic teller machine (ATM), using banks, cell carriers, and increasingly, hybrid bank–cell phone companies

- Sending and receiving remittances,with superior delivery and reduced transaction costs

- Retail purchasing and bill paying, both at preselected outlets

Microfinance institutions, given their symbiotic relationship with cell phone companies in certain countries, are also beginning to experiment with the delivery of microloans through the cell phone, although microlending remains a very high-touch business. In general, the technique of making financial transactions by sending text messages on a cell phone has been started by people who don't have much money and who are not connected to banks. Such mobile banking is likely to be the second cell phone application, after prepaid cards, that first takes root in poor countries and then migrates to rich countries.

The Birth of Mobile Banking in the Philippines

Mobile banking first took root in the Philippines. Although the Philippines is clearly a poor country, its per capita GDP of $1,123 ($4,920 PPP) makes it richer than most of sub-Saharan Africa (excepting South Africa) and Bangladesh. That extra cash in hand has put a little more zip in the m-commerce transformation in the Philippines.

The fact that texting (SMS, or short message service) is more prevalent in the Philippines than anywhere else in the world has also helped drive m-commerce. The first day texting was available in 1998, 50 million messages were sent (in a country of 80 million); the average Filipino cell phone user now sends 20 text messages a day; the 20 million subscribers to the Philippine mobile service provider Smart Communications send 500 million text messages a day. In January 2001, Philippine president Joseph Estrada was overthrown in a bloodless coup four days after hundreds of thousands of protestors massed in Manila to demand his ouster. Antigovernment mobilizers had sent this text message to every number they had: "Full mblsn tday Edsa": that is, "full mobilization today at the Edsa shrine in Manila."[3]

The innovative evolution of Smart Communications in the Philippines shows how the combination of texting with a prepaid system has quickly turned phones into cashless ATMs–cum–debit cards. Smart started business in 1999, as a wholly owned subsidiary of the state-owned Philippine Long Distance Telephone Company (PLDT), courting the lower end of market. This unusual strategy was necessary to offset the head start of Globe Telecom (44 percent owned by Singapore's SingTel, which has since bought a significant minority stake in Bangladesh's CityCell), the only other major cellular player, which was targeting the high end of the market and the urban elite. This was essentially the situation GrameenPhone encountered with CityCell in 1997. By reaching out to a broader market, as GrameenPhone had done, Smart quickly moved past Globe and now holds a 58 percent market share. (Globe, unlike CityCell, is still a strong number two.) In addition to the strategy of tapping an underserved market, much of Smart's success resulted from developing innovative services to attract that market.

Smart's first product was Smart Buddy, introduced in 2000, which allowed subscribers to buy prepaid SIM cards in various voice-and-text combinations and in increments as low as $5. But a sluggish economy in 2002 caused a high churn rate even at these low rates, so Smart introduced PureTxt 100—prepaid text-only cards in increments as low as $1.80. This was "to encourage subscribers to stay in the system even in a limited capacity, instead of churning and resubscribing at a later time," notes a case study by Digital Dividend (a project of the World Resources Institute). "When PureTxt was introduced, it opened up an entire subset of the BOP (bottom of the pyramid) market for Smart."[4] A text message cost only two cents, versus seven or fourteen cents for a voice call.

Smart Money, introduced in late 2000 in partnership with First e-Bank (later acquired by Banco de Oro) and MasterCard, allows transfer of money from a bank account to a Smart Money account. It was the "world's first reloadable electronic cash wallet," according to Smart's current CEO, Napoleon L. Nazareno. A subscriber can use Smart Money like a debit card at retail outlets, transferring money via texting (SMS) to the cell phone of another Smart Money subscriber, such as a taxi driver or fast-food outlet. Although Smart Money requires the user to have a bank account and is thus aimed at upmarket users, its value-loading technology set the stage for what was to follow.

Expanding Distribution and Access to Mobile Banking

In 2003, Smart Load, based on Smart Buddy, enabled electronic transfer of airtime from resellers to subscribers. Prepaid text-and-call combo packages were sold in increments as low as fifty-four cents—what Smart called "telecom in sachets" (in small packages). To cut transaction costs, Smart shortly thereafter eliminated the physical card and went to electronic-only transfer. Thus, Smart had essentially integrated the Smart Money value-loading technology into the prepaid reseller system, and a subscriber could use it even if he or she didn't have a bank account. "With electronic loading, the system becomes borderless, as it can be distributed all over the country via 700,000 outlets within seconds," says CEO Nazareno.[5]

Now, Filipinos who practice *tingi-tingi* (purchasing food in small amounts) from *sari sari* (neighborhood shop) owners can buy *telecom in sachets* from Smart distributors, even if they don't have money. *Sari sari* owners depend on relationship marketing—and extend credit for phone minutes as they do for staples. Smart has essentially transformed *sari sari* retailers into electronic microlenders! Out of necessity Smart has replicated a form of group lending, as the *sari sari* owners know their customers and could make life difficult in the community if a customer were to default on the "loan," thus enforcing payback.

These new microlenders don't charge interest, but they have added a whole new service to their inventory of goods—for which they earn a 15 percent commission from Smart. Of Smart's 700,000 retailers, 90 percent are *sari sari* owners (the rest are housewives and students), who need only a bank account and phone to get into the business. They are given a retailer's SIM card (less than $2) and an initial load of 300 pesos ($5 or $6). Some retailers make $20 a day from selling phone services, as much as they make from selling all other goods combined. On its Web site Smart advertises for more resellers—"Earn extra money! Start a business with SmartLoad!"

The story of Smart's outreach to poor people on the outside looking in, like that of GrameenPhone's outreach to the phone ladies in Bangladesh, exemplifies inclusive capitalism. As the World Resources Institute's case study notes, the business model is "BOP [bottom-of-the-pyramid] driven." Smart is creating jobs and income opportunities in its quest to reach as broad a market as possible, even if people need to borrow to buy prepaid packages costing as little as fifty cents. The social and economic dynamic is so complex and the product so perfectly designed, it could only have been executed by local businesspeople who listened to their customers and tinkered with their product until they hit on a workable win-win solution. For example, by moving to electronic transfer of phone minutes in order to avoid the costs associated with using SIM cards, Nazareno estimates Smart saves $20 million a year.

Meanwhile, Smart's revenues and profits have spiraled upward since its inception. At the end of 2005, Smart counted 21 million subscribers, revenues of 74 billion pesos (about $1.4 billion), and profits of 50 billion pesos (about $900 million), with margins of 66 percent. Targeting the low end of the market is not always a risky business proposition.

Globe's G-Cash

In 2004, Globe Telecom, which is Smart's only major competitor, introduced G-Cash. Like Smart Money, G-Cash "turns your cellphone into a wallet." With G-Cash, however, you don't need a bank account but can bring cash to Globe business centers or certain resellers. You can then text cash to another Globe subscriber, certified retailers (such as 7-Eleven and McDonald's), and pay bills and taxes.

G-Cash is not a revolutionary product (how quickly we adapt!), although the fact that the user doesn't need a bank account made it a new idea in the m-commerce arena. (Globe operates a clearinghouse facility that records transactions and settlements.)[6] But G-Cash is also noteworthy for two other reasons. It is being used in conjunction with the Rural Bankers Association of the Philippines for making loan repayments, and experiments are under way to advance microloans through microfinance institutions. More important, it exhibits a radical shift in Globe's perception of the market. Having initially aimed at the high end of the market in the mid-1990s, Globe realized that to continue growing it had to develop what amounts to an innovative banking product—even though many of its new customers may not even have bank accounts.

"We saw a segment of the market that was underserved by the formal financial system," says Gerardo C. Ablaza, president and CEO of Globe Telecom. "With G-Cash, we have minimized barriers to entry that we have seen in other m-Commerce implementations; for example, the requirement to have a bank account or a credit card."[7]

Another innovative Globe product aimed at low-income customers is Txt Bak Mo, Libre Ko, a messaging service that allows the
sender to shoulder the cost of the text reply, ensuring two-way communication even if one person has no value in his or her phone.
The sender essentially prepays for a response, without any transaction occurring—an extremely innovative solution. In Kenya, Safaricom subscribers have developed their own solution: *flashing*. Callers
ring someone they want to speak with, then hang up almost immediately and wait for a callback. The practice is so widespread that
phone-booth operators charge customers five cents to flash—cheaper
than making a call.

Mobile Banking in Africa

South Africa is by far the richest country in Africa (with per capita
GDP of $3,534, $12,346 in PPP), but the income is not very evenly
distributed and only half of South Africans over age sixteen have
bank accounts. In many rural areas you can drive 100 miles without seeing a bank. When you do find one, fees are high. But MTN
Group, the leading cell phone operator in Africa, has partnered
with Standard Bank to deliver banking services to customers who
have never before had bank accounts. Their joint venture, like that
of Smart Communications and Banco de Oro in the Philippines,
could become a model for a corporate marriage of convenience that
extends formal banking to millions of people.

MTN Banking, like the Filipino cashless transaction systems,
involves a virtual bank accessed by inserting a special SIM card into
a phone. MTN Banking customers, in effect, are customers of Standard Bank but with limitations on their monthly transaction totals
and amounts held in accounts. There are no monthly charges, but
a bank fee for each transaction and a texting fee for each message
provide a revenue stream for each partner. All you need is a cell
phone and a government-issued identity number to subscribe. In
addition, the government expects to use MTN Banking to distribute

pensions, which will lower its transaction costs and save people a sometimes lengthy trip to a distribution center.

An unusual twist to MTN Banking is that it gives people who have never had bank accounts an ATM card—which is upgradable to a MasterCard debit card. "We believe that this very simple but very well-designed product has the potential to revolutionize banking on the African continent," says Herman Singh, director of technology engineering at Standard Bank.[8]

To encourage new customers, South African regulators waived the provisions of the Financial Intelligence Centre Act that require proof of identification and address for all account holders. Similarly, in Malawi the Opportunity Bank of Malawi accepts fingerprint biometrics stored on a smart card, as many potential new customers don't have the driver's license or passport typically required to open an account.[9]

Other virtual banks are sprouting up in Africa. WIZZIT is a new mobile bank that operates as a division of the South African Bank of Athens. Customers use phones to make person-to-person payments, transfer money, and buy airtime. WIZZIT does not have its own physical branches or ATMs but gives customers a Maestro branded debit card to use at ATMs and retail outlets.

Celpay, a former subsidiary of Celtel that is now owned by First Rand Bank of South Africa, issues SIM cards through cell phone companies, and these cards allow customers to make bill payments, store value, and transfer money. Its Web advertising aptly describes the informal cash economy of Africa: "Until now, many customers in Africa have had little choice but to use cash for all their purchases. They have had to plan ahead, stand in line, count and recount. They have forgone interest, faced the embarrassment of not having enough money, and taken a security risk. Celpay puts an end to all this."

Like Smart Money, Celpay requires that customers have a bank account, from which they *load* money onto their phone. They can then send it to pay bills and buy gas and groceries from selected merchants, which meets a need in areas where point-of-sale outlets don't offer debit card payments. Celpay is currently operational in Tanzania and Democratic Republic of the Congo (DRC). As DRC banks count a mere 35,000 account holders out of a population of 56 million, tapping into the 1 million mobile phone subscribers holds great potential. Because cell phones work well even in rural parts of the DRC, notes a 2006 research report by the Consultative Group to Assist the Poor (CGAP), they may be an ideal tool to help the country quickly develop a national network for retail payments. "Mobile phone payments may help countries with underdeveloped payment systems leapfrog traditional paper-based ways of making payments."[10]

In fact the cell phone is already being used as a credit card terminal. Very few outlets in Africa offer credit card payments, due to the relatively high cost of point-of-sale systems, irregular electricity to run them, faulty phone lines to process charges—and the overriding fact that most purchases are too small to justify the transaction costs.

But thanks to a solution devised by iVeri Payment Technology, a South African company, small business owners can now take credit cards, even for very small purchases, and dial the iVeri access number via cell phone. The seller manually enters the buyer's credit card number and the transaction amount. That data journeys via Internet to a gateway in Johannesburg, then to a Lebanese processing center, then to the cardholder's bank—and back—in less than twenty seconds.[11] The service is available in South Africa, Namibia, Rwanda, Kenya, Nigeria, and Ivory Coast, and merchants need neither electricity nor fixed phone lines.

Remittances: Foreign Aid via Cell Phone

The mobile banking phenomenon is much less pronounced in Bangladesh than it is in South Africa and the Philippines, where income levels are considerably higher, virtually all subscribers are prepaid, and the prevalence of bank accounts is much higher. In addition, the literacy rate in Bangladesh hovers around 40 percent, and texting is relatively new, which stymies the growth of cell phone add-on services. GrameenPhone, however, has entered into an agreement with the Bangladesh Rural Advancement Committee (BRAC) Bank, which serves the gaping midmarket hole between big commercial banks and microfinance institutions, allowing subscribers who are bank customers to check bank account data and order checks through their cell phones. This could be the precursor to a more full-bodied mobile banking network at a later time.

But even without this transacting activity, the cell phone has improved the flow of remittances in Bangladesh, which are by far the largest source of foreign currency in most poor countries, outstripping aid and investment combined (see Figure 8.2). The World Bank puts the remittance total at around $200 billion a year, but unreported flows may put the actual number closer to $300 billion.

"Fairly rapid increase in the use of cell phones is a good indicator of social progress. The fact that these phones are also being used

Figure 8.2. Remittance Flows: Remittances Are an Important Source of External Financing in Developing Countries.

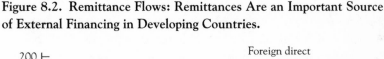
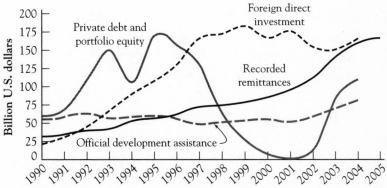

Source: Global Economic Prospects 2006: Economic Implications of Remittances and Migration; The International Bank for Reconstruction and Development/The World Bank.

widely by the rural people is a happy trend in the reduction of distance in urban-rural communication," read a 2006 editorial in Dhaka's *The Independent*. "The large expatriate community living in distant lands can now communicate with their families and relatives more easily through these phones."[12]

Bangladesh, for example, receives about $3.5 billion a year from its émigrés, compared to about $2 billion in aid and investment. In a country with a per capita GDP of $415, a small remittance in U.S. dollars, British pounds, or Euros goes a long way. By reducing transaction costs, the cell phone radically improves the flow of information and money, allowing people to call overseas from remote villages if and when they need money, and allowing Western Union to call recipients when the money arrives so that they can pick it up. A study of village phones by Canada's Telecommons Development Group determined that 42 percent of village phone calls concerned remittances (overall, 86 percent of all calls discussed money) and explained why the phone is so important to the transaction:

> Bangladesh is a labour-exporting country with many rural villagers (predominantly men) working in the Gulf States. The Village Phone acts as a powerful instrument to reduce the risk involved in remittance transfers, and to assist villagers in obtaining accurate information about foreign currency exchange rates. Transferring cash from a Gulf State to a rural village in Bangladesh is fraught with risks; remittances are thus a key factor in demand for telephone use.
>
> Reducing the risk of remittance transfers from overseas workers has important micro-implications for rural households and villages. At the micro level, remittances tend to be used for daily household expenses such as food, clothing and health care. Remittances are thus an important factor in meeting household subsistence needs, and can make up a significant portion of house-

hold income. Remittance funds are also spent on capital items including building or improving housing, buying cattle or land, and buying consumer goods such as portable tape/CD players and televisions. Once subsistence needs are met, remittances tend to be used for "productive investments," or for savings.[13]

Remittance flows overall have increased steadily as wiring costs have dropped, but in some cases, depending on the amount of money sent, transaction costs can still total 30 percent of the transfer. Western Union charges hefty transaction costs and large international banks have typically focused on large-value remittances; in addition, both sender and receiver have to travel to make the transaction, which is an opportunity cost for both parties. It's clear that the extension of m-commerce into remittance flows will cut transaction costs by reducing time and fees.

In the Philippines both Globe Telecom (G-Cash) and Smart Communications (Smart Padala) offer international cash remittance services that are extensions of their domestic mobile banking services. Remittances make up 17 percent of the Philippines' GDP, so these services are a natural extension of Globe's and Smart's existing mobile banking products. Rather than waiting three or four days for physical delivery, money can be sent via SMS for instantaneous delivery to Smart or Globe business centers.

Sam Pitroda, Redux

A slight twist on these remittance approaches is offered by UAE Exchange's UAE Exchange Wallet, engineered by Sam Pitroda, architect of India's digital fixed-line and village phone system. (India is the global leader in remittances received, with more than $21 billion a year; Mexico is second with $20 billion.) UAE Exchange allows Indian expatriates in the United Arab Emirates to wire money home to Indian banks using their cell phones, and neither the sender nor recipient needs to visit a bank. The sender calls up Exchange Wallet on his phone, enters a PIN number, indicates whether the funds should be sent to a bank, Western Union office, or another Exchange Wallet customer, and sends the money over the Internet to its destination.

Exchange Wallet steps beyond previous remittance vehicles in that the money can be wired directly to another cell phone. But Pitroda's real breakthrough with OneWallet software, developed and patented by his new company, C-SAM (based in Chicago and in Mumbai and Vadadora, India), is turning cell phones into virtual leather wallets that can contain multiple credit and debit cards, bank accounts, photographs, and even visas—as well as pay bills and transfer funds. More sophisticated than one-trick ponies such as G-Cash or Smart Money or even PayPal, which tie customers to one vendor, OneWallet probably has more potential appeal in developed markets where people have multiple relationships with financial institutions. But Pitroda, who is licensing OneWallet to companies such as Motorola, predicts global acceptance. "Worldwide, there are 2 billion cell phone users, but not 2 billion checking accounts," says Pitroda, who has received seven patents for OneWallet (with twenty-three more pending). "In India, there are more than 200 million phone users, the majority of them cell phone users, but not 200 million bank accounts. So there's a big potential for banks if they can get more people to open accounts, even if it's just $50 or $100."

C-SAM is yet another representation of the external combustion engine. Pitroda, a native of India, is importing information technology backed by foreign investors. In this case he is both entrepreneur and investor, having invested more than $10 million of his own money to kick-start his firm. He has been working on OneWallet since 1994, when he returned to the United States from India and asked a lawyer to dig up all the patents on credit cards. Pitroda read through a stack of 140 patents and discerned that they all concerned plastic, magnetic stripes, and putting a chip on plastic. "What would happen if a credit card were on an LCD?" he asked. "What if your cell phone could call up multiple accounts, like an ATM?" Answers to those questions led to patents for OneWallet.

"I've always been interested in paradigm shifts," says Pitroda, who sports long locks and a thick, elegant mustache. "I like the disruption. Just as digital switches were a disruption to analog switches and cell phones to fixed lines, this presents a disruption to the entire financial market—but people haven't understood this yet. Today, a credit card comes in the mail. C-SAM's credit card comes over the air into your phone. Banks used to build huge buildings, but a new bank in Africa doesn't need an edifice—it needs trust. Nor does the bank need to print money. The whole banking model has changed."

Microloans by Phone

Now that mobile banking via cell phones has been successful, targeting underserved communities where very few people have had bank accounts, the obvious natural progression is to electronically connect microfinance institutions with this emerging *m-commerce* platform. "The village phone builds off microfinance," says Alex Counts, president and CEO of Grameen Foundation USA. "The question now is how microfinance can build off the village phone." Vodafone Group CEO Arun Sarin, speaking at the Eradicating Poverty Through Profits Conference in San Francisco in December of 2004, noted that only a small fraction of the world's population who could benefit from microfinance are actually able to access it. "We think mobile technology will help change this. It allows extension of financial services into previously unprofitable areas and increases the financial products available to the customer."[14] If there are no banks in remote regions but there are cell phones, then the infrastructure is in place for mobile banking. There is a beautiful symmetry to this, of course, but also some hurdles to surmount.

Globe Telecom in the Philippines, as noted before, is working with the Rural Bankers Association of the Philippines to provide loan repayment by cell phone to small banks with widespread clientele.

Globe is also working with Grameen Foundation USA to set up village pay phones (modeled on GrameenPhone), which would then set up the possibility of distributing loans through the phones. There are more Grameen-style microfinance institutions in the Philippines than anywhere else in the world. "At the end of the day, you need a way to get money into and out of the phone," says Tim Wood, a Grameen Foundation USA technology expert working to develop village phone products with Globe in the Philippines. "That's a real problem in remote areas."

In Kenya, Safaricom is conducting trials of a service called M-Pesa, which seems to offer a solution to the vexing cash-in–cash-out problem. Working in partnership with the Commercial Bank of Africa and a microfinance institution operating in rural markets (Faulu Kenya), M-Pesa allows cash deposits, transfers, and withdrawals. Faulu is experimenting with microloans, crediting money to a borrower's mobile M-Pesa account, which can then be converted into cash at a Safaricom dealer. Conversely, loans can be repaid through the dealer, who texts Faulu to indicate repayment.[15]

Like many other cell phone companies, Safaricom allows prepaid users to transfer funds from one subscriber to another, which can in effect be a form of domestic remittance, typically from an urban worker to a relative in a village. Once the money has been transferred, it can be exchanged for cash or goods.

In addition to the cash-in–cash-out problem, mobile banking in rural areas must surmount several other impediments. One is the small number of phones in many villages. In the village phone model, as pioneered in Bangladesh and now being replicated in Uganda and Rwanda by MTN, and the Philippines, the typical village has just one or two phones. Although it's conceivable that villagers could all use the same phone for transactions by having their own SIM cards with private PINs and swapping them as needed, this has not yet taken place on a wide scale.

A World Bank and International Finance Corporation study addresses this issue and concludes: "There is a concern that some of the solutions link a specific user to a specific phone through the use of a purpose-configured SIM. This has the effect of preventing another registered user from 'borrowing' a phone in order to arrange a transaction. This could pose a significant barrier in poor communities where one phone may be shared among several users."[16]

MTN has tried to circumvent this problem by selling prepaid SIM cards to people to use in borrowed phones. But because prepaid accounts expire within a certain number of days, people who wait until they need to make a transaction might run past the expiration date. Globe Telecom has tried to assist users to acquire their own phones through microfinance, which of course offers the fastest route to spreading microlending by phone.

Formalizing Microfinance

A second impediment to microfinance-based m-commerce is that the various microfinance institutions (MFIs) do not have standardized computing and accounting systems. Most depend on one-off custom systems, which makes it difficult for them to tie into the networks of commercial banks or cell phone systems. Manual or spreadsheet-based systems cannot provide the comprehensive information needed to scale operations and connect to other more formal capital providers.

Grameen Foundation USA and Hewlett-Packard combined to develop the Rural Transaction System (RTS) through a pilot project in Uganda. RTS, an open-source system, allows microfinance clients to deposit and withdraw cash through a network of accredited third-party merchants (such as gas stations or grocery stores) in rural areas. A secondary benefit is that RTS allows microfinance institutions to capture transaction data, which can then be reported to credit bureaus, helping clients to develop a credit rating.

Another ambitious open-source initiative is the Mifos (Microfinance Open Source) project (www.mifos.org), which aims to develop open-source architecture for the back-end management of microfinance information systems. The goal is to increase capacity, standardization, and information exchange possibilities among the different stakeholders in the industry—MFIs, funding agencies, software vendors, banks, rating agencies, and regulators.

Banking on a Younger Generation

A third impediment to mobile financial transactions in countries such as Bangladesh, Kenya, and even South Africa is lack of an SMS culture. Arun Sarin, CEO of Vodafone Group, which has stakes in several African cell providers, cites surveys showing that African voice calls in general outnumbered text messages three to one and that that ratio increased to thirteen to one in rural communities.[17] High rates of illiteracy, a tradition of oral communication, and lack of familiarity with phones and computers—and with the Latin alphabet—contribute to this reality. But as a younger generation grows up with phones, and as keyboard conventions for languages such as Bangla are developed, texting and other innovative phone habits are slowly being introduced to cultures that have never had phones or computers.

In a late 2005 runoff between contestants on the knockoff TV hit *Bangladesh Idol*, 1.5 million votes were cast by SMS (with more than half going to winner Nolok Babu, a twenty-year-old "penniless slum dweller"). That indicates that as phones are adopted by young Bangladeshis, who are more likely than their parents to be educated and tech savvy, texting may slowly permeate the culture. As it is, SMS produces a mere 3 percent of GrameenPhone's revenues, compared to rates of 13 to 15 percent in Malaysia and even higher in the Philippines, according to Erik Aas, CEO of GrameenPhone.

Despite Bangladesh's relatively undeveloped texting and mobile banking culture, GrameenPhone has introduced CellBazaar, a new m-commerce product that is dependent on texting but does not involve the transfer of money. CellBazaar is kind of a "craigslist for cell phones," says its founder, Kamal Quadir, who developed the concept while earning an MBA degree at MIT's Sloan School of Management. Kamal, who is Iqbal's youngest brother, is backed by U.S. investors (including eBay founder Pierre Omidyar), which of course makes him another exemplar of the external combustion engine.

People list goods for sale or trade by sending a text message such as "HONDA 2001 DHAKA T500000" ("2001 Honda in Dhaka selling for Taka 500,000"). People looking for goods can search by category or locale or both. Other than the Tk2 charge to send a text message, there is no fee to list or to search. GrameenPhone and CellBazaar split the texting revenues. Kamal Quadir admits that unless you are conversant with the listing technique, it could take as many as five text messages to post a product for sale, but he notes that a Tk10 or Tk15 charge is likely to be a minimal fee for a sale that cuts out a middleman.

"CellBazaar is a very good idea," says Grameen Telecom's Khalid Shams. "Those in any wholesale business will be able to cut through layers of intermediaries. A pineapple sells for Tk15—but the producer only gets Tk3 or Tk4. CellBazaar has the potential to increase the producer's take."

In a country with limited Internet access, CellBazaar fills a huge void. For GrameenPhone, which is facing intense competition from Middle Eastern newcomers Orascom and Warid, CellBazaar is potentially a value-added service that will lock in customers and prevent churning as price wars accelerate. (GrameenPhone has a three-year exclusivity agreement with CellBazaar.) And although texting itself is catching on slowly, cell phones in Bangladesh are in fact being used primarily to conduct business and financial transactions, so CellBazaar offers a high-powered means to do what is already being done. "Rather than making as many calls as you can to determine market prices, which by definition is limited by your time and the strength of your network," says Kamal Quadir, "you can search more and larger markets very quickly."

Grameen Telecom, which runs the village phone program, is also touting CellBazaar as a new income opportunity for phone ladies and other phone owners who can charge fees to list items or search for items for sale for those who don't have phones. That of course also helps to introduce the service to those who may be unfamiliar with texting. GrameenPhone is banking on the potential income opportunities being a goad to people to learn texting. Notes Syed Yamin Bakht, general manager of information at Grameen-Phone, "You don't need to know the Queen's English to text."

Where's the Money?

The spread of m-commerce in developing countries raises more questions than it answers right now. How far will it spread? Will banks make enough from transaction fees to justify the small amounts transferred? Will banks find a way to replace the face-to-face credit checks that microfinance institutions have mastered? Grameen Bank, for example, has 6 million clients—and a bank representative meets with every one once a week. No commercial bank could, or would want to, do that.

There is clearly a latent demand for banking services that few could have predicted, a replay of the early misperceptions about cell phones. The banking system in developing countries is very stratified, with large banks catering to urban customers, microfinance institutions to rural clients, and little middle ground. But if there really is demand for formal banking or mobile banking in poor, rural areas, the big question is, How are people living on $2 a day going to get the money to enter the formal financial system, even if that system is accessible through quasi-banks powered by cell phones?

Possible answer: through the cell phone.

9

Wealth Creation and Rural
Income Opportunities

That cell phones are extending into areas where electricity and banks are fantasies—and bringing with them income opportunities—is a revolutionary occurrence far larger in scope than the introduction of personal computers to the U.S. economy in the 1980s. The spread of cell phones in developing countries is more akin to the industrial revolution in the West, which started the steady economic separation of the West from most of the rest of the world. Khalid Shams calls the unexpected chain of economic activity unleashed by GrameenPhone and its competitors a *silent revolution*.

As information technology rampages through the South, it is creating wealth and producing millions of new income opportunities in rural areas that translate into billions of dollars in new national income. The unlikely symbiotic relationship between corporate profits and income opportunities for the rural poor is what business theorists refer to as *inclusive capitalism*—a capitalism that spreads wealth as it creates wealth, that empowers the poor as it generates returns for investors, a win-win capitalism.

Neither the distribution of money nor the creation of wealth necessarily leads to widespread economic development or the eradication of poverty. Certainly, the wealth of some oil-rich nations that have relatively low levels of human and economic development, such as Saudi Arabia and Nigeria, confirms that point. Similarly, foreign investors that generate wealth by extracting minerals or labor from poor countries do not contribute to development.

But income—or an opportunity for income—is development. Income allows people to move beyond subsistence living and to save, invest, and produce. Income allows people to make decisions about where and how they live. Income frees people from an often small and unproductive plot of land that has provided bare subsistence. And in developing countries with miniscule formal job sectors and large informal sectors, these income opportunities come largely through self-employment (see Figure 9.1).

Income opportunities spell a higher order of development in all countries, no matter how rich. President Reagan's acknowledgment in the mid-1980s that small business was "the engine of the economy" was a tacit recognition that the United States was a better place with millions of small-company jobs than with thousands of corporate jobs. (Many of those small-company jobs were in fact created by self-employed independent consultants who had been fired from large corporations.) With a few fat cats and lots of small cats and nothing in between, a country develops a stratified society, like the oil-wealth societies of Saudi Arabia and Nigeria.

In South Asia and sub-Saharan Africa it would be folly to suggest that information communications technology (ICT) is building a stable, income-earning middle class. But it would also be an oversight to ignore the huge jolt toward a sustainable cash economy that cell phones are providing to millions of people.

ICT Drives GDP

When Ode magazine asked Muhammad Yunus in 2005 to describe the relative impacts of Grameen Bank and GrameenPhone on Bangladesh, he replied, "Grameen Bank has an impact on the poor, GrameenPhone on the entire economy."[1] Wealth created by productively serving millions of customers daily gives the whole economy a huge lift. Not only are tens of thousands of direct and indirect

Figure 9.1. Self-Employment and Wage Income Are the Ways Out of Poverty.

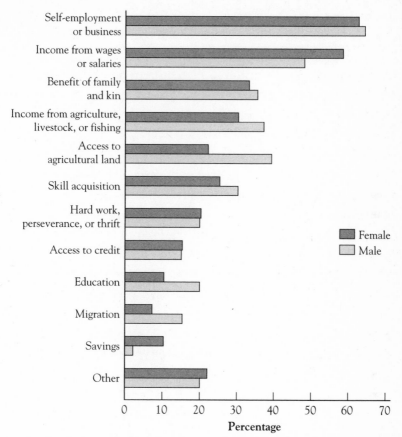

Source: World Bank, *World Development Report 2005* (New York: Oxford University Press, 2004), fig. 1.15.

jobs and income opportunities created but the reinvestment of a significant proportion of profits creates yet another lift for the economy.

Without the corporate profits and reinvestment that fuel further growth, there would be no rural income opportunities. A 2006 study by the research firm Ovum, *The Economic and Social Benefits of Mobile Services in Bangladesh,* concludes that the mobile phone industry in Bangladesh created a total value added of $812 million in 2005, of which $256 million was retained by the operators and used to pay employee wages and taxes. The remaining $650 million, about 1 percent of GDP, went to dealers, terminal manufacturers, equipment suppliers, fixed operators, support services, and equipment suppliers. In all, the report estimates that the mobile industry contributes directly or indirectly to more than 250,000 income opportunities (not including the work of the village phone operators).[2] This is in line with the impact of telecom on GDP around the world (see Figure 9.2).

The logic behind the International Telecommunications Union calculation that Iqbal Quadir used in the mid-1990s, which showed that adding a phone to a country with Bangladesh's GDP would add $6,000 to GDP, is still valid. However, because the figure was a multiple of the cost of connection, which is considerably lower now, today's value added per new phone is probably in the $1,000 to $2,000 range, depending on where the phone is placed. This theory is bolstered by econometric research from the London Business

Figure 9.2. The Relationship Between GDP per Capita and Mobile Penetration Among "Lower Income" Countries, 2005.

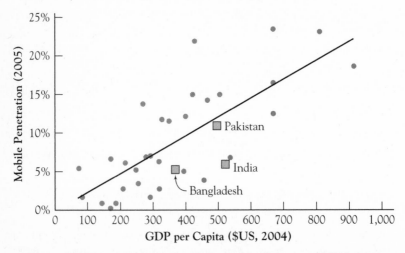

Source: GSM Association and Frontier Economics, *Taxation and Mobile Telecommunications in Bangladesh* (London: GSM Association, 2006), fig. 7.

School, which concludes that adding ten phones per hundred people in a low-income country would increase GDP by .59 points. That study suggests that "long-run growth in the Philippines (with 27 phones per 100 in 2003) could be as much as 1 percent higher than in Indonesia (with nine phones per 100 in 2003)," if the Philippines maintains its advantage in mobile phones.[3]

Another study confirming the theory that ICT drives GDP was conducted by Kuwait-based MTC, which bought Celtel in 2005. In Jordan, mobile revenues accounted for 5 percent of the increase in Jordan's GDP (2002–2004). In Egypt, the study concluded, every job created in the mobile sector generates eight others, and the study authors predicted that if Egypt's ICT investment were doubled, 1.3 million jobs would be created and the GDP growth rate would rocket from 4 to 8 percent.[4] (Egypt headed in that direction by auctioning off a third GSM license in 2006, for which there were ten bidders, including MTC, South Africa's MTN, and Norway's Telenor. UAE Etisalat, in partnership with Egyptian partners, won the license with a $2.9 billion bid.)

One needs to take widespread extrapolations from any one statistical study with a grain of salt, but the preponderance of evidence certainly supports the notion that mobile phones directly contribute to significant GDP growth in all countries—and produce most growth in poor countries with previously low levels of phone penetration. GrameenPhone, for example, has 4,000 employees in Bangladesh (the vast majority Bangladeshis) and calculates that another 70,000 people (in addition to the 250,000 phone ladies) derive indirect income as agents, resellers, dealers, and suppliers. Income received by these 50,000-plus beneficiaries contributes directly to the country's national income figure—not to mention the fact that many of these jobs are the high-quality, white-collar, service sector jobs that signify an evolving economy. But in Bangladesh and throughout vast swaths of Asia and Africa, it is in the forgotten rural sector of the population that the impact of ICT is the greatest.

Rural Income Opportunities

Roughly half the world's population, about 3 billion people, lives on less than $2 a day, according to World Bank statistics. And roughly 3 billion people live in rural regions. The locales may not be far from major urban centers, and they may not look rural in the conventional sense. But they are cut off from urban markets, not to mention global markets, by lack of communications, dangerous and often impassable roads (or lack of bus fare), lack of electricity—and lack of phones.

Not everyone living in a rural region is poor, but there is a very high degree of correlation. True, $2 a day needs to be viewed in context. In such informal, untaxed, and untracked economies—with high levels of barter, not to mention remittances from overseas—actual income levels are often higher and costs are fungible, from a Western perspective. Because people without property are not extended credit, they have no debt. They often eat well and, because of hard work, maintain good health. But the fact that their poverty does not precisely fit an outsider's perception does not mean they are not poor and particularly susceptible to disease and natural disasters, not to mention economic stress.

Exhibit A in creating rural income opportunities is Grameen-Phone's village phone project. After a slow start over the first two years, the number of village phones has increased to nearly 250,000. Village phones provide phone access to more than 100 million people. You'd be hard pressed to find any other program with such reach and effectiveness or one that has brought the benefits of digital technology to so many previously disenfranchised people. "I know of no other social venture even close to this magnitude," says Josh Mailman, the first investor in GrameenPhone, who has been an active social investor for more than twenty-five years.

Given 250,000 phones in 68,000 villages, some villages clearly have multiple phones, which has led to more competitive pricing. Village phone ladies are given suggested call pricing by Grameen

Telecom, but as long as they hold a monopoly in a village, there's nothing to stop them from charging what the market will bear. And as several studies have shown a clear consumer surplus on the cost of a call—meaning that people perceive the value to be higher than the cost—there's plenty of room for higher prices. (An analysis by the Telecommons Development Group of Canada determined that the cost of a trip to Dhaka was two to eight times the cost of a phone call, resulting in savings of $2.70 to $10 on a call that replaces a trip to the city.[5])

Quadir was once asked if the call tariffs (prices) for village phones were too high, as many in Bangladesh have suggested. "If you think this is a problem, try no service," he replied, harking back to his "connectivity is productivity" theme. "No service is very costly." Economist Leonard Waverman of the London Business School looked at the issue of price and determined that for mobile phones in developing countries, "demand increases much more than in proportion to either increases in income or reductions in price."[6] In short, whatever the cost of a phone call, it's worth it to most people.

The issue of cost is fading into the sunset, as GrameenPhone's rapid growth in subscribers, along with increased competition from other carriers, has created downward pressure on prices. "The average revenue per user is coming down, which was bound to happen," says Grameen Telecom's Shams. "But village phones are still a good business that provides 20 percent of GrameenPhone's overall revenues." Says GrameenPhone's CEO, Erik Aas, "Now that villagers can buy subscriptions from any operator, buy a new SIM card for Tk100 and a phone on the black market, and choose to pay prepaid or postpaid, the village phone ladies can no longer count on 100 percent market share. For the end user, I see this as healthy competition."

More phones and pricing wars generate more usage and productivity for villagers, more revenues for GrameenPhone, and more income opportunities for the phone ladies—as well as opportunities for *more* phone ladies. This is inclusive capitalism, reminiscent in some ways of Henry Ford's operating principle from Model T days: pay workers enough so they can afford to buy the cars they produce, which will create more jobs, which will sell more cars.

Quantifying the Impact of Village Phones

It is widely accepted that village phone ladies can make anywhere from $750 to $1,200 a year, compared to an average per capita income of $415. Some, such as Laily Begum, the first Grameen Bank borrower who became the first phone lady (and made the initial cell phone call to the prime minister), have moved into another realm altogether. Begum has parlayed her phone business into a mini-business empire. With her husband she owns five shops and a restaurant, and together they earn $2,500 or so a year.[7] A woman who once borrowed money from Grameen Bank to buy a cow now lives with her family in a brick home with two color TVs and a fridge.

But Begum, a national icon, is an anomaly. To be extremely conservative, assume phone ladies make $400 more per year than they would without the phone. Multiply that by 250,000 village phones, and that's $100 million in new annual income for the villages. But that doesn't account for savings from productive use of the phone or income generated by selling goods and services through the phone. For farmers and fishermen, or anyone looking to sell goods, the ability to check market prices and choose a buyer has increased their income. It's difficult to quantify the value of this disintermediation, but anecdotal evidence leads to an estimate that the phone increases by 10 to 20 percent the amount farmers and fisherman receive for their produce, on top of the aforementioned time savings. In many cases, they sell direct and cut out the middleman. Finally, the increased flow and reduced costs of remittances, the largest source of foreign income in Bangladesh, is attributable to cell phones. It's conceivable that the total of these income and cost-savings streams is $1 billion in rural Bangladesh alone. Nationwide the income gains top $2 billion, between 2 percent and 3 percent of GDP.

The fact that village phone operators are primarily women rather than men has contributed to the success of the program, somewhat by chance. Women were selected to own phones because the village phone program selected credit-worthy Grameen Bank borrowers, and virtually all Grameen Bank borrowers are women. That has led to two fortuitous spin offs. First, because many men are away from home working in Dhaka or the Middle East (or even New York or London), they naturally want to communicate with their families. Both Yunus and Quadir have noted that were the phones controlled by men, women, especially those whose husbands were away, would be unlikely to feel comfortable dealing directly with men to place or receive calls.

The enhanced status of women accruing from their business success needs to be factored into any discussion of economic gain, however intangible that status. Because phone ladies have become among the top earners in their villages, and present a new role model for other women and young girls, they have given momentum to a wave of potential new earners in the economy. Before Grameen Bank helped solidify the notion that women were fiducially responsible and knew how to put money to work, economic matters were by and large the domain of men. "Women cannot transact with the market as men can," Yunus said in a 2006 speech at the Fletcher School at Tufts University. "But Grameen has led to a dramatic change in women's status and empowerment; and their participation in the labor force has increased much faster in rural areas than in urban."

Quantifying the Impact of *Sari Sari* Resellers

In the Philippines the story is different because the culture and the economic ecosystem are different, but the 700,000-plus *sari sari* resellers of prepaid phone-and-text *sachets* (packages) are comparable in many ways to the phone ladies. The resellers are tailoring a low-cost product to their poor clientele. Even though they are typically dealing with individual phone owners rather than shared phones, they are selling very small sachets and often extending credit. They also generate around $100 million in income annually, according to this conservative math: 700,000 × $20 × 52 × .15

(700,000 people, selling $20 worth of prepaid calls every week, at a 15 percent commission).

New national income of $100 million is not impressive by Western standards; it *is* impressive in a country with a per capita income of $1,000. And that $100 million in the Philippines and in Bangladesh is sustainable, productive, and growing every year.

What's much more impressive is this math: 700,000 *sari sari* resellers plus 250,000 phone ladies equals nearly 1 million new income opportunities for the rural poor—all developed in the last eight years. And these micro-entrepreneurs are not selling lottery tickets; they are selling information communications technology, a proven productivity booster.

A New Retail Class in Africa

The mobile-to-mobile concept (GP-GP) pioneered in Bangladesh by GrameenPhone has been replicated to perfection in Africa. Fixed-line networks are better for copper, which is routinely stolen, than for phone calls. But unlike GrameenPhone, which made a mission of delivering universal service even to remote and poor regions of its country, African cell providers by and large have not made special provisions to reach distant villages. The main exception to this rule is in South Africa, where Nelson Mandela's post-apartheid government mandated in 1995 that cell phone companies deliver phone lines to disadvantaged areas. That year Vodacom pioneered a franchise system by fitting used container cars with five or more phones, and delivering these ready-made phone shops to franchisees, who then charge phone users to make calls. MTN has since done the same, and sometimes moves into territory that Vodacom has staked out.

The Vodacom project has delivered access to 4 million customers who would otherwise probably not have had phone access. Franchisees pay a fairly hefty up-front fee of $3,500 to get a container delivered to a mutually agreed upon location, but thereafter they own and operate the business. BBC News, reporting on a man who owned seven shops with twenty-eight employees, said: "The introduction of community telephone shops by the multinational company, Vodacom, is having a dramatic impact in a place where 40 percent of the people are unemployed and living conditions are cramped and crowded."[8]

These franchisee entrepreneurs, charged discount rates for phone time, prepay Vodacom for phone minutes and end up keeping one-third of the call revenues. A case study by Digital Dividend (a project of the World Resources Institute) found that the typical well-located phone shop with five lines would log about 100 hours a month, generating revenues of $3,550, with owners pocketing $1,190 a month ($14,280 a year).[9] Today Vodacom has about 5,000 outlets, and MTN 2,000. Multiply 7,000 by $14,280, and you are just short of $100 million in new income opportunities.

The most explosive phone-related entrepreneurial opportunity in Africa involves the resale of prepaid cards and the *topping up* of existing cards. Ninety-eight percent of Africa's subscribers are prepaid, whether they are businesses or consumers, rich or poor. Celtel's Dr. Mo estimates that the business of selling prepaid cards across the continent is worth $3 billion. That business, largely run by indigenous entrepreneurs, didn't exist five years ago; Celtel alone has more than 120,000 outlets. With a 10 percent commission for resellers, that translates to $300 million in new income at the grass roots. Divide that by an estimated 200,000 outlets (including those other than Celtel's), and the result is $1,500 per outlet per year. In sub-Saharan Africa, that's big money.

International Calls at Domestic Prices

Another major economic and social contribution African cell phone companies have begun to force is the reduction of international calling rates between contiguous areas that are ethnically or tribally connected. For example, "the Banyambo in Kagera [Tanzania] probably have more in common with the Bachiga and the Batoro of Uganda than they do with the Wazaramos of Dar es Salaam, but it costs them 420 shillings per minute to call neighboring Uganda to speak to a relative. Calling Dar es Salaam, more than 1,000 kilometers away, costs 314 shillings," says Omari Issa, COO of Celtel.[10] Similarly, calling internationally from the Ugandan border to nearby Kenyan towns costs three times more than long-haul domestic calls.

Although these anomalies have yet to be corrected, Celtel subscribers can now call across the Congo River between the Democratic Republic of the Congo (DRC) and Republic of the Congo. Calls previously routed through satellite connections in Europe at international long-distance rates now travel through direct microwave links at the cost of a local call. Before, people would take a ferry across the river rather than call. In 2002, after negotiating with both governments, Celtel received permission to install a microwave link. Per minute pricing dropped from one dollar to twenty-eight cents and traffic jumped twentyfold in the first few weeks.

"Kenya, Uganda, and Tanzania should be one big calling zone," says Dr. Mo. "The boundaries cut right through tribal areas and don't reflect society."

But there may be an even bigger business sprouting. A South African company called SharedPhone is marketing a SIM card for low-cost Motorola phones that turns the phone into a pay phone and allows entrepreneurs a low-cost way to start a new business. The operator deposits funds into a designated bank account and can preset the profit margin to generate immediate call charges.

"The SIM-based payphone allows operators on the streets of Africa and India to manage and grow their payphone businesses at a fraction of the standard price," says Warren Steyn, marketing manager at SharedPhone, which competes with more traditional pay phone outlets, such as those run out of Vodacom container cars. Steyn estimates that 200,000 pay phones will be sold within the next two years, noting that the application is designed for informal business owners, such as taxi operators, hairdressers, and hawkers, and for students. The airtime recharge application provides advantages for the rurally located, unsophisticated operator, who may not have a bank account, as it allows an operator to transfer funds between phones.

"The product is best suited to countries with high unemployment rates and low tele-density," says Steyn. SharedPhone ("business in a pocket") has launched in DRC, Togo, India, South Africa, Mozambique, Kenya, Tanzania, and Lesotho.

"While there is a lot of focus on absolute rates of mobile penetration, this underestimates the real impact that mobile is having through the innovative and entrepreneurial ways in which the technology has been extended beyond the model of individual ownership," says Arun Sarin, CEO of Vodafone; as head of the world's largest cell phone company, Sarin has emerged as a leading spokesperson for the social and economic benefits of cell phones. "Thousands of jobs have been created and some very successful indigenous companies have emerged. It's a clear success story in commercial terms but one that also has a profound impact on the development of the economy and society."[11]

Repatriating or Reinvesting Profits?

The connection between commercial success and social impact is lost on many sovereign governments, including the Bangladeshi government, which wonders whether a telecom company owned in whole or part by foreigners will just suck money out of a country such as Bangladesh. To be sure it's a valid concern, although it's quite possible the government has its eye on the money at the expense of social impact.

In March 2006, the Bangladesh Telecommunication Regulatory Commission (BTRC) threatened to withhold approval for any private phone company expansion unless the money was raised by floating shares on the capital markets, saying that bank loans were straining currency reserves.[12] This seems more of a political maneuver to develop capital markets than a valid concern about capital fleeing the country, but it is indicative of a long-held xenophobia in South Asia that dates back to the time of the East India Company.

Take GrameenPhone, which is 62 percent owned by Telenor AS, a Norway-based company. In 2004, GrameenPhone recorded aftertax profits of $125 million, which means that $77.5 million could have been repatriated to Telenor AS. But the shareholders have typically reinvested profits in the company, or the country. In 2004, for example, GrameenPhone invested $196 million in Bangladesh, doubling the number of cell towers to 1,400 and laying another 250 kilometers of fiber-optic cable. In 2005, with profits of $162 million, GrameenPhone reinvested another $300 million. Since it started in 1997, the company has invested about $1 billion in Bangladesh—which makes Josh Mailman's $125,000 initial seed capital look pretty sharp from an impact perspective.

True, much of this reinvestment was paid to foreign suppliers, such as Ericsson, which means currency leaves the country. When GrameenPhone earns money in takas (and sometimes borrows money from local banks in takas) and then turns those takas into Swedish kronor to buy from Ericsson (or Euros or dollars to buy from other vendors), that does put pressure on Bangladesh's foreign currency reserves. This in turn limits the government's ability to maintain a stable exchange rate for the taka by buying its own currency on exchange markets. Historically, the taka has been steady against the U.S. dollar, especially compared to other emerging market currencies, such as the Thai baht, but it has depreciated considerably in the past few years.

Ignoring the currency concerns, the cell towers and related infrastructure represent a fixed capital investment that will pay dividends in-country for years to come. And of course GrameenPhone's financial success has attracted a number of deep-pocketed competitors, most recently Egypt's Orascom and UAE's Warid, both of which are investing heavily to build networks. In all, GrameenPhone and other cell phone companies invest far more than they extract from

Bangladesh, even without counting the jobs and income opportunities their products and services provide.

"GrameenPhone re-invested $300 million in the company in 2005," says CEO Aas. "Some people think that most of it went to foreign vendors. But half that money remained in Bangladesh and goes to tens of thousands of people providing services, a new set of entrepreneurs and engineers. Our base stations, for example, are manufactured in Bangladesh."

Celtel is reinvesting even more heavily in its African companies. By the end of 2005, Celtel had signed up 8 million subscribers, was generating $1 billion in annual revenues—and had invested $1.2 billion in Africa. "When we started in 1998, commercial banks told us there was a total of about $200 million looking to invest in sub-Saharan Africa," says Dr. Mo, noting the fast-changing investment climate. In June 2006, Celtel quintupled that with one investment, buying 65 percent of Vmobile, one of Nigeria's leading cellular service operators. Celtel International CEO Marten Pieters said the agreement marked "Celtel's most important expansion in Africa to date." In 2006, $700 million of Celtel's $1 billion plus in revenues will be reinvested in its territories, and $350 million will be paid to local governments in taxes and duties, according to Dr. Mo.

When I first heard Dr. Mo speak in Washington, D.C., in May 2005, it was shortly after he had sold Celtel for $3.4 billion, creating fifty new millionaires, many in Africa. He was a happy man, oozing equal parts charisma and chutzpah as he spoke to a group of venture capitalists at the International Finance Corporation's annual Global Private Equity meeting, chiding them for overlooking the profit potential in Africa. "And you call yourselves capitalists?" he questioned, with a grin.

The success of GrameenPhone and Celtel, among others, in creating wealth in poor countries and producing an extended supply chain that delivers income opportunities to millions begets an obvious question: Can this fortuitous approach to problem solving be replicated while addressing other unmet human needs?

10

Beyond Phones
In Search of a New "Cow"

The model for delivering credit and banking services to the poor has been developed and replicated around the globe. Likewise, the model for delivering communications to the poor has been developed and replicated, sometimes appearing in new mutations through prepaid cards. The models can and will be improved to reach more people, but the basic models are proven to work.

That both these classic models for the delivery of services to the rural poor were initially forged in Bangladesh may be surprising. The outside world has heard nothing from Bangladesh but tales of woe. But necessity is the mother of invention—or in this case innovation. And innovation that solves local problems is much more likely to be developed by local players, even though they may need external combustion to get their solutions airborne and to cross-pollinate in other cultures. "Ten years ago, the probability of an idea from Bangladesh affecting a community in Brazil, Poland, or the U.S. was very limited," says Bill Drayton, the founder of Ashoka, which promotes social entrepreneurship globally. "Now it is common (the best-known example being Muhammad Yunus's impact on the global spread of microcredit) and becoming more common every year."[1]

Although hundreds of millions if not billions of people are yet to be served by microcredit or telecommunications systems, the success rate to date bodes well for future delivery of such systems. By the end of 2005, 100 million families had taken out microloans, and half had been lifted out of poverty. An estimated 400 million families, requiring $400 billion, could still benefit from microloans or related financial services. Similarly, phone penetration in poor countries has spread to serve tens of millions of people, although the overall rate is still abysmally low by Western standards. But in both cases it's clear that the current hurdles to success are mere technical problems that numerous people in different countries are working to surmount. The pace of delivery is speeding up every year; the GSM Association claims the new, low-cost Motorola handset (spawned by the GSM Association's Emerging Markets Handset initiative) is selling at the rate of 31,000 a day, more than 11 million a year. Given the widespread practice of sharing phones, this translates to access for tens of millions of new users.

Can the self-sustaining business models that meet the previously unmet human needs for credit and communications be transferred or transmuted to meet other glaring unmet needs? Consider electricity—many of the rural areas that don't have phones don't have electricity either. An estimated 1.6 billion people in the world have no source of electricity beyond old car batteries. In fact, the same satellite image of tele-density that would radiate "dangerously low" would likely show darkness at night in many of the same areas. No phones, no lights. Enter Iqbal Quadir, stage left.

Gonofone Exits GrameenPhone

Quadir, a true entrepreneur in that he prefers creating businesses to managing them, had quit working at GrameenPhone in 1999. He had put in six years, helping to develop the concept, persuading all the key players to join the consortium, raising the money and serving on the board. Managing the company's growth was not nearly as challenging or rewarding.

He returned to the United States with the idea of lecturing about the role of entrepreneurship and technology in development—particularly technology that empowers people at the grass roots, from the bottom up. He had been well paid in Bangladeshi terms, but hadn't made any money off GrameenPhone, which in 1999 was still two years away from profitability.

At the World Economic Forum in 1999, where he was named World Leader of Tomorrow, he caught the eye of Joseph Nye, the dean of Harvard's Kennedy School of Government, who later offered him a post as a lecturer. Quadir used that platform to speak throughout the world about his GrameenPhone experience, captivating audiences at universities and conferences with his "cell phone as cow" story.

As GrameenPhone grew exponentially and the phone ladies turned up more often in the international press, Quadir was on a bit of a victory lap. People loved the cow story. It is of course a brilliant conceit. The first time I met Quadir, I heard the cow story. It was how you got to know him and get a glimpse of his upside-down thinking—and it's not a story you forget. He even appended another metaphor to the story for the paperback edition of Thomas Friedman's *The Lexus and the Olive Tree:* "The phone may be a 'cow' for the lady who operates it, but it acts as a horse for the village, pulling the whole village out of poverty."[2] Cell phone as horse?

Quadir's victory lap preceded the spoils. It wasn't until late 2004 that he engineered an exit from GrameenPhone, turning Gonofone's $1.7 million investment into a $33 million return (before legal and transaction expenses) for its twelve American shareholders. Unlike the other shareholders in GrameenPhone, which were institutions, Gonofone was a collection of individual investors.

By the end of 2002, at the end of Grameen Telecom's six-year "right of first refusal" should any shareholder want to dispose of shares, some of the Gonofone shareholders were restless. There was no sign that GrameenPhone was considering a public offering, and Gonofone, as the smallest shareholder (4.5 percent) and which didn't hold a board seat, had absolutely no say in the company.

Quadir approached Marubeni with the idea of buying that company's 9.5 percent stake, which included a board seat. The Japanese economy had been weak and Marubeni had sold its telecom assets in Indonesia. Marubeni agreed to sell its stake for $22 million, a nice return on its initial investment of around $5 million. Gonofone didn't have the cash, but approached a major New York investor, an individual who agreed to put up the money in exchange for a 7 percent share. Thus, after buying Marubeni's stake, Gonofone would increase its stake from 4.5 percent to 7 percent (14 percent minus 7 percent), without expending any cash.

When Marubeni notified the other two shareholders of its intent to sell, they were vehemently opposed. Telenor sent two corporate officers to Boston to meet with Quadir and contest the deal. Gonofone then proposed that Telenor buy Gonofone's stake (plus its option to buy another 2.5 percent before an initial public offering) for $22 million, money Gonofone would then use to buy Marubeni's stake. Again without expending cash, Gonofone would end up with 9.5 percent and a board seat, an upgrade over the initial deal. Grameen Telecom was also upset that Marubeni hadn't offered its shares to Grameen Telecom. Nor did it like the idea that both Telenor and Gonofone would increase their stakes while Grameen Telecom's stake remained stagnant.

After six months of negotiations and multiple price changes, it was agreed that Telenor, Grameen Telecom, and Gonofone would divvy up the Marubeni shares at the valuation Gonofone had negotiated. Then, given the company's rapid growth and rosy prospects (the number of subscribers had jumped from 600,000 in 2002 to 5 million by the end of 2004), Telenor offered to buy Gonofone's new and existing shares plus its pre-IPO option at a higher valuation, for a total of $33 million. Grameen Telecom declined to participate in this shareholder exchange. As a result, Telenor now owns 62 percent of GrameenPhone and Grameen Telecom owns 38 percent.

The complexity of the deal shows the difficulty posed by investing in countries without well-formed capital markets; the results demonstrate the rewards.

Quadir spent nearly two years orchestrating the deal; he and Josh Mailman, representing founder's sweat equity and early equity, respectively, took the lion's share of the proceeds. With that grand exit Quadir now was truly ready for something new.

Quadir Meets Dean Kamen

In 2002, while Quadir was teaching at Harvard, he met inventor Dean Kamen through the Lemelson Foundation, a nonprofit dedicated to the innovative application of technology around the world, with a special interest in developing countries. Quadir's reputation for delivering products to the poor was in some circles legendary, as was Kamen's reputation as an inventor. Kamen and Quadir together were a potential dream team.

Kamen, the founder and president of DEKA Research & Development Corporation, is best known in the popular press for designing and marketing the Segway Human Transporter, which is touted as a great way to traverse short distances without driving or walking. Sales for this "self-balancing transporter" never took off, however, despite the exhilaration of riding it—perhaps due to its cost ($5,000), perhaps because it doesn't have an engine. Nonetheless, the Segway has since found niche markets where it excels. It has achieved a high degree of popularity in Paris among tourists who use it as a sightseeing vehicle; in Arizona and other places, riding a Segway has become an alternative to riding a golf cart or walking around golf courses.

For all the fascination the Segway attracted, it was merely using robotic technology that Kamen had designed for an advanced, high-tech wheelchair that can actually walk up and down stairs—as well as elevate so that a disabled rider can talk face to face with standing people (the chair is marketed as the Independence IBOT Mobility System, by Johnson & Johnson). Kamen holds more than 150 patents, mostly for medical devices. He designed the first wearable infusion pump and the first insulin pump. Kamen is a very serious and successful technologist and inventor who is driven to meet human needs.

When Kamen met Quadir, he had already designed a water purification device that he wanted to use in the developing world. The Slingshot, as he calls it, distills water at the rate of 40 litres per hour. The instruction sheet is simple—"just add water"—intended to show that the device does not require scarce chemicals, filters, or expertise. "Not required are engineers, pipelines, epidemiologists, or microbiologists," says Kamen. "You don't need any -ologists. You don't need any building permits, bribery, or bureaucracies."[3]

Each Slingshot prototype had cost $100,000 to build, but certainly with mass production the cost would drop to an affordable level for villagers. At least that was a theory worth testing.

For Quadir there were several problems with deploying the Slingshot in Bangladesh. The rural areas of Bangladesh typically didn't have electricity to run the Slingshot. And even if electricity were available, the real problem is arsenic in the water, which affects close to 40 million people. But there may be cheaper ways to solve that problem. He recommended to Kamen that the Slingshot might be more appropriate in urban slums, which are more likely to have electricity and polluted waters.

The real problem in Bangladesh, Quadir told Kamen, is lack of electricity. Three-quarters of the population lives without a reliable supply of electricity. In fact Quadir and his brothers, Khalid and Kamal, had been researching an energy business in Bangladesh off and on for years, even before Iqbal got involved in the phone business.

Kamen had something for that too. He was redesigning the Stirling engine, a nineteenth-century external combustion engine. Its main virtues are simplicity of use and an ability to run off any power source—oil, gas, methane, solar heat, you name it. (An American company, Stirling Energy Systems, is building a 4,500-acre *sun farm* in California to generate energy from solar panels; mirrors focus light beams on Stirling engines to heat hydrogen that drives pistons to generate power.[4]) Kamen had redesigned the engine to make it more reliable and cost-effective. The new Stirling is quiet and efficient and pumps out 1 kilowatt of power when running—enough to light about seventy to eighty energy-efficient light bulbs.

Quadir liked this. He had put the idea of an electricity business aside a decade earlier because Moore's law had made cell phones more compelling and because of the entrepreneurial opportunities cell phones provided. The small, easily manageable Stirling engine might provide similar entrepreneurial opportunities. He could see the Stirling working nicely in the marketplaces and residential areas of villages. Plus, since many villagers already cooked with biogas, he could identify a good, readily available, power source: cow dung. "I haven't forgotten about my cows," says Quadir.

The Myth of Appropriate Technology

In theory the Stirling engine is an appropriate technology for generating electricity in a Bangladeshi village. Quadir has formed a company, Emergence Bio-Energy, based in Lexington, Massachusetts, to test that theory. But many products that have appeared to be appropriate technology for the developing world have been abject failures. Yet the cell phone, which was considered a luxury tool totally inappropriate for developing countries, has hit the trifecta. In fact, despite good intentions and some small-scale successes, the so-called appropriate technology movement has turned out to be somewhat of a bust.

The appropriate technology movement crystallized with the publication of E. F. Schumacher's *Small Is Beautiful* in 1973, during the first energy crisis.[5] It followed several years of publication of Stewart Brand's popular *Whole Earth Catalog*, which glorified low-cost, high-quality tools for individuals and communities and became a bible of the back-to-the-land movement.

The theory of appropriate technology essentially holds that any technology should be *right sized* and designed for the people who will actually use it. The technology should be small, apt, sustainable, and productive—aimed at the grass roots. Poor countries don't need state-of-the-art technology, the thinking goes; they need practical basics, like simple stoves. In developing countries the "right" technology is an inexpensive to own and operate tool or machine that has been designed to address local needs. As a Teleplan consultant had once told Grameen Bank, "Bangladesh doesn't need the Mercedes of cellular technology, it needs the Volkswagen."

To the extent that there is an actual theory or overriding philosophy behind this movement, it isn't a bad one. There certainly are examples of successful, small, and simple technologies, such as the motors for Bangladeshi fishing boats and the natural gas–driven three-wheelers in Dhaka, that have had a huge social, economic, and environmental impact. At the same time, efforts to build Internet kiosks in the jungle for people who had never before used computers have by and large been abject failures, for a host of reasons everyone should have foreseen, lack of reliable electricity and phones being paramount, followed by high rates of illiteracy. The current big bet on appropriate technology is the $100 laptop, developed by Nicholas Negroponte's One Laptop Per Child nonprofit organization, whose fate is yet unknown.

Historically, new-fangled ideas have been imposed from the outside to meet a developing country's or region's perceived needs, rather than evolving from the inside out to meet actual needs. Consider the solar cooker, promoted by Westerners for use in Africa as a simple way to generate cooking heat that didn't require women to collect firewood and denude forests. But solar cookers were expensive in local terms, didn't cook food the way people liked it, and required cooking to be done during the heat of the day, when the big meal was traditionally at night.[6] The solar cooker may have been apt and sustainable somewhere, but was an expensive cultural misfit in Africa.

"The appropriate technology movement placed too great an emphasis on time- and labor-saving technologies," says Martin Fisher, the cofounder of Kenya's KickStart, which manufactures the very successful MoneyMaker foot-powered irrigation pumps for farmers.[7] Fisher was an early protégé of the appropriate technology movement and had even named his company ApproTEC (Appropriate Technologies for Enterprise Creation) before coming up with the name KickStart. He eventually concluded that the movement's emphasis on time- and labor-saving devices was not applicable to the rural poor, who don't have much but do have a surplus of time and labor. Nor do money-saving devices make sense unless they cost less than the "local price of a chicken," because few have the cash to invest in saving money. You can't save money you don't have. And time is cheap if you don't have work. But money-making devices, that's a different story. Income is development.

This brings us back to the cell phone, a triple-threat tool that does save time and money but also generates income. Why did it succeed? "To succeed and scale in the developing world without subsidies, it helps to have some Western interest and an effective means of distribution, which drives down the price," says Quadir. "Beyond that, it must attract local interest, show a clear economic gain, and empower individuals. This last point is key, because it means that people will find a way to use the technology, such as through sharing, even if it is seemingly out of reach. The cell phone checks all those boxes and may be the best example of an empowering technology. But it's certainly not the only one."

In addition, while the cell phone certainly costs more than "local price of a chicken," microloans made purchases possible in Bangladesh; not every poor country has such a well-established microcredit system. Microloans clearly lower the investment threshold barrier that might make otherwise appropriate technologies unaffordable.

Emergence Bio-Energy

The success of GrameenPhone's village phone program is easy to take for granted. Why wouldn't it have worked? People need phones, and if they can use them à la carte without owning them, why wouldn't they come up with a few takas to call people they might not otherwise communicate with? But the company's success belies the complexity of the model, or at least the amount of effort that went into designing the model—including the unusual for-profit–nonprofit partnership. So I was curious to watch Quadir in the lab, as it were, with a new company in search of a new model.

When Quadir formed Emergence Bio-Energy to test whether or not the Stirling engine was a profitable route to delivering electricity to Bangladeshi villages, he started with a few givens. Of the 100 million people living in rural Bangladesh, 70 million do not have access to the electric grid; of the 30 million who do, only 10 percent have access to reliable electricity.[8] "Right now, the entire Bangladesh sleeps as soon as the sun goes down," says Abdul-Muyeed Chowdhury, executive director of the Bangladesh Rural Advancement Committee (BRAC), the NGO that functions as the in-country sponsor and distribution vehicle for Emergence Bio-Energy. "People burn expensive kerosene to provide light at night for children's homework and other unavoidable needs. They also burn firewood and cow dung for cooking. In a densely populated country they lose valuable tree cover and huge amounts of valuable organic fertilizer."

Just as BTTB's Dhaka-centric phone system had left the vast majority of the population without access to phones, the centralized urban electric grid means 40,000 of 68,000 villages have no access to electricity. The Rural Electrification Board (REB) supplies access to 20,000 villages, but delivery is highly unreliable. To make things worse, REB has doubled its customer base in the last five years and can supply only one-quarter of the demand, for which it charges customers roughly the same price as before. (The price for rural electricity is about the same as in concentrated urban areas, despite the increased costs of distribution, so it is in effect subsidized.)[9] Even in Dhaka, electricity is extremely unreliable, and garment manufacturers say the frequent brownouts threaten their industry's future as a competitive exporter.

Bangladesh's current electricity production capacity stands at 4,000 megawatts; projections indicate a need for an additional 10,000 megawatts over the next ten years. Even if this extra supply is delivered, it will only bolster the existing concentrated supply in urban areas and is unlikely to extend into virgin territory. "The tragedy in Bangladesh is that what is available from Mother Nature, such as vast reserves of natural gas, is not distributed," says Quadir. "And what is distributed by Mother Nature, such as cow dung, is not properly utilized."

As for alternative methods of power generation, some villagers now use batteries or solar panels, distributed through Grameen Shakti ("Energy"), BRAC, and ten other organizations. Grameen Shakti started selling solar panels through microloans in 1996 before Grameen-Phone started business, but as electricity is the lifeblood of cell phone ecology they have been a useful accessory to cell phones. To date the consortium has sold more than 75,000 solar panels, making this effort one of the fastest-growing renewable energy programs in the world. After making a small initial down payment for a solar panel loan, buyers make installment payments of Tk500 a month for three years. They pay about what they would pay for kerosene over that time, but once the loan is paid off they own a solar panel good for twenty-five years. (Grameen Shakti also provides loans and technical information to villagers who want to build underground biogas chambers to produce cooking gas.)

However, the solar business is commercially viable only because the microlenders have refinanced their loans through the Dhaka-based Infrastructure Development Company Limited (IDCOL), a nonprofit infrastructure finance firm, backed in part by the World Bank, that encourages private sector investment in Bangladesh. "What's the cost of keeping someone in the dark for fifty to sixty years?" asks Fouzul Kabir Kahn, IDCOL's CEO, explaining why he considers the subsidies vital, while also noting that solar home systems will be more commercially viable when solar-cell efficiency increases from 15 to 50 percent or when prices drop from $3 a watt peak to $2 per watt peak.

In short, close to 100 million people need electricity, there is no indication that the government will meet that need, and the only alternative source (aside from old car batteries) is expensive and limited in output. Wind power is not a viable option in a country with soft winds most of the year.

As for fuel, Bangladesh has 21 million head of cattle, so cow dung is plentiful and capable of producing 200 million cubic feet of methane per day—enough to produce 2,000 megawatts of electricity eight hours a day, or half the country's current output. The warm climate is favorable for biogas production. Many villagers already cook either by burning cow dung (which has negative health and environmental impacts) or by using biogas stoves, so this fuel is culturally acceptable. As the Stirling engine is an external combustion engine that will run on any fuel, and because it is less susceptible to the effects of impure fuels, which leave harmful deposits in an internal combustion engine, methane (biogas) converted from cow dung is a perfect fuel.

With a clear market need, a retooled technology, and a ready-made fuel source, Quadir could see a business opportunity. Like GrameenPhone, this new business could create a whole new class of micro-entrepreneurs. In any village, one entrepreneur would collect cow dung, feed it into a biodigester, and produce biogas (methane). He or she would sell the biogas to another entrepreneur, a micro-power-plant operator, who would purchase and operate a Stirling engine and sell electricity to villagers (see Figure 10.1). Both businesses would be driven by microloans, as before. However, the Stirling engine would cost a lot more than a phone. How much more, and how much people would be willing to pay for electricity, were total unknowns.

Market Testing Biogas as an Energy Source

As he did when laying the foundation for GrameenPhone, Quadir moved methodically to address one issue at a time, always on the

Figure 10.1. Two-Entrepreneur Model.

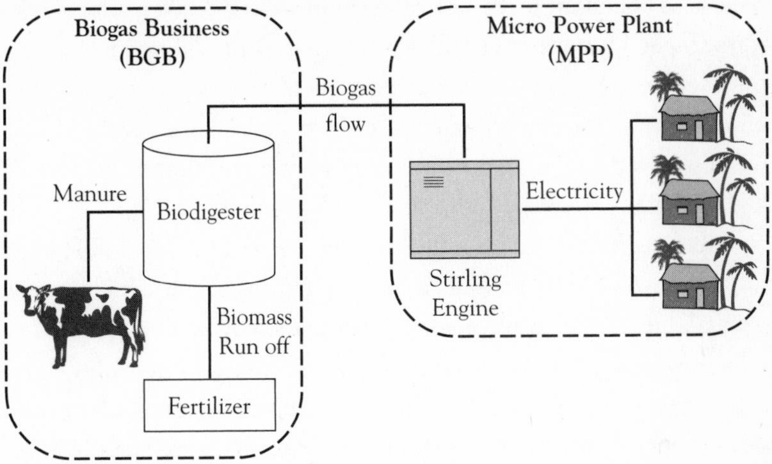

Source: Emergence Bio-Energy.

lookout for bricks he could put in place. The first brick was Tawfiq-
e-Elahi Chowdhury, Bangladesh's former secretary of energy and
a hero of the Liberation War, whom Quadir had first met when
researching his phone idea. Chowdhury knew energy issues, and
he had worked in government circles for nearly thirty years and
so had valuable contacts. Chowdhury was to serve as Emergence
Bio-Energy's director of operations in Bangladesh, while Quadir
worked on the overall plan and investment in the United States.

Instead of turning back to Grameen Bank as a distribution partner in developing the electricity business in the villages, Quadir
teamed with BRAC. BRAC is older than Grameen Bank, having
been started shortly after independence, and operates in virtually
all 68,000 villages, offering microcredit as well as education and
health services. BRAC, a nearly self-sufficient NGO, generated
77 percent of its $330 million operating budget in 2006, according
to executive director Abdul-Muyeed Chowdhury.

During 2005, Emergence Bio-Energy managed a six-month
experiment in two villages chosen by BRAC. The trial was overseen

by Tawfiq Chowdhury and funded by a $100,000 loan from the Lemelson Foundation. Two Stirling engines—$100,000 prototypes—were shipped from Kamen's DEKA office, an old mill building along the Merrimac River in Manchester, New Hampshire. External combustion in the form of an external combustion engine! Each village was also given a biodigester, designed by graduate students at BRAC University.

I had visited one of the villages with Quadir and Tawfiq Chowdhury on my first trip to Bangladesh. The Stirling engine had not yet arrived, but the team was picking a future site in conjunction with village leaders, who were young men. It was in the center of the village, right next to the school, and children were jumping in and out of the windows to watch the activity. Old men sitting and chatting outside shops across the street seemed disinterested. Looking at TV antennas strapped to tall bamboo poles (the black-and-white TVs run off car batteries), I imagined how their village life might be about to radically change. I asked Tawfiq if the villagers were ready for change. "Of course they are," he said. "They want to be connected to the way of life in the rest of the world. It's hard for fathers to marry off daughters who have never lived with electricity." Simply stated, a girl from a family with access to electricity would not marry into a family without electricity.

Talking Cow Dung

The eventual six-month test confirmed that the Stirling engines run efficiently and quietly when burning cow-dung methane. They provide enough electricity to power seventy to eighty energy-efficient bulbs (new 8-watt bulbs produce the equivalent illumination of an old 60-watt bulb) for five to eight hours a day in a small neighborhood.

More important, the business model showed promise. It was clear that the biogas provider would be able to easily recover the cost of the biodigester (approximately $500) by selling fertilizer (a by-product)—making income from the sale of biogas pure profit. Because biodigesters turn the dangerous greenhouse gas methane into water and carbon dioxide (methane is much more damaging to the environment than CO_2), their owners would also earn a methane consumption credit. Quadir estimates there is the potential to establish 500,000 micro power plants in Bangladesh, which would require 500,000 Stirling engines. If Emergence reached its goal of selling 500,000 biodigesters, it would recover an estimated $23 million in methane credits, more than enough to run a centralized repair and maintenance operation and leave plenty to return to the owners.

As for cow dung, a million households in Bangladesh have more than five head of cattle. To produce enough biogas, an entrepreneur would need to collect manure from twelve to thirteen head of cattle. Stocking quality cow dung turns out to be more complex than it would first appear. "There's a trade-off between building up a big stockpile that dries out quickly and keeping a just-in-time supply of fresh manure that provides more gas," says Tawfiq Chowdhury.

During the test period, villagers proved willing to pay more for electricity than urban customers do. As with phones, customers perceived a *consumer surplus* in electricity, which they currently don't have access to. Despite this price elasticity, Quadir didn't trust it as something he could depend on to scale a business. A small test in one village might attract novelty-seekers who would eventually balk at paying more than their urban relatives paid. At any rate, for commercial viability the calculus was dependent on building a Stirling engine that would sell for $1,000. To date, the engine is not manufactured commercially. "Moore's law made the phone business so compelling we survived and plowed through all obstacles," says Quadir about the startup of GrameenPhone. "The energy business is not subject to Moore's law. Say it takes $1 of capital to generate 1 watt of power. That is true for both large plants and small plants. But a large plant may depreciate its capital investment over a thirty- to forty-year period. We're talking about a machine that lasts five years, which means the capital costs are higher." And even if a $1,000 engine is possible, it isn't clear the power-plant owner could make a business of it.

Fine-Tuning the Bio-Energy Plan

After the six-month trial, the Stirling engines were returned to New Hampshire, but BRAC paid to buy new engines from China, knowing how cruel it would be to plunge the villages back into darkness. (The Chinese engines have proved to be noisier than the Stirling engines.) Quadir and his brain trust analyzed findings and their implications, trying to assess the viability of two entrepreneurs running successful businesses *and* providing electricity at an affordable price. This modeling exercise was similar to Inge Skaar's computer modeling that eventually showed that GrameenPhone could profitably deliver affordable phone service to remote villages.

Initially, results seemed to indicate that the cow-dung provider would be able to succeed but that the power-plant operator would struggle to make a profit. This conundrum made Quadir consider the possibility of selling generators to individuals in Dhaka at a higher rate than in the villages, thus using the elite urban market to subsidize the poorer village market. The lucrative urban market was what had attracted outside telecom investors and made the village pay phone scheme work.

Dhaka's electricity is highly unreliable, and Quadir thought many people might purchase a quiet, clean, and efficient Stirling engine as a backup source. Because the Stirling runs on any kind of fuel, you wouldn't have to carry cow dung into urban apartments but could use natural gas or other fuels.

Another possible option is to find a way to redesign the Stirling engine to capture waste heat, 85 percent of which is now lost in the conversion to electricity. That heat could be used to produce more power, possibly enough to drive appliances, or to develop other side businesses dependent on heat. Quadir and engineers are confident they can find a way to derive economic value from the lost heat.

Emergence Bio-Energy

Emergence Bio-Energy hypothesizes that if more power could be generated from the same amount of methane, an entrepreneur could conceivably develop other income streams. At the least, he or she could charge batteries several hours a day, a valuable service that would obviate the need for villagers to travel into market centers to recharge them. Like the cell phone, rechargeable batteries would save villagers time and money. With the added income streams from monetizing the waste heat, the power-plant owner would be much more likely to run a profitable business.

But this business is significantly more complex than the village phone business. The basic Emergence model presumes two entrepreneurs—one selling gas, one selling electricity. What if the biogas producer decides to sell his gas elsewhere, perhaps to individuals for their stoves? What if he sees that the power-plant owner is making better money with more services, and holds out for a higher price? Electricity is a valued commodity to the extent that it is reliable and consistent; if you can't plan your evening because you don't know whether you'll have light, you might begin to balk at paying four or five times what urban customers pay. The biogas producer is in the driver's seat, with an unregulated monopoly on the production of methane. The entrepreneurs are part of a self-regulated supply chain that could easily break.

Substituting another fuel for village-produced methane, such as bottled propane, might simplify the business. But it would also reduce income opportunities in the villages, which is a key element of the overall plan. Plus, importing another fuel would make the business dependent on an undependable transportation system.

The technical expertise required also differentiates this energy business from the village-phone business. The learning curve to use a phone is relatively short, as the complex brains of the communications system are housed in a central switching station. All phone ladies really need to do is provide the phone and collect a usage fee, although calculating overseas rates can be difficult and keeping the phone charged can be frustrating. The Emergence Bio-Energy model supposes a decentralized business, where the entrepreneurs are responsible for the production of gas and the generation and distribution of electricity, both technically challenging production tasks.

Quadir realizes these issues need to be worked out, but says, "It's important to recognize that this is the nature of building a more complex economy." Plus there are higher hurdles to clear.

Internal Combustion: Domestic Manufacturing

Martin Fisher concluded that KickStart could provide affordable MoneyMaker pumps in Kenya by manufacturing them in China and importing them. Quadir thinks that Emergence Bio-Energy might build Stirling engines more cheaply in Bangladesh than overseas— given the low cost of labor and the avoidance of import duties. He hasn't proved this yet because he would have to build a manufacturing plant, but he looks to a major international engineering firm as a likely candidate to take advantage of Bangladesh's low-cost and hard-working labor force.

In addition to avoiding import taxes, domestic manufacturing would begin to create a more skilled workforce in Bangladesh. Knowledge transfer from a world-class supplier (imagine a Bosch or a Honda) to the overall manufacturing sector, currently dependent on light industries such as apparel, would help move Bangladesh up the manufacturing food chain. Given Bangladesh's large supply of low-cost labor, moving into heavier manufacturing would give the country a chance to develop a new export industry, which is the first spark of internal combustion.

Proposing domestic manufacturing is also a good political move, as the government would like to keep as much foreign exchange in the country as possible. Already, the government is concerned that the cell phone businesses are exporting capital to buy equipment and handsets—not to mention expatriating profits (see Chapters Nine and Eleven).

More Revolutionary Than GrameenPhone?

Emergence Bio-Energy's business model and plan is likely to mutate further as Emergence moves closer to full implementation on the ground. The company has raised another round of capital from foreign investors to continue testing and refining the model. But conceptually, at least, Emergence believes that microloans can help scale an electricity business as they do communications, even if there are unsolved problems.

At first blush, Emergence Bio-Energy does not appear to be as scalable as cellular telephony, an information communications technology with seemingly limitless possibilities. That's because the Stirling engine is a mechanical engine designed 200 years ago, one that is not dependent on digital switches or software for operation. Moore's Law does not hold, and even though the manufacturing price may drop with scaled-up production, it will not drop because an integrated circuit has doubled its density.

But Quadir has deep belief in the transformative power of technology, any technology. And on closer examination, the full-blown model holds huge potential. Emergence Bio-Energy is looking to establish 500,000 one-kilowatt power generators running eight hours a day. That's an average of seven micro power plants per village, and it would increase Bangladesh's current generation by 500 megawatts, or about 12 percent. It might actually increase it by more, as virtually all power will be distributed without loss, whereas power distributed over larger areas typically dissipates with transmission. And because that electricity will flow to villages that now have no electricity, the marginal productivity of every megawatt is much more than is obtainable by adding a similar new capacity to the city.

Just as capital in the form of microloans is more productive where there is no capital (that is, banks), and cell phones are more productive where there are no fixed-line phones, electricity where there is no electricity will add years to villagers' lives. The impact on children's ability to absorb knowledge through extended study time alone is of incalculable value. And who now knows how the captured lost heat might be deployed? Certainly in a country with a very long wet season, that heat will be a valuable resource. And if each of 500,000 micro power plants requires two operators, that's 1 million new income opportunities. Finally, processing manure into methane that is burnt off will prevent vast amounts of this harmful gas from escaping into the atmosphere.

Says Tawfiq Chowdhury, sipping a cool yogurt drink on a hot day in a hip Dhaka cafe, "Emergence Bio-Energy is potentially more revolutionary than GrameenPhone. These villages have been dark since time immemorial."

11

Eyeing the Dhaka Stock Exchange

I revisited Bangladesh about fifteen months after my first foray. I was curious to see how GrameenPhone was faring against the new competition, and whether Bangladesh was changing with all the new phones—about 5 million more since my first visit. I wanted to reexperience a country in transformation through its silent revolution.

When I got off the plane I was looking forward to the gratifying experience of turning on my phone and seeing GrameenPhone pop onto the screen. Surprise! It was Aktel, the Malaysian carrier! Competition! As I walked toward customs I passed GrameenPhone ads seemingly every fifty feet, with instructions on how to switch over to GrameenPhone for international roaming. This was like Hertz reasserting its airport dominance in the United States. As a brand loyalist, I switched immediately and sent my wife a text message to test the system.

Within seconds I received a text: "Dear Cingular subscriber. GrameenPhone welcomes you to Bangladesh! No of USA Embassy is 02-824700." I thought this was useful, if somewhat ominous. A month before the Peace Corps had suspended operations indefinitely in Bangladesh, fearing possible terrorist reprisals for the arrest of several leading Islamic fundamentalists (who were to be sentenced in May 2006 to death by hanging). Seconds later, I got another text: "Dial 2007 for updated currency exchange rate. 2222 for News. 933 for Police. . . ." Police? I listened to the news on my phone, which had an Edward R. Murrow feel, with a clicking tele-type sound in the background. There was a *hartal* in progress, chaos in the streets.

My next anticipated touchstone was the handmade "Welcome, Foreign Investors" sign that had caught my eye before as I was going through the passport check. The sign had been upgraded to an official electronic welcome for "Diplomats and Foreign Investors." It was a more serious entry notice that foreign investors are becoming part of the landscape. Many of these investors are in the garment trade, as Bangladesh has established a foothold in the global garment industry as a manufacturer of both knitwear and woven wear. Turkish textile executives, among others, were in Dhaka talking abut relocating textile plants and setting up joint ventures. A wall-sized promotion touted Bangladesh as "the best investment opportunity in South Asia." This bold and somewhat contentious affirmation was supported by several bullet points:

- Most liberal investment regime in South Asia
- Conducive and congenial business environment
- Facilitative economic governance
- Competitive and viable cost of doing business
- Diligent and productive human resources
- Widest range of sustainable investment sectors

Bangladesh was talking the talk, if not yet walking the walk, of a government with an open-door investment policy. I think the government wants to believe that all these points are accurate and defensible, and perhaps that if people believe in them hard enough they will become true, in fairy-tale fashion. But points two and three in particular are just not true. The business environment is not "conducive and congenial" because of political strife that leads to strikes and corruption. And the economic governance at the micro level is not "facilitative."

In the case of cell phones the government levies some of the highest industry taxes in the world on the sector; in the case of textiles, the leading export sector and the main source of foreign currency, electrical system brownouts hamper production. The good news is that the cell phone industry, like the country as a whole, continues to grow faster and faster despite the government and its governance, which gives one hope that one day the government will get on the bandwagon, walk the talk, and facilitate growth.

I called Tawfiq-e-Elahi Chowdhury to set a time to meet, and mentioned the *hartals* in progress as a hindrance. "We live in a kakistocracy," he said. I asked for clarification. "It means 'governed by the worst.' That's us."

Bloody Hartals Cripple Business

The intractable political situation and the hatred between the two main parties dominate public life in a very negative way, and the strife was on full display during my visit as the two parties headed toward their fourth electoral contest since 1991. Voters were preparing to choose between Sheikh Hasina's opposition Awami League and Prime Minister Zia's ruling Bangladesh National Party.

The day before there had been a violent antigovernment protest by the Awami League, and police had baton-charged the crowd and had set off tear gas, resulting in injuries to several ranking opposition officials. "Sealed city turns into battlefield" and "City cringes in fear," were the lead stories in the *Daily Star* ("Journalism Without Fear or Favour").[1] *The Independent* ("Where Truth and Ethics Matter") countered with, "Police foil opposition's sit-in using rubber bullets, tear gas."[2]

The highly charged protests were in response to the killing of twenty villagers by police the week before in a remote northwest corner of the country, near the Indian border. The villagers had been protesting the low supply and high price of electricity. For that they were shot dead in broad daylight. They could with equal reason have been protesting the low supply and high price of fertilizer or natural gas, even though Bangladesh sits on huge gas reserves. The government's response was inhumane, as the Bangladesh Human Rights Commission pointed out. Why should people who have the least be penalized the most? Why should they be shot? One can only imagine how maddening it must be to know that these commodities exist in ample supply around the world, even in a city perhaps only fifty kilometers distant, when you have nothing.

In response to the police crackdown on their protest, the Awami League had called for a nationwide *hartal,* which would pause for Friday prayer and the Saturday holiday, then resume Sunday. This effectively scotched the planned meetings I had set up, but at least I was able to contact people on their cell or home phones. Bangladeshis are so proud to have phones they put every conceivable number on their business cards, including home phones. All day long the steamy, sultry air was filled with the jarring sound of men inciting unrest through loudspeakers—soothed later by the soft sound of incanted evening prayers cutting through the haze. No one was killed, but 200 were injured.

The political paralysis (no new political leaders for more than fifteen years) and consequent corruption (as bureaucrats are rarely replaced, they consolidate inordinate power) remain a serious brake on the country's economic development. "The government . . . yesterday betrayed nothing less than this administration's utter contempt for the interest of the people of the capital city, and by extension, the nation at large. . . . Just to stop the demonstrations, the economic clock was brought to a grinding halt," read an editorial in the *Daily Star* that appeared to be indicative of popular opinion.[3]

I asked Shams to explain the political situation. "People in politics today didn't grow up with any institutions. They have to coerce people to vote; they need the Mafia to get people to vote for them. It's like Tammany Hall in the United States. Except in our case these two ladies are trapped in the past and have been forced into playing certain roles. It's become very personal."

A few months before, in early 2006, Muhammad Yunus had delivered a remarkable speech at the celebration of the fifteenth anniversary of the *Daily Star* (which was started after Bangladesh elected its first civilian leader in 1991). Yunus called for new open-door policies that welcomed the world into Bangladesh, new blood into politics, and an end to corruption. "Our non-stop political bickering does not give a respite to celebrate our enormous successes to prepare ourselves to reach out to still higher levels of accomplishments. Our biggest worry is corruption. There is no way out but to eliminate corruption in politics, from where the infectious disease of corruption spreads around."[4]

Corruption is the topic *du jour* wherever you go in Dhaka, with economists and hotel clerks uniformly agreeing that the country's growth rate would soar if the disease could be quelled. Almost everyone agreed that Yunus would not and could not have given this speech ten years earlier, when there was truly no "countervailing force" to counteract the government. In all this, it's worth remembering that Bangladesh is a young country (born in 1971) with an even younger democracy (effectively started in 1991).

Taxes Impede Industry Growth

Corruption may be the biggest worry, but it is not the only drag on growth. Economic governance is far from "facilitative," as the airport promotion would have you think, especially if you're the biggest foreign investor and competing with a government entity, as Telenor finds itself pitted against the Bangladesh Telephone and Telegraph Bureau (BTTB). GrameenPhone also competes against Aktel, Banglalink, CityCell, and Warid—but at least it's on an even playing field with the other cell phone operators, who are all fighting uphill against BTTB. Their collective gripes against BTTB and the Bangladesh Telecommunication Regulatory Commission "regulators," some of whom used to work for BTTB, are threefold:

1. Interconnection with BTTB's fixed-phone network is still an inadequate, expensive, one-way deal—BTTB callers do not pay to connect to the cell phones, but cell phone callers pay to connect to BTTB phones. Hard to believe, more than ten years later, that the difficulty Iqbal Quadir foresaw before GrameenPhone won its license is still a bone of contention.

2. All international calls go through BTTB, so that service is more expensive and unreliable for cell phone users than it needs to be, and cell phone operators are denied a potentially huge new revenue stream. "The interconnection system subsidizes the less productive and more expensive fixed-line system, whilst harming the more productive and cheaper mobile industry," research firm Ovum concluded in a study.[5]

3. Industry taxes levied on the cell phone operators—import duties and connection fees—are among the highest in the world, which has created an unregulated black market in phone sales that ends up depriving both suppliers and the government of revenue.

The only thing that makes this particular form of economic governance tolerable is that BTTB is still a moribund player that provides virtually no competition. And the lack of reliable interconnection becomes less of an issue as cell phones become more and more dominant (85 percent of all phones) and operators establish interconnection agreements with each other. But the tax issue is a real detriment to growth.

The link between private commercial success and overall economic growth—the relationship between corporate profits and GDP—is one that telecom executives in poor countries are forced to continually promote. In the West the tenet that successful businesses create jobs and generate tax revenues is widely understood and accepted. In the South the notion that corporate profits (especially those earned by foreign actors likely to take money out of the country) are beneficial to the nation is antithetical to most people's experience. In Bangladesh this perception of unfairness is creating tension between the government—which on the one hand is desperate to attract foreign investors but on the other hand levies industry taxes that reduce growth—and foreign investors—who feel that they have been courageous to enter poor, corrupt Bangladesh and that their profits and investments are contributing to the country's growth.

In 2004, for example, GrameenPhone contributed $160 million to the government through a combination of taxes, import duties, interconnection fees to BTTB, and the leasing of the fiber-optic cable from Bangladesh Railway. Overall in 2004, the mobile industry in Bangladesh contributed nearly $260 million in direct and indirect (flowing from related sectors) taxes.[6]

Cheap Phones, Costly Connections

At a time when the GSM Association, through its Emerging Markets Handset initiative, and handset manufacturers are looking to produce ultra-low-cost phones to meet high demand in countries such as Bangladesh, Nigeria, the Philippines, Russia, and South Africa, all of which have high import duties, one of the most contentious issues for cell phone operators in developing countries is the high import tax rates and connection fees for handsets. In Bangladesh the government essentially charges a $16 royalty on each new connection—25 percent in form of an import tax and 75 percent in the form of a tax on the SIM, the technology that makes the phone actually work. If you buy a Motorola 113 or 113A phone, which costs less than $30, the connection "royalty" adds 50 percent to the cost of the phone.

In Bangladesh a majority of phones are sold on black market. "With reduced handset taxes, more handsets will be legally imported," says GrameenPhone CEO Erik Aas. "High cost is still the main barrier for people to get connected. Any reduction in handset and connection taxes will increase the number of new subscribers and government will end up with more tax revenues. Countries with lower entry costs, like India, Sri Lanka, and Pakistan, have grown the industry faster." (See Figure 11.1.)

Bangladeshis are not alone on this boat. "Taxes are a huge issue for us," Phuthuma Nhleko, CEO of MTN in South Africa, told the *International Herald Tribune*. "The government sees us as a sort of secondary treasury that they can go to when they need to solve financial issues. The governments need to carefully think about the decisions they make on taxes because that will dictate how much people are willing to invest in their country."[7]

"There is a great irony in the way governments tackle the digital divide," Rob Conway, chief executive officer of the GSM Association commented in a press release about the 2005 GSM report *Tax and the Digital Divide*. "They say they want more of their people to have access to communications and yet they impose high taxes on mobile phones and usage."[8]

Figure 11.1. Percentage Change in Tax Revenues Following the Removal of Mobile-Specific Taxes.

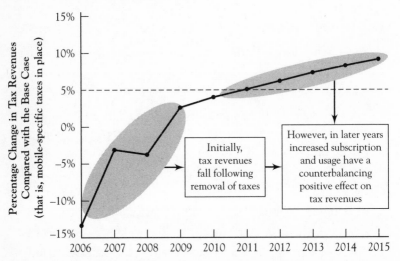

Source: GSM Association and Frontier Economics, *Taxation and Mobile Telecommunications in Bangladesh* (London: GSM Association, 2006), fig. 4.

Foreign Investors Under the Gun

In Bangladesh, the government's regulatory bodies have erred by letting multinationals operate in the country without paying license fees, and these agencies are now trying to play catch-up by levying taxes on products and services. GrameenPhone, for example, paid zero for a license. A few years later, cellular licenses were being sold for hundreds of millions of dollars in other poor countries, in what would become a kind of Internet-like frenzy that left many investment banks carrying a lot of debt. "This was a huge break, because if the government had charged several hundreds of millions, Grameen Bank wouldn't have been able to play," says Josh Mailman, Grameen's first investor. But even today, as the sector attracts more competition, license fees in Bangladesh are abnormally low. UAE's Warid bought a license in Bangladesh in 2005 for $50 million—just several months after paying $291 million for a license in Pakistan. Licenses in Afghanistan, a much smaller and more difficult market, go for $40 million. Thus some in government are looking to make up for the lost revenue. "I have asked the commission to increase revenue from the mobile phone companies that have been doing businesses randomly for the past several years," Saifur Rahman, minister of finance, told the *New Age*. "The mobile phone companies are doing businesses without giving any license fee, which is not possible in other countries."[9]

In addition to imposing excessive taxes the government is using its clout to try to force foreign multinationals to list public equities on the stock exchange. Whatever the government's intent, it would allow Bangladeshis to participate in the profits. The minister of finance, among others, argues that when foreigners borrow from Bangladeshi banks and then convert that loan into foreign currency to buy equipment, the local currency is put under pressure. Hence the counterargument from GrameenPhone that at least half its investment stays in Bangladesh (see Chapter Nine).

India's Tata Group, a $20 billion conglomerate that proposes to invest up to $3 billion in Bangladesh to produce steel, power, and fertilizer (see the following box), was clearly cognizant of the government's contentious debate with the cell phone operators over repatriation of profits when negotiating with the government. After agreeing to triple the price paid for natural gas, as well as to supply all the steel Bangladesh could use, Tata's revised proposal to the government also offered 10 percent ownership of Tata projects to the government and offered to float another 10 percent of all projects in the local stock market. The *Financial Express*, Dhaka's only English-language daily financial paper, used these improved terms to take a pot shot at the cell phone companies. "The investment to be made by the Tata is not an ethereal one as has been witnessed in the case of the telecom sector. Taking advantage of weak deals, the so-called foreign direct investors have borrowed from the local money market, made investments and at the end of the year repatriated huge profits back home."[10]

New Foreign Direct Investment (FDI) from India

For the last decade China has driven so-called South-South investment. As China attracts more business and wages rise—not to mention a steady $50 to $60 billion in foreign investment—it outsources manufacturing throughout Asia. And now India, which has historically struggled to attract foreign investment (its $5 to $10 billion a year is much closer to Bangladesh's level of FDI than China's) is beginning to export capital.

Tata Group, a huge Indian conglomerate with ninety-three companies and nearly $20 billion in revenues, recently indicated it planned to invest $3 billion in Bangladesh—in steel, power, coal mining, and fertilizer. This would be by far the biggest single investment in the country's history, and is indicative of the new trend toward South-South investment. "The main objective of these investments is to expand our business to all South Asian countries including Iran, Pakistan, and Afghanistan," T. Mukherjee, deputy managing director of Tata, told the *Daily Star*.[11]

It's hard to make a direct link between the cellular investments of the previous decade and this aggressive play by a huge conglomerate with a voracious appetite for natural resources, but let's be frank. First, if you can't make a phone call into a country to check on your people and your money, you're not going to send in money. Second, without a track record of successful foreign investment, it would have been psychologically difficult for India to be the first mover into Bangladesh, given the history of social and economic tension between the countries. But seeing successful European, Asian, and Middle Eastern investors certainly makes the water more appealing.

To List or Not to List

From the outset GrameenPhone's stated intent was to list a public offering to buy shares in the company. All shareholders signed a statement to this effect in their original Memorandum of Understanding. In part this was a feel-good statement to help win the license, but it was also in keeping with the Grameen Bank tradition, where every borrower is a shareholder in the bank. Ideally, every GrameenPhone customer, along with shareholders of Grameen Bank, could become a shareholder in the largest company in the country.

The 1999 annual report, which outlines the company's "in the hands of people" philosophy about cell phone distribution, notes that "even the ownership of GrameenPhone is planned to be in the hands of people. Once its economic viability is proven, the company will be listed so that ordinary people can buy shares and be a proud owner of GrameenPhone."[12] But there has been no movement toward an IPO, which is one reason why Gonofone orchestrated its own exit in order to liquefy its holdings at the end of 2004.

There are emotional, financial, and political aspects to consideration of an IPO for GrameenPhone, and all are pretty easily understood. *Emotionally*, it's unsettling to Bangladeshis that the largest company, and one so important to the economy's future, is majority owned by Norway-based Telenor AS, even given Telenor's superior track record as a corporate citizen and pillar of the national community. *Financially*, it would be a huge boost to the Dhaka Stock Exchange to attract the country's most vibrant sector. From GrameenPhone's perspective, however, the company is fueling its own growth and investment organically (with more than 60 percent market share and steady, high profit margins), and it probably doesn't feel any urgency to sell shares to the public. Perhaps the increased competition from Warid and Orascom will change the dynamic and force GrameenPhone or one of the others to list on the capital markets. Finally, *politically*, for the government (which within the last few years has forced domestic banks and insurance companies onto the stock exchange), adding telecoms to the stock market would be a huge coup that would hide many of the government's other shortcomings. (The actual government may be different as you read, with elections scheduled for 2007.)

In 2005, IPOs on the Dhaka Stock Exchange hit a record high, and most were oversubscribed. This is in keeping with the explosive growth of emerging market stock indices from 2003 on; overall returns have dwarfed those of the S&P 500, Dow Jones 30, Nikkei, and FTSE. The Dhaka Stock Exchange is not near the top of the pack in this surge, but the fact that it is being pulled along is indicative of a new reality in global capital markets.

Grameen Telecom, the minority shareholder (at 38 percent), strongly favors a listing. "I've been advocating this at board meetings, trying to persuade Telenor to go public, to give people a sense of ownership," says former Chairman Shams, wearing a Grameen Check shirt and sitting under a three-bladed fan in his office on the Grameen campus. "Otherwise, it's a Norwegian company. I think it would be a good move."

Shams suggests that if Telenor doesn't need to raise money, it might consider listing a smaller portion of the company shares, which would bypass lockup regulations and give majority shareholders the ability to take away profits in hard currency more quickly. "There's a lot of money in Bangladesh just waiting to invest, because right now people don't have good places to invest. Every IPO is oversubscribed. And you can bet that the listing of Grameen-Phone would put the Dhaka stock market on fire!" Analysts put the value of GrameenPhone in the $1 billion range, which would add at least 25 percent to the total stock market capitalization.

Silent Revolution

Despite its self-involved politicians, despite undeveloped capital markets that still struggle to attract investors, despite the cancerous corruption that eats at the country's soul, Bangladesh has changed dramatically in the last ten years. The forces of regeneration are outpacing the forces of degeneration. The silent revolution is transforming the country in spite of the government.

The GDP growth rate, which had been plugging along at a steady 5 percent, is projected to hit 6.5 to 7 percent in 2006—shrugging off the high oil prices that are putting a strain on costs and foreign reserves (in a country with vast natural gas reserves). The rate of growth would be even faster were it not for the corruption and *hartals* that generate uncertainty. World Bank vice president Praful Patel noted in the spring of 2006 that according to the World Bank study *Sources of Growth and Productivity in Bangladesh*, the growth rate of Bangladesh could be 2 to 2.8 percentage points higher if corruption were reduced to the level of the least corrupt countries. The economy also loses about 3 to 4 percent of GDP annually on average because of *hartals*, he said, referring to another study by the United Nations Development Programme.[13]

Social changes are equally impressive. The birth rate and the death rate are down; the number of children completing school, particularly girls, is up. In a country of rivers, where ferries were not long ago the primary mode of transport, you can get anywhere in the country from Dhaka within ten hours, traveling mostly on roads. Thanks to mechanized irrigation, rice production has tripled over the past thirty years, despite significantly less land under cultivation, and vegetables are exported. Thanks primarily to advertising by cell phone operators, Dhaka has ten private television stations. Rickshaw drivers carry cell phones, just as car drivers do, which not only enhances their productivity but saves their customers time. Numerous Internet wireless networks pop up on computer screens, although many are line-of-sight and don't work particularly well in the city. Today uninterrupted wireless broadband is spreading from Dhaka out into the countryside. It's easy to understand how Muhammad Yunus could have been so optimistic in his comments on the fifteenth anniversary of the *Daily Star:* "We are ready to launch ourselves into a path to cross USD 1,000 per capita income, 8 percent GDP growth rate, and reducing poverty level to under 25 percent in the near future."[14] A recent World Bank study on the economies of South Asia echoes this point, predicting that a 7 percent growth rate between now and 2013 will reduce poverty in Bangladesh to 20 percent (see Figure 11.2).

One of the more notable new wireless providers is bracNet, a joint venture between BRAC's existing BRAC BDMail Network (BBN) and GNet, a U.S.-based company. Khalid Quadir, Iqbal's brother who had performed early reconnaissance on Grameen Bank, came up with the idea for a nationwide wireless network and approached BRAC, bringing along investors from the United States, Europe, and Japan. I visited bracNet's offices, high up in the twenty-one-story BRAC building, and they reminded me of worksites in the go-go Internet days of the late 1990s in the United States—full of young engineers working feverishly to beat another office of young engineers working feverishly. But they were looking out on Dhaka, where barefoot construction workers hung from bamboo scaffolds thirty stories high, below which ferrymen delivered

Figure 11.2. Poverty Reduction in South Asia Associated with Higher Growth Rates.

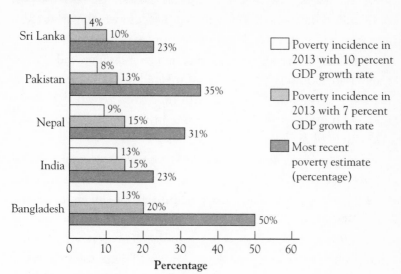

Note: The method used for computing growth elasticity varies among countries.
Source: S. Devarajan and I. Nabi, *Economic Growth in South Asia: Promising, Un-Equalizing, . . . Sustainable?* (Washington, D.C.: World Bank, June 2006), fig. 3.

big boatloads from island shantytowns onto city streets. In addition to the wireless network, bracNet also offers a Bangladesh-based portal, which speeds access to information for local Internet users, who no longer have to wait for data to traverse the world via satellite, and Kinko's-style print shops and computing centers.

A People-Based Company

The biggest change to the country and the heaviest artillery of the silent revolution may result from connection to an international submarine cable. In the spring of 2006, Bangladesh connected to the SEA-ME-WE 4 (South East Asia–Middle East–Western Europe 4) transoceanic submarine cable, wiring Bangladesh directly into the world's information superhighway for the first time. Bangladesh should have been connected a decade earlier, but bureaucrats feared losing the nation's "secrets," and thus Bangladesh had been the only nonlandlocked country of its size that didn't have submarine cable access, remaining dependent on the more expensive and less reliable satellite service for both Internet and long-distance calls. "From today Bangladesh is going to be connected with the global information superhighway," proclaimed Prime Minister Zia. "We have reached our target through different initiatives by the grace of Almighty Allah."[15]

ISPs (Internet service providers) immediately noted a vast improvement in data-transfer speeds, and many hope that the broadband pipeline opens new possibilities for call centers, telemedicine, e-commerce, e-government activities and services, and even software exports. The country also will conserve valuable foreign exchange, as over time less money will go to foreign-owned satellite services; the flip side is that the money will go to BTTB, which controls operation of the cable.

How quickly the cable becomes a practical contributor to communications depends on BTTB, which is not unlike sending a fox to guard a chicken coop. BTTB plans to implement four nodes off the main trunk, to which wireless networks can connect. This excites the relentlessly optimistic Khalid Shams, who wants to bring broadband wireless to the same remote rural communities now served by GrameenPhone.

"I want to move fast, that's why I've been experimenting with EDGE technology," says Shams, speaking of GrameenPhone's cell phone–based Internet option. "We can easily have 60,000 Internet kiosks that handle VOIP calls, passport applications, visas, secondary school exams, and so on." Grameen Telecom already has several rural Internet kiosks (with computers and printers) running, despite having no broadband connection. Run by "unschooled young men" funded by Grameen Bank microloans, they are making money. "Just like the phone, this will have a snowball effect," says Shams.

The possibility of widespread Internet kiosks brings Grameen Telecom full circle, back to the original concept papers written by Quadir in 1995 for a "people-based information company," playing off the Bangla translation of Gonofone ("phones for the masses"). In addition to cellular phones, Quadir envisioned a data network with Grameen Information Centers, which would provide e-mail and fax services as well as money transfer services. All that is now happening in Bangladesh, not just because of GrameenPhone but in large part because GrameenPhone has shown people the possibilities and value of spending precious takas to communicate.

They may say you cry twice in Bangladesh, but now you can begin to smile.

Epilogue

On August 5, 2006, Iqbal Quadir was awarded the Rotary SEED Award by the Rotary Club of Metropolitan Dhaka for pioneering universal telephony in Bangladesh during 1993–1999 and helping to create self-employment opportunities for 250,000 poor women in rural Bangladesh. The distinguished SEED award, one of the most prestigious in Bangladesh, recognizes outstanding contributions made by Bangladeshi citizens in the fields of science, education, and economic development. Trustees of the Rotary Club recognized Quadir's "original and outstanding contribution in the field of economic development," noting that his "idea of the 'mobile ladies' and initiative to bring GSM mobile phone technology to Bangladesh brought in tremendous possibilities and ushered in a new era of lasting economic development."

Quadir was the twelfth recipient of this award. Muhammad Yunus, whose already impressive list of awards was capped by the 2006 Nobel Peace Prize, received the first SEED Award in 1995 for developing the Grameen Bank concept. These awards are fitting bookends to an unusually successful business initiative that has become a global model for rural distribution and a key part of Telenor's global portfolio.

In the second quarter of 2006, when Telenor's revenues jumped 37 percent over the previous year and earnings increased 35 percent,

GrameenPhone was singled out as a top performer by Telenor's CEO, Jon Fredrik: "We are very satisfied that several of our mobile operations are performing so well in their markets. In particular, GrameenPhone improved its market position by increasing its customer base by more than 30 percent during this quarter alone." GrameenPhone added more than 2 million subscribers in the second quarter, taking its base to nearly 8.5 million and a market share of 63 percent. Meanwhile, cellular subscriptions in Norway *decreased* by 11,000 during the same period.

Given the success of GrameenPhone and other market share leaders such as Kyivstar in Ukraine (Telenor owns 56.5 percent), Telenor is looking to increase its exposure in emerging markets. It bid for but lost out on the third GSM license in Egypt (which sold for $2.9 billion in an auction), then won a ten-year license and 100 percent of Mobi 063, a cellular operator in Serbia, by paying an astounding $1.9 billion. Telenor, which also has operations in nearby Montenegro, outbid Mobikom of Austria, Orascom of Egypt, and a consortium of Austrian investors. In 2005, for the fourth consecutive year, Telenor was one of three telecom firms (out of 250 total firms) listed on the Dow Jones Sustainability Index.

On the heels of its success with Telenor, Grameen Bank has started another partnership with a multinational firm. Grameen has partnered with France-based Groupe Danone to deliver infant formula and fortified yogurt to pregnant women and nutrition-deprived youngsters in the Bogra region, where Danone is building a $1 million plant. Unlike GrameenPhone, which is a for-profit business with a nonprofit arm (Grameen Telecom), Grameen Danone Foods is structured as a "social business" or "nonloss" business that aims to maximize benefits, not profits. But like Grameen-Phone, it engages local people as part of the farming, processing, and distribution chain. Farmers produce milk that is converted into yogurt and then distributed in the same community, a closed-loop system that provides both income and a nutritious end product.

Groupe Danone will use solar energy and biogas to drive production and hopes to use this initial plant as a model it can replicate all over Bangladesh. Such a distributed manufacturing model would keep jobs in the region.

Quadir left his post at Harvard in 2005 to become the "founder director" of the Program in Developmental Entrepreneurship at the Massachusetts Institute of Technology (MIT). He also used some of the proceeds from divestment of his shares in GrameenPhone to set up an annual global competition in his father's name to develop the best ideas for economic development in Bangladesh. The annual $25,000 prize is administered by Harvard's Center for International Development.

Dr. Mo, chairman of Celtel, has announced his intention to create his own $100 million foundation to fund development projects in Africa. He calls his new private-sector initiative "investment with a heart," to be distinguished from Western-funded aid efforts such as Tony Blair's Commission for Africa. In addition, the new Mo Ibrahim Foundation announced a $5 million prize for African leaders who are elected fairly, improve their country's standard of living, and hand over power peacefully. Recipients of the Mo Ibrahim Prize for Achievement in African Leadership will be awarded $500,000 a year for their first ten years out of office, and $200,000 a year thereafter as long as they live. "The message is that we, Africans, need to take charge of our own issues," said Ibrahim on announcing the prize. "It is our responsibility to look after our continent, to look after our kids." Ibrahim notes that his financial models assume leaders will live twenty-five years after leaving office, making the estimated net prize worth $8 million.

Finally, Josh Mailman, who turned his $125,000 seed capital investment in Gonofone into a multi-million dollar payday, is in on the ground floor again with seed investments in bracNet, the broadband wireless company run by Khalid Quadir. (CellBazaar, the cell phone–based "classified advertising" system started by Kamal

Quadir, has also attracted U.S. investors.) Whether lightning strikes twice or thrice remains to be seen, but the presence of Mailman and other foreign investors backing Bangladeshi-Americans importing and implanting information technology shows that the forces of external combustion are still in play in Bangladesh. M-commerce via wireless broadband, unconceivable in Bangladesh just a few years ago, is taking hold.

Notes

Preface

1. S. Devarajan and I. Nabi, *Economic Growth in South Asia: Promising, Un-Equalizing, . . . Sustainable?* (Washington, D.C.: World Bank, June 2006), p. 1.

2. C. K. Prahalad, *The Fortune at the Bottom of the Pyramid: Eradicating Poverty Through Profits* (Upper Saddle River, N.J.: Wharton School Publishing, 2005).

3. C. K. Prahalad and S. L. Hart, "The Fortune at the Bottom of the Pyramid," *strategy + business*, First Quarter 2001.

4. W. Easterly, *The White Man's Burden: Why the West's Efforts to Aid the Rest Have Done So Much Ill and So Little Good* (New York: Penguin Press, 2006).

5. W. Easterly, *The Elusive Quest for Growth: Economists' Adventures and Misadventures in the Tropics* (Cambridge, Mass.: MIT Press, 2001).

Introduction

1. The term *bottom of the pyramid* was coined by C. K. Prahalad and Stuart Hart in their article, "The Fortune at the Bottom of the Pyramid," *strategy + business*, First Quarter 2001, which provided the first articulation of how business could profitably serve the needs of the four billion poor in the developing world.

2. A. Islam, "A Bangladeshi Helena and Her Magic Lamp of ICT," 2004, retrieved from www.grameentelecenter.org.

3. A. Shafiq, "Mobile Rings Changes for World's Poor," *Sydney Morning Herald*, Apr. 22, 2005, retrieved from www.smh.com.au.

4. E. Sylvers, "Connecting Developing Nations," *International Herald Tribune*, Feb. 17, 2006.

5. S. Pitroda, "Development, Democracy and the Village Telephone," *Harvard Business Review*, Nov./Dec. 1993, p. 66.

6. A. Perry, "Rebuilding Bangladesh," *Time Asia*, Apr. 3, 2006.

7. J. Sachs, *The End of Poverty: Economic Possibilities for Our Time* (New York: Penguin Press, 2005), p. 73.

8. D. S. Landes, *Wealth and Poverty of Nations: Why Some Are So Rich, and Some So Poor* (New York: Norton, 1998).

9. The term *disruptive technology* was coined by Clayton M. Christiansen in his book *The Innovator's Dilemma* (Boston: Harvard Business School Press, 1997).

10. Pitroda, "Development, Democracy and the Village Telephone," p. 66.

11. C. Gibbs, *MTN: 10 Years of Cellular Freedom: 1994–2004* (Sandton, South Africa: MTN Group Corporate Affairs, 2004), p. 20.

12. M. Ibrahim, speech at the IFC Global Private Equity conference, Washington, D.C., May 2005.

13. Transparency International, *Corruption Perceptions Index 2005* (London: Transparency International, 2005).

14. J. J. Novak, *Bangladesh: Reflections on the Water* (Dhaka: University Press Limited, 1994), pp. 77–83. (Originally published by Indiana University Press, 1993.)

15. M. Ali, *Brick Lane* (New York: Scribner, 2003), p. 214.

16. Novak, *Bangladesh*, p. 4.

17. C. K. Prahalad, *The Fortune at the Bottom of the Pyramid: Eradicating Poverty Through Profits* (Upper Saddle River, N.J.: Wharton School Publishing, 2005).

18. "The Real Digital Divide," *The Economist*, Mar. 12–18, 2005.

19. L. Waverman, M. Meschi, and M. Fuss, "The Impact of Telecoms on Economic Growth in Developing Countries," *Vodafone Policy Paper Series*, no. 2, Mar. 2005, pp. 10–19.

Chapter One

1. World Bank, World Development Indicators, 1995.

2. A. Lawson, "Phone Wait Over for Dhaka Man," BBC News, June 23, 2005, retrieved from www.bbc.co.uk.

3. See generally, P. Bowring, "The Puzzle of Bangladesh," *Financial Times*, May 7, 2005, retrieved from www.ft.com.

4. J. Baez, "Song of Bangladesh" on "Come From the Shadows" LP, 1972, A&M Records, Santa Monica, CA.

5. "Conversation with Iqbal Quadir: Bottom-Up Economics," *Harvard Business Review*, Aug. 2003, pp. 18–22.

6. T. Wolfe, *Bonfire of the Vanities* (New York: Farrar, Straus & Giroux, 1987).

7. R. Solow, "A Contribution to the Theory of Economic Growth," *Quarterly Journal of Economics*. Feb. 1956, 70, 65–94; and, "Technical Change and the Aggregate Production Function," *Review of Economics and Statistics*. Aug. 1957, 39, 12–20.

8. I. Quadir, "The Bottleneck Is at the Top of the Bottle," *The Fletcher Forum of World Affairs*, Summer/Fall 2002.

9. A. Islam, "A Bangladeshi Helena and Her Magic Lamp of ICT," 2004, retrieved from www.grameentelecenter.org.

10. M. Jordan, "It Takes a Cellphone," *Wall Street Journal*, June 25, 1999, pp. B1–B4.

11. Dominic Wilson and Roopa Purushothaman, *Dreaming with BRICS: The Path to 2050*, Goldman Sachs Global Economics Paper No. 99 (New York: Goldman Sachs, Oct. 2003).

12. Jim O'Neill, Dominic Wilson, Roopa Purushothaman, and Anna Stupnytska, *How Solid Are the BRICs*, Goldman Sachs Global Economics Paper No. 134 (New York: Goldman Sachs, Dec. 2005).

Chapter Two

1. Microcredit Summit Campaign, *State of the Microcredit Summit Campaign: Report 2005* (Washington, D.C.: Microcredit Summit Campaign, Dec. 2005).

2. M. Yunus and A. Jolis, *Banker to the Poor: The Autobiography of Muhammad Yunus, Founder of the Grameen Bank* (London: Aurum Press, 1998), p. 4.

3. Yunus and Jolis, *Banker to the Poor*, p. 24.

4. Zenit News Agency (Madrid), "Banker for the Poor: Exclusive Interview with Recipient of the 1998 Prince of Asturias Award," June 22, 1998.

5. A. Singh, "An Empire Built on Poverty," *Bloomberg Markets*, Nov. 2005, p. 123.

6. Grameen Bank, "Key Information of Grameen Bank: For the Years 1995 and 2001 to 2005," Table, June 2006.

7. "The Hidden Wealth of the Poor: A Survey of Microfinance," *The Economist*, Nov. 3, 2005, special Survey section.

8. Yunus and Jolis, *Banker to the Poor*, p. 152.

9. M. Yunus and A. Jolis, *Banker to the Poor: The Autobiography of Muhammad Yunus, Founder of the Grameen Bank* (New York: Public Affairs, 2003), pp. 107–109.

10. M. Chu, "Commercial Returns and Social Value: The Case of Microfinance," paper presented at the Harvard Business School Conference on Global Poverty, Cambridge, Mass., Dec. 1–3, 2005, p. 8.

11. Chu, "Commercial Returns and Social Value."

12. V. Khosla, "Microlending: An Anti-Poverty Success Story," presentation at the Global Business and Global Poverty Conference, Stanford Graduate School of Business, May 2004.

13. MicroCapital, "Microfinance Funds Universe," June 28, 2006, retrieved from www.microcapital.org. See www.microcapital.org and www.cgap.org for current information on funding, ratings, and returns for MFIs.

14. Chu, "Commercial Returns and Social Value," pp. 8–10.

15. Microcredit Summit Campaign, *State of the Microcredit Summit Campaign*, p. 7.

16. S. Pitroda, "Development, Democracy and the Village Telephone," *Harvard Business Review*, Nov./Dec. 1993, pp. 66–79.

17. Pitroda, "Development, Democracy and the Village Telephone," p. 72.

18. Pitroda, "Development, Democracy and the Village Telephone," p. 66.

19. M. Chhaya, *Sam Pitroda: A Biography* (Delhi: Konark, 1992).

20. Pitroda, "Development, Democracy and the Village Telephone," p. 66.

21. J. Greenwald, "Dish-Wallahs," *Wired*, May/June 1993, retrieved from www.wirednews.com/wired/archive.

22. Greenwald, "Dish-Wallahs."

Chapter Three

1. Grameen Bank, "Key Information of Grameen Bank: For the Years 1995 and 2001 to 2005," Table, June, 2006.

2. M. Yunus and A. Jolis, *Banker to the Poor: The Autobiography of Muhammad Yunus, Founder of the Grameen Bank* (New York: Public Affairs, 2003), p. 225

3. O. F. Younes, "Dialing for Dollars the Grameen Way," *The WorldPaper*, Summer 1998 white paper, pp. 4–5.

4. I. Quadir, "Some Thoughts on Grameen Telecom," Memo, July 13, 1995.

5. "The Richest People in America," *Forbes*, Oct. 6, 2003, retrieved from www.forbes.com/lists.

Chapter Four

1. J. Salacuse and N. Sullivan, "Do BITs Really Work? An Evaluation of Bilateral Investment Treaties and Their Grand Bargain," *Harvard International Law Journal*, Winter 2005, 46(1), 69–130.

2. UBS, "Bangladesh: Waiting for the Elections," Global Research Report (New York: UBS, May 1995), p. 2.

3. I. Quadir, "To Invest or Not to Invest," Memo, July 28, 1995.

4. M. Goedhart and P. Haden, "Emerging Markets Aren't as Risky as You Think," *McKinsey Quarterly*, Special Edition, Spring 2003, retrieved from www.mckinseyquarterly.com.

Chapter Five

1. GrameenPhone Ltd., "Offer for Establishing Operating and Maintaining Cellular Mobile Radio Telephone Services in Bangladesh," submitted to the Bangladesh Ministry of Post and Telecommunications, Nov. 6, 1995.

2. M. Yunus, "Financing," Memo to Iqbal Quadir, n.d.

3. K. Shams, Letter to Amin Khan, Bangladesh Telegraph and Telephone Board, Apr. 13, 1996, p. 1.

4. Shams, Letter to Amin Khan, p. 4.

5. "Interview with Muhammad Yunus," *Daily Star*, Jan. 1, 1995.

Chapter Six

1. GrameenPhone, *Annual Report 1998* (Dhaka: GrameenPhone Ltd., 1999), pp. 2–42.

2. GrameenPhone, *Annual Report 1998*, p. 39

3. O. F. Younes, "Dialing for Dollars the Grameen Way," *The World-Paper*, Summer 1998 white paper, p. 5.

4. GrameenPhone, *Annual Report 1999* (Dhaka: GrameenPhone Ltd., 2000), p. 33.

5. M. Yunus, "IT Can Be Bangladesh's Road to Prosperity," in GrameenPhone, *Annual Report 1999* (Dhaka: GrameenPhone Ltd., 2000), pp. 34–35.

Chapter Seven

1. C. Gibbs, *MTN: 10 Years of Cellular Freedom: 1994–2004* (Sandton, South Africa: MTN Group Corporate Affairs, 2004).

2. Gibbs, *MTN: 10 Years of Cellular Freedom*, p. 19.

3. Gibbs, *MTN: 10 Years of Cellular Freedom*, p. 20.

4. Gibbs, *MTN: 10 Years of Cellular Freedom*, p. 22.

5. Gibbs, *MTN: 10 Years of Cellular Freedom*, p. 27.

6. Gibbs, *MTN: 10 Years of Cellular Freedom*, p. 20.

7. "Judgement Day," *The Economist*, Oct. 8, 1998, retrieved from www.economist.com.

8. S. Robinson, "2002 Global Influentials: Strive Masiyiwa: Founder of Econet Wireless," *Time*, Nov. 30, 2002, retrieved from www.time.com/time/2002/global influentials.

9. Robinson, "2002 Global Influentials: Strive Masiyiwa."

10. S. LaFraniere, "Cellphones Catapult Rural Africa to 21st Century," *New York Times*, Aug. 25, 2005, p. 1.

11. J. Sachs, *The End of Poverty: Economic Possibilities for Our Time* (New York: Penguin Press, 2005).

12. LaFraniere, "Cellphones Catapult Rural Africa to 21st Century," p. 1.

13. "Wireless Warriors," *The Economist*, Feb. 14, 2002, retrieved from www.economist.com.

14. "The New Pharaohs," *The Economist*, Mar. 10, 2005, retrieved from www.economist.com.

15. A. Allam, "Egyptian Mobile Phone Provider Treads Where Others Dare Not," *New York Times*, Feb. 13, 2006, retrieved from www.nytimes.com.

16. M. Rao and L. Mendoza (eds.), *Asia Unplugged: The Wireless and Mobile Media Boom in the Asia-Pacific* (New Delhi: Sage, 2005), pp. 354–372.

17. "Lex Column," *Financial Times*, Nov. 16, 2004, retrieved from www.ft.com.

18. Allam, "Egyptian Mobile Phone Provider Treads Where Others Dare Not."

19. Associated Press, "Cell Phone Use Changes Africa," Oct. 16, 2005.

Chapter Eight

1. "The Hidden Wealth of the Poor: A Survey of Microfinance," *The Economist*, Nov. 5, 2005.

2. "Thank You for Your Purchase: A Mobile Phone Turns Into a Credit Card Terminal," allAfrica.com, Dec. 20, 2005, retrieved from http://allafrica.com.

3. "Fewer Buffaloes, Livelier Democracy," *The Economist*, Nov. 10, 2001, p. 45.

4. S. Smith, *What Works: Smart Communications—Expanding Networks, Expanding Profits*, Digital Dividend Case Study (Washington, D.C.: World Resources Institute, Sept. 2004), p. 7.

5. Information for Development Program, International Finance Corporation, and GSM Association, *Micro-Payment Systems and Their Application to Mobile Networks*, an *info*Dev Report (Washington, D.C.: Information for Development Program, Jan. 2006), p. 17.

6. Information for Development Program, International Finance Corporation, and GSM Association, *Micro-Payment Systems* . . . , p. 21.

7. Information for Development Program, International Finance Corporation, and GSM Association, *Micro-Payment Systems* . . . , p. 24.

8. N. Itano, "Africa's Cellphone Boom Creates a Base for Low-Cost Banking," *Christian Science Monitor*, Aug. 26, 2005, retrieved from www.csmonitor.com.

9. Itano, "Africa's Cellphone Boom . . ."

10. G. Ivatury, *Using Technology to Build Inclusive Financial Systems*, Focus Note No. 32 (Washington, D.C.: Consultative Group to Assist the Poor, Jan. 2006), p. 11.

11. "Thank You for Your Purchase . . ."

12. "Spread of Cell Phones," *The Independent*, Apr. 22, 2006, p. 22.

13. D. Richardson, R. Ramirez, and M. Haq, *Grameen Telecom's Village Phone Programme: A Multi-Media Case Study*, Telecommons Development Group (Ottawa: Canadian International Development Agency, Mar. 2000).

14. *Eradicating Poverty Through Profit*, Conference Summary Report (Washington, D.C.: World Resources Institute, Apr. 2005).

15. Ivatury, *Using Technology to Build Inclusive Financial Systems*, p. 5.

16. Information for Development Program, International Finance Corporation, and GSM Association, *Micro-Payment Systems . . .* , p. 42.

17. *Africa: The Impact of Mobile Phones,* Vodafone Policy Paper Series, No. 2 (Newbury, England: Vodafone Group, Mar. 2005), p. 2.

Chapter Nine

1. M. Visscher, "How One New Company Brought Hope to One of the World's Poorest Countries," Jan. 2005 (Issue 22), retrieved from www.odemagazine.com.

2. B. Lane and others, *The Economic and Social Benefits of Mobile Services in Bangladesh* (London: GSM Association and Ovum, Apr. 2006), p. 1.

3. L. Waverman, M. Meschi, and M. Fuss, "The Impact of Telecoms on Economic Growth in Developing Countries," in *Africa: The Impact of Mobile Phones,* Vodafone Policy Paper Series, No. 2, Mar. 2005, pp. 10–19.

4. T. Schellen and T. El Zein (eds.), *Mobility for One Language, Diverse Cultures,* An MTC Report (Kuwait: MTC, Feb. 2006).

5. D. Richardson, R. Ramirez, and M. Haq, *Grameen Telecom's Village Phone Programme: A Multi-Media Case Study,* Telecommons Development Group (Ottawa: Canadian International Development Agency, Mar. 2000).

6. Waverman, Meschi, and Fuss, "The Impact of Telecoms on Economic Growth . . ."

7. GrameenPhone, "The Village Phone," 2006, retrieved from http://www.grameenphone.com/

8. R. Hamilton, "Community Phones Connect SA Townships," BBC News, Dec. 2, 2003.

9. J. Reck and B. Wood, *What Works: Vodacom's Community Cell Phones,* Digital Dividend Case Study (Washington, D.C.: World Resources Institute, Aug. 2003).

10. E. Toroka, "Celtel Confirms Its Commitment to Africa," BSC Times.com, Oct. 21, 2004, pp. 17, retrieved from www.bcstimes.com.

11. *Africa: The Impact of Mobile Phones*, Vodafone Policy Paper Series, No. 2 (Newbury, England: Vodafone Group, Mar. 2005), p. 2.

12. Z. Islam, "BTRC Not to Allow Mobile Phone Network Expansion on Bank Loan," *New Age*, Mar. 23, 2006.

Chapter Ten

1. B. Drayton, "Everyone a Changemaker," *Innovations*, Winter 2006, p. 82.

2. T. L. Friedman, *The Lexus and the Olive Tree* (New York: Anchor Books, 2000), pp. 359–362.

3. E. Schonfeld, "Segway Creator Unveils His Next Act," *Business 2.0*, Feb. 16, 2002, retrieved from www.money.cnn.com.

4. P. Sharke, "Sun Rises on Solar," *Design News*, Jan. 9, 2006.

5. E. F. Schumacher, *Small Is Beautiful* (New York: HarperCollins, 1973).

6. M. Fisher, "Income Is Development," *Innovations*, Winter 2006, p. 12.

7. Fisher, "Income Is Development," pp. 9–30.

8. I. Quadir, *Emergence Energy Inc.: Refining the Franchise Model and Other Preparations*, company document, June 2006.

9. S. Khan, "REB Subscribers Victims of 'Unusual' Expansion," *Daily Star*, Apr. 21, 2006, p. 10.

Chapter Eleven

1. "Sealed City Turns into Battlefield," *Daily Star*, Apr. 20, 2006, p. 1.

2. "Police Foil Opposition's Sit-In Using Rubber Bullets, Tear Gas," *The Independent*, Apr. 20, 2006.

3. "Capital Put Under Lockdown," *Daily Star*, Apr. 20, 2006.

4. "Yunus Spells Out Nation's Rosy Future," *Daily Star*, Feb. 5, 2006.

5. B. Lane and others, *The Economic and Social Benefits of Mobile Services in Bangladesh* (London: GSM Association and Ovum, Apr. 2006), p. 12.

6. Lane and others, *The Economic and Social Benefits of Mobile Services in Bangladesh*, p. 12.

7. E. Sylvers, "Connecting Developing Nations," *International Herald Tribune*, Feb. 17, 2006.

8. "Developing Economies Held Back by Taxes on Mobile Phones," GSM Association Press Release, 2005.

9. A. Islam, "BTRC Not to Allow Mobile Phone Network Expansion on Bank Loan," *New Age*, Mar. 23, 2006.

10. S. H. Zahid, "Tata's Investment: Now a Different Ball Game," *Financial Express*, May 8, 2006.

11. R. Hasan, "Coalmine Project to Pust Tata Investment up to $3b," *Daily Star*, Sept. 17, 2005.

12. GrameenPhone, *Annual Report 1999* (Dhaka: GrameenPhone Ltd., 2000), p. 5.

13. "Hartals Eat Up 4pc of GDP," *Bangladesh Observer*, June 15, 2006.

14. "Yunus Spells Out Nation's Rosy Future."

15. "Snaking In from Under the Seas: Submarine Cable Link Launched by Bangladesh," Association for Progressive Communications, May 31, 2006, www.apc.org.

Resources

This bibliography contains some supplemental sources of information, in addition to those listed in the Notes.

Bullis, K. "Generating Hope." *Technology Review*, Oct. 5, 2005.

Butler, R. "Cell Phones May Help 'Save' Africa." Mongabay.com, July 18, 2005. Retrievable from http://news.mongabay.com/2005/0712-rhett_butler.html.

Cohen, N. *What Works: Grameen Telecom's Village Phones*, Digital Dividend Case Study. Washington, D.C.: World Resources Institute, June 2001.

Grameen Bank. "Grameen Bank Performance Indicators & Ratio Analysis." Dhaka: Grameen Bank, Oct. 2005.

Grameen Foundation USA. "Growth Guarantees Fact Sheet." Washington, D.C.: Grameen Foundation USA, Dec. 2005.

GrameenPhone. *Annual Report 2000*. Dhaka: GrameenPhone Ltd, 2001.

GrameenPhone. *Annual Report 2001*. Dhaka: GrameenPhone Ltd. 2002.

GrameenPhone. *Annual Report 2002*. Dhaka: GrameenPhone Ltd., 2003.

GrameenPhone. *Annual Report 2003*. Dhaka: GrameenPhone Ltd., 2004.

GrameenPhone. *Annual Report 2004*. Dhaka: GrameenPhone Ltd., 2005.

GrameenPhone. *Annual Report 2005*. Dhaka: GrameenPhone Ltd., 2006.

GrameenPhone. *Transmission, Continuous Coverage and the Use of Fiber*. Dhaka: GrameenPhone Ltd., July 1999.

Ibrahim, M. "Connecting Africa to the Global Economy." Connect-World. Retrievable from http://connect-world.com/Articles/old_articles/MohamedIbrahim.htm.

Ibrahim, M. "Getting the Message." *The Economist*, Mar. 4, 2006.

Kabushenga, R. "Who Is Iqbal Quadir?" *Sunday Vision*, Dec. 21, 2003, retrievable from http://newvision.com.co.ug.

Pfanner, E. "New Markets Call to Millicom Bidders." *International Herald Tribune*, Jan. 23, 2006. Retrievable from http://www.iht.com/articles/2006/01/23/yourmoney/millicom.php.

Reed, S. "Helping the Poor, Phone by Phone." *New York Times*, May 26, 2002.

Sarin, A. "Mobile Penetration Will Boost African Business." *Financial Times*, July 29, 2005.

"South African Farmers Use Weather SMS." *Business Day*, Aug. 22, 2005.

"Twenty Great Asians: The Lender: Muhammad Yunus." *Asiaweek*, June 2, 1995. Retrievable from http://www.grameen-info.org/agrameen/profile.php3?profile=3.

Vasagar, J. "Talk Is Cheap and Getting Cheaper." *The Guardian*, Sept. 14, 2005. Retrievable from www.guardian.co.uk/kenya/story/0,12689,1569469,00.html.

Index

102, 186; new service connections from, 45; questions GrameenPhone licensing, 82, 83–84; rejects proposal to lease fiber, 80; relations with Alcatel, 62; resists fiber leasing, 91; role in submarine cable operations, 196; uninterested in cellular business, 49; Yahya tries to lease fiber-optic cabling for, 48–49
Businesses: BOP model for, xvii, 129, 130, 203; domestic manufacturing and, 178–179; microfinance in solar, 171–172; model of village phone vs. biogas electrical, 177–178; startup times required for, xxviii; sustainability of, xx; wealth creation and small, 146. *See also* Microfinance; Wealth creation
Business Week, 93

C

Cable & Wireless, 110
Capital: development of MSI's venture, 115–117; flight, 62; initial plans for GrameenPhone, 74; overestimating risk of foreign investment, 68–69; Pitroda's vision of improving, 28; Quadir raises phone system investment, 42–44; raising U.S. venture, 42–43
Capitalism. *See* Inclusive capitalism
Carter, Jimmy, 18
Cash-in–cash-out problem, 140
CDC Capital Partners, 116
CDC (Commonwealth Development Corporation), 74, 97, 99
CDMA (Code Division Multiple Access) services, 121
C-DOT (Centre for Development of Telematics), 28–30
Cell, C, 118
CellBazaar, 142–144, 201
Cellnet, 113, 114
Cell phones: airtime of rural callers, 93, 94, 95; banking with, 125–128, 132–134; borrowed phones and SIM cards, 140–141; buying min-

utes on credit, 130; bypassing fixedline network, 97–99; call pricing, 83–84, 151; "cell phone as cow" concept, xviii, 39–42; cellular operators in Bangladesh, 124; CityCell service, 53, 55, 84, 128, 185; climbing trees for better reception, 118; correlation between GDP and, 148; as credit card terminals, 134; development in Scandinavia, 51–55; as disruptive technology, xxiii; features of GSM, 56–57; flashing, 132; growth in MTN subscribers, 123, 124; handset costs of, xxxiv, 11; international calling rates, 155–156; international roaming agreements, 101; licensing tender in Zimbabwe, 112; loading money onto, 133–134; modeling network for, 79–80; MOPT floats tender for licensing, 53, 64; more voice than text calls in, Africa, 142; Mugabe's opposition to, 111, 112; myths about poor and, 38; opinions in South Africa of, 109; PHS, 72–73; Pitroda's development in India, 26–31, 55; prepaid subscriber cards for, 125–126; prepaid village service, 101; remittance flows via, 134–137; rise in African subscribers, 122–124; silent revolution of, 145; Skaar's viability model for, 66–67; social impact of mobile credit, 133; subscriptions in India, 121; taxes in Bangladesh, 186–187; texting cash to cell subscribers, 131; texting rates for Philippines, 128; universal appeal of, xxxii; use during emergency flooding, 97. *See also* Costs; Village pay phones
Celpay, 133–134
Celtel International BV: about, xix; begins operations as MSI-Cellular Investments, 115; capital raised by, 116; Celpay owned previously by, 133; corruption policy at, 117; costs of operation for, 119–120; foreign